Shah Alam Granting Diwani Right to the East India Company

HISTORY
THAT
INDIA
IGNORED

HISTORY THAT INDIA IGNORED

PREM PRAKASH

Vitasta

Published by
Renu Kaul Verma
Vitasta Publishing Pvt Ltd
4348/4C, Ansari Road, Daryaganj
New Delhi-110 002
info@vitastapublishing.com

ISBN 978-81-19670-32-1
© Prem Prakash
First Edition 2025

MRP ₹ 625

All Rights Reserved.
No part of this publication may be reproduced, stored in a retrieval system, or transmitted in any form, or by any means—electronic, mechanical, photocopying, recording or otherwise—without the prior permission of the publisher. Opinions expressed in this book are the author's own. The publisher is in no way responsible for these.

Editor: Oswald Pereira
Layout & Cover Design by Rohit Gautam
Printed by Chaman Enterprises, New Delhi

PRAISE FOR THE BOOK

In India, only a handful of carefully selected episodes and individuals are part of the official narrative that relates to our resistance to foreign domination. Prem Prakash has taken up an alternative view in this book.

—**Sanjeev Sanyal**
Writer and Economist

A Powerful Narrative of India's Unsung Heroes
They may kill me, but they cannot kill my ideas. They can crush my body, but they will not be able to crush my spirit.

—**Bhagat Singh**

Growing up in the UK as a second-generation Indian, I was captivated by the stories of India's Independence struggle, which have influenced generations of Indians in mind and spirit.

I worked with Prem Prakash on this book, discussing chapters, and did meticulous research and fact-checking with the British Library's India Office Collection.

This book offers more than just a historical timeline. It weaves a powerful narrative of how the unsung heroes of India's Independence movement contributed to the nation's freedom. The author captures their stories of sacrifices, resilience, and unyielding determination that underpin India's journey to Independence.

More than a chronicle of the past, this book is a living testament to the spirit of Independence and the ideals that continue to inspire us.

The book should be a textbook for schoolchildren to learn from and for university students to analyse, ensuring that the sacrifices and triumphs of the Independence movement remain etched in our collective memory as we work for a more just and equitable future.

–**Dr Hari Mann**
Visiting Fellow, *University of Cambridge*,
Dean, *Ashridge Business School*

An Expose of the Savage British Raj

Prem Prakash vividly portrays the sacrifices and battles of heroic revolutionaries who wanted to build an India where ignorance, injustice, hunger and poverty ended.

The author narrates the journey of revolutionaries to eliminate the perpetrators of loot, subjugation and exploitation of India. The book is an expose of the most dastardly torture, killings, hangings, deportations, and unjustified long prison terms of vocal revolutionaries by the British Raj.

Bhagat Singh, Ajit Singh, Chapekar Brothers, Prafulla Chaki, Khudiram Bose, Barin Ghosh, Madan Lal Dhingra, Veer Savarkar, Rash Behari Bose, Shreesh Ghosh, Basant Kumar, Vishnu Ganesh Pingle, Kartar Singh Saraba, Udham Singh, among many others faced savage, inhuman treatment by the British Crown.

In the author's eyes, the unsung heroes remain great martyrs whom history has forgotten.

–**Dr Archana Verma**
Retired Professor, *Hindu College,*
Department of History

CONTENTS

Foreword — xi

Preface — xv

Bharat: Early India, Alexander, Arrival of Muslims — 1

A State in the Guise of a Merchant — 18

The Callous East India Company — 36

Company Rule Amidst Uprisings — 50

The Heroic 1857 Mutineers — 65

Queen Victoria and the Cosy Indian National Congress — 82

Ajit Singh, Madan Lal Dhingra, Veer Savarkar — 99

The Ghadar Movement and Rash Behari Bose — 118

Revolutionaries Hanged — 133

Bhagat Singh Hanged — 153

Indian Republican Army Attacks the British Raj — 169

Quit India-1942, Netaji Escapes and Takes Over Indian National Army	188
India Inches Closer to Independence	206
India is Free but Partitioned	222
Goa is Liberated	239
Supplement	*247*

PROCLAMATION
of the
Provisional Government
of
AZAD HIND

AFTER their first defeat at the hands of the British in 1757 in Bengal, the Indian people fought an uninterrupted series of hard and bitter battles over a stretch of one-hundred years. The history of this period teems with examples of unparalleled heroism and self-sacrifice. And, in the pages of that history, the names of Sirajuddoula and Mohanlal of Bengal, Haider Ali, Tippu Sultan and Velu Tampi of South India, Appa Sahib Bhonsle and Peshwa Baji Rao of Mahrashtra, the Begums of Oudh, Sardar Shyam Singh Atariwala of Punjab and last, but not least, Rani Laxmibai of Jhansi, Tantia Topi, Maharaj Kunwar Singh of Dumraon and Nana Sahib—among others—the names of all these Warriors are for ever engraved in letters of gold. Unfortunately for us, our forefathers did not at first realise that the British constituted a grave threat to the whole of India and they did not therefore put up a united front against the enemy. Ultimately, when the Indian people were roused to the reality of the situation, they made a concerted move—and under the flag of Bahadur Shah, in 1857, they fought their last war as free men. In spite of a series of brilliant victories in the early stages of this war, ill-luck and faulty leadership gradually brought about their final collapse and subjugation. Nevertheless, such heroes as the Rani of Jhansi, Tantia Topi, Kunwar Singh and Nana Sahib live like eternal stars in the nation's memory to inspire us to greater deeds of sacrifice and valour.

Forcibly disarmed by the British after 1857 and subjected to terror and brutality, the Indian people lay prostrate for a while — but with the birth of the Indian National Congress in 1885, there came a new awakening. From 1885 till the end of the last World War, the Indian people, in their endeavour to recover their lost liberty, tried all possible methods—namely, agitation and propaganda, boycott of British goods, terrorism and sabotage —and finally, armed revolution. But all these efforts failed for a time. Ultimately, in 1920, when the Indian people, haunted by a sense of failure, were groping for a new method, Mahatma Gandhi came forward with the new weapon of non-co-operation and civil disobedience.

For two decades thereafter, the Indian people went through a phase of intense patriotic activity. The message of freedom was carried to every Indian home. Through personal example, people were taught to suffer, to sacrifice and to die in the cause of freedom. From the centre to the remotest villages, the people were knit together into one political organisation. Thus, the Indian people not only recovered their political consciousness, but became a political entity once again. They could now speak with one voice and strive with one will for one common goal. From 1937 to 1939, through the work of the Congress Ministries in eight provinces, they gave proof of their readiness and their capacity to administer their own affairs.

Thus, on the eve of the present World War, the stage was set for the final struggle for India's Liberation. During the course of this War, Germany, with the help of her Allies, has dealt shattering blows to our enemy in Europe—while Nippon with the help of her Allies has inflicted a knockout blow to our enemy in East Asia. Favoured by a most happy combination of circumstances, the Indian people today have a wonderful opportunity for achieving their national emancipation.

For the first time in recent history, Indians abroad have also been politically roused and united in one organisation. They are not only thinking and feeling in tune with their countrymen at home, but are also marching in step with them, along the path to Freedom. In East Asia, in particular, over two million Indians are now organised as one solid phalanx, inspired by the slogan of "Total Mobilisation." And in front of them stand the serried ranks of India's Army of Liberation, with the slogan "Onward to Delhi," on their lips.

Having goaded Indians to desperation by its hypocrisy and having driven them to starvation and death by plunder and loot—British rule in India has forfeited the goodwill of the Indian people altogether and is now living a precarious existence. It needs but a flame to destroy the last vestige of that unhappy rule. To light that flame is the task of India's Army of Liberation. Assured of the enthusiastic support of the civil population at home and also of a large section of Britain's Indian Army, and backed by gallant and invincible allies abroad — but relying in the first instance on its own strength, India's Army of Liberation is confident of fulfilling its historic role.

Now that the dawn of freedom is at hand, it is the duty of the Indian people to set up a Provisional Government of their own, and launch the last struggle under the banner of that Government. But with all the Indian leaders in prison and the people at home totally disarmed — it is not possible to set up a Provisional Government within India or to launch an armed struggle under the aegis of that Government. It is, therefore, the duty of the Indian Independence League in East Asia, supported by all patriotic Indians at home and abroad, to undertake this task—the task of setting up a Provisional Government of Azad Hind (Free India) and of conducting the last fight for Freedom, with the help of the Army of Liberation (that is, the Azad Hind Fauj or the Indian National Army) organised by the League.

Having been constituted as the Provisional Government of Azad Hind by the Indian Independence League in East Asia, we enter upon our duties with a full sense of

(Continued on page 2)

FOREWORD

I am not a historian myself. My exposure to history, for a time, has been limited merely to textbooks. Though I was forced to read in my school years, my interest in subjects was, frankly, lukewarm. However, as I moved ahead, I slowly began to realise that I needed to read history, not just to memorise names of kings and rulers but to understand where I, and of course others, stood at that point of time, how we came to be there, and where we may go from there. And I also realised that history was not just about a nation and its politics, but everything had a history—matters, objects, plants, humans and other living beings; man's acquired knowledge and beliefs; our creations and expressions in literature and other arts. So, history became for me, the root of all kinds of knowledge.

Yet, not being a historian by training, I was in two minds about writing a preface for Mr Prem Prakash's book, *History that India Ignored*. On reading the book, however, my hesitation took a back seat, prompting me to write something as an ordinary reader, not as a specialist.

What I found in Mr Prakash's book is a thorough understanding of India's history, including the various kinds of foreign onslaughts and occasional dominations the country had gone through. His focus has been both on the centre and the capital, as on the margins. Alongside Delhi, where most of the events took place, Punjab, Goa, and the South were not forgotten. And he covered Bengal in depth, as this was another margin of India, which came to acquire a centrality for a period, under the last foreign rulers, the British.

The author has a very defined objective. He wants to challenge and correct the somewhat skewed view of the historians of the Indian freedom struggle: that 'India's fight for freedom was...just led by Mahatma Gandhi and the Indian National Congress.' He wants to point out that there were other important 'forces that fought the British.' And these 'forces,' for him, are the 'unsung heroes.'

Who are they, one may ask. For him, they are 'martyrs who went to the gallows for the motherland'. He says, 'It is tragic that independent India has erased the names of most revolutionaries from the history of India's fight for freedom.' Not only that, luminaries like Bal Gangadhar Tilak, Bipin Chandra Pal and Lala Lajpat Rai have been pushed into oblivion, and Netaji Subhash Chandra Bose and his heroic Indian National Army have been somewhat marginalised. His book 'aims to bring out a brief history, the sacrifice and fight of those countless freedom fighters who pushed their head fearlessly for the nation right from the day Prithviraj Chauhan lost Delhi.'

This Mr Prakash has done with excellent results. His research has been deep, wide and varied. I hope readers as well as scholars of Indian history will appreciate, as I do, Mr Prakash's commendable attempt at redressing the imbalance of the recorded and familiar history of India's freedom struggle.

Prof Pabitra Sarkar
Former Vice Chancellor
Rabindra Bharati University, Kolkata
24 February 2025

PREFACE

On 15 August 1947, India achieved Independence from British colonial rule. A new victorious India emerged on the world scene. It was now going to be a country ruled by its own people elected by them. Emperors, monarchs and colonial power were part of history that was best forgotten as rule that was not people-friendly.

I have spent a fair amount of time in Bengal on different occasions as a journalist. I learnt that Bengal's contribution in the fight for India's Independence was as substantial as Punjab.

The first foreign attacks on India in recorded history were by Darius in 536 BC and by Alexander in 327 BC when the country was known as Bharat, spread across South Asia with many kingdoms. In Alexander the Great's campaign to capture the land of Bharat, he crossed the Jhelum river to face King Porus. It was a heavily fought battle in which Porus lost his son and the Greeks suffered heavy casualties. Folklore and some historians have noted that when Alexander faced a defeated Porus, he asked him how he wished to be treated? Porus replied 'the way one king treats the other king.' Alexander did not execute King Porus but settled with him, restoring his kingdom though under his sovereignty.

After moving from Greece into Bharat, a long and arduous journey, Alexander's soldiers refused to go further. They had heard of the powerful Nanda Empire with a huge army that lay ahead if they were to march further into India. Alexander decided to turn back. Folklore has it that a young Chandragupta Maurya had managed to come face to face with Alexander and asked him to leave India. Chandragupta escaped before he could be arrested by Alexander's men.

Soon after Alexander's departure, Chandragupta under the guidance and advice of Chanakya began to attack and free the areas ruled by the governors that Alexander had left behind. Chanakya's pen name was Kautilya. He was an authority on politics and economics. He wrote the great treatise on statecraft *Arthashastra* that covered politics and economics. This treatise of statecraft guides how a king should rule and keep his people happy.

As advisor to Chandragupta, Chanakya guided him in his campaign to free the areas under the Greeks. Chandragupta's toughest fight was against Seleucus which lasted almost two years, but he was finally able to free the areas right to the high mountains of Hindu Kush (including today's Afghanistan). In a settlement, Chandragupta is said to have married the daughter of Seleucus.

After freeing the area under Greek occupation, Chandragupta began expanding his empire with Chanakya's guidance. He defeated the powerful Nanda dynasty and extended his rule all over today's South Asia. This has been the biggest Indian empire in history which was extended by his successors. The greatest of his successors was Emperor Ashoka. The Mauryan empire is considered to have been the best ruled state in the world, a model fit for today's democratic political rulers.

The foreign rule in India began long after the Mauryan empire. Almost 1,500 years after the end of the Mauryan empire, Prithviraj Chauhan who ruled his kingdom from Delhi was defeated by Muhammad Ghori. Earlier Prithviraj had defeated Ghori, but instead of executing him as was the custom in that era, he asked him to go back where he came from and never dare to return. But Prithviraj was betrayed by Jaichand who incited Ghori to attack Prithviraj. The traitor ensured the defeat of Prithviraj. Thereafter, Delhi was ruled by Muhammad Ghori's men from 1206 to 1526 AD. They were followed by Babur, ruler of Ferghana who established Mughal rule in India. The atrocities of Babur are well recorded in the four hymns of Guru Nanak. The great Guru had seen what the foreigner from Ferghana was doing. One of the hymns when translated describes Babur as messenger of death.

Atrocities on Sikh Gurus continued later on by other Mughal rulers after Babur. The great Gurus spoke always for the cause of the suffering people. The torture and killing of fifth Guru Angad Dev followed by the torture and killing of ninth Guru Tegh Bahadur and his disciples by Aurangzeb are all part of history. Later, Guru Gobind Singh's two young sons were buried alive and two others killed in the battle of Chamkaur. However, in the end, the atrocities of Aurangzeb brought his end, while fighting the Marathas. He himself had predicted that after him there would be a void.

The history of the capture of India by the East India Company is a long story by itself. But the British formally succeeded the Mughals after the Mutiny of 1857 when Queen Victoria took control of India. The Union Jack rose over the front minarets of the Fort facing Chandni Chowk. A contingent of the British troops was always based in the Red Fort. The Union Jack came down at sunset on August 14.

At midnight of August 14-15, India's Independence was ushered in as the day turned to August 15. The country was still a dominion with Lord Mountbatten as the first Governor General.

As the sun rose on the morning of August 15, General Shah Nawaz of the Indian National Army raised the National flag of India as confirmed by Adil Shah Nawaz, grandson of the general. This fulfilled a promise that Netaji Subhash Chandra Bose had made when giving the call 'Chalo Dilli.' The great Fort was adorned with the tricolour National flag of India. The next day on the morning of August 16, Jawaharlal Nehru, the first Prime Minister of India raised the National flag from the ramparts of the Fort and addressed the nation and the vast crowd assembled below. Since then the Prime Ministers of India have raised the National flag every Independence day, followed by an address to the nation.

Significantly, Netaji Subhash Chandra Bose, Supreme Commander of the Indian National Army (Azad Hind Fauj) and head of the Provisional Government of India raised the tricolour on the Indian soil on 30 December 1943, during World War II at Andaman Islands, Port Blair.

On 15 August 1947, while India was free of foreign rule, some enclaves of the country like Pondicherry, Yanam, Karaikal, Chandernagore, Goa, Daman and Diu were still under the control of the French and Portuguese. India's fight for independence was led by Mahatma Gandhi and the Congress Party in what is known as a non-violent non-cooperation agitation. There were other forces too—revolutionaries who did not believe in this Gandhian approach. There were those who were fighting and sacrificing their lives long before Gandhiji appeared on the scene. Many young revolutionaries including Bhagat Singh and his revolutionary friends laid down their lives fighting the British. Prominent among the revolutionaries was Netaji Subhash Chandra Bose who raised the Indian National Army (INA) to fight the British.

The demand of the Congress Party till 1930 was only for home rule under the status of a Dominion of the British empire as were countries like Australia and Canada. The Head of the State in this system had to be the British monarch who would appoint a Governor General to head the Dominion. Revolutionaries did not believe in this concept. Bhagat Singh and his revolutionary friends who were on trial in 1930 in Lahore for the killing of police officer Saunders had not only raised the demand for complete independence, but forced the British to recognise them as political prisoners. For this, they had gone on fasts unto death. Their logic was simple: that the British as a foreign power were ruling their land and they as Indians were fighting them to leave their country. And that Saunders was killed for he was responsible for using violence against Lala Lajpat Rai that led to his death. Thus, they argued that they were not criminals but political prisoners held by the British. They needed to be treated as such.

The contribution of revolutionaries in the cause of India's Independence was well accepted by Clement Attlee under whose Premiership India achieved independence. He was asked why Britain could not have continued to rule over India? Were the British not able to handle Gandhi and the Congress Party he was specifically asked. This question was asked by P N Chakraborty who was the Chief Justice of the Calcutta High Court, but acting as Governor of Bengal. Attlee was staying with him at the Governor's house during his visit to India. The reply that Attlee gave to Chakraborty was categorical. As for the role of Gandhi and Congress, he considered it as 'minimal' in their decision to leave India, as there was no agitation by them on the horizon.

The real factor that spurred the British to leave India was the first Indian National Army led by Subhash Chandra Bose that was leading the fight into India at Imphal. Significantly, the Japanese who were marching towards India were not ahead, but it was the Indian National Army that was leading their Japanese allies entry into India. Bose had laid down the condition to the Japanese that the march into India would be led by the Indian National Army, not the Japanese army. As many as 26,000 of INA's men were killed in this march.

The second factor that made the British consider leaving India was that sailors of the Royal Indian Navy in Bombay had gone on mutiny. The sailors were going around Bombay carrying portraits of Bose and shouting slogans of *Jai Hind* and Indian National Army. Large crowds were joining the sailors in these demonstrations in Bombay. A similar rebellion by airmen took place in what was the Royal Indian Air Force. The British were apprehensive and not prepared to face a 1857-like conflagration when the sepoys of the East India Company revolted.

The Indian Army had played a major role in keeping the British Empire intact through its period of existence. During World War II, it was the Fourth Indian Armoured Division which turned the tide of war against Germany in the battle of tanks in North Africa where German forces were led by Germany's famous General Rommel. It was no small task for the Fourth Indian Division to push Rommel back in the famous battle of El Alamein.

Yet another factor that made the British think that their days in India were numbered was the trial of three officers of the Indian National Army, General Shah Nawaz Khan, P K Sahgal and G S Dhillon in the Red Fort of Delhi. The trial received massive publicity all over India. The sympathy of the people lay with the three INA officers. Defence of the three officers had been organised by the Indian National Congress. Jawaharlal Nehru also wore his legal clothes to join the team of lawyers defending the three. People were enthused as they read the proceedings of the trial each day. There was massive support all over India for the three officers. Despite the sympathy and demand all over India that the three INA officers be released, the three were sentenced to death. But without any delay, the Commander-in-Chief of the Indian Army, Field Marshal Claude Auchinleck, commuted the sentence and the three INA officers were released.

They received a huge welcome at the Gandhi grounds of Delhi, where this author then a school boy, was present. I had a narrow escape as I fell down in the huge stampede that took place there. Hundreds walked over me and others who were pushed down. It was a lathi charge by the police that pushed back the people and rescued those who had fallen down.

Today, New Delhi's Central Vista near the famed India Gate is adorned with a statue of Netaji Subhash Chandra Bose under a Royal canopy that once had the statue of King George. This gives recognition of the fact that India's fight for freedom was not just led by Mahatma Gandhi and the Indian National Congress but also by armed forces that fought the British. The Indian National Army apart, there were so many other unsung, unknown martyrs who went to the gallows for their motherland. It is tragic that Independent India has erased the names of most revolutionaries from the history of India's fight for freedom. Not just that, little is said even about the great men like Bal Gangadhar Tilak, Bipin Chander Pal, Lala Lajpat Rai and many more.

During my student days, I would hear of such

revolutionary acts as the Chittagong Armoury Raid or Robbery on Kakori train. To understand such acts, one must go back to what happened in India after the Mutiny of 1857 had been crushed. Bahadur Shah Zafar was put on trial in the Red Fort and sent to the farthest corner of the subcontinent to Rangoon. That ended the rule of the Mughal dynasty.

As Queen Victoria took over the reins of India from the East India Company following the Mutiny of 1857, the first task that the British government in India resolved to do was to disarm the country. It was a very successful operation in which the British gathered whatever weapons were available in a vast country like India. No individual was to own any weapon. Licensed arms dealers were established who could sell certain types of guns used for *shikar* (hunting). The gun owner had to keep a record of the number of bullets used and where. Thus, the revolutionaries had no other option but to raid or snatch weapons from armed police, or as happened in the Chittagong raid of the armoury.

When Bhagat Singh and his revolutionary colleagues decided to take revenge for the killing of Lala Lajpat Rai, they faced the problem of acquiring the right pistol. All they could get was what is known as a country pistol, made by the local hardware mechanics and sold clandestinely. The pistol did the job required of it. However, Bhagat Singh and his friends asked for a device that could be thrown into the well of the Assembly in Delhi to make enough noise without injuring any one. The British gave it the name of a crude bomb. The explosive used in making this device was the same as that for manufacturing bullets for the pistol that killed Saunders, the forensic team of the police was able to prove in the court. This led to the conviction of Bhagat Singh and his friends for murder of police officer Saunders.

Most historians have treated the Mutiny of 1857 as the first war of Indian Independence. They have either ignored or failed to recognise the role played by South India. The first war of Independence, if a mutiny is to be known as that, was not in 1857 but in 1806 at Vellore in South India. As was the case in 1857, here too something similar was being forced both on Hindu and Muslim sepoys on their dress and religious practices. Both Hindu and Muslim sepoys were told of other rules they must follow. Hindu sepoys were told that they could not have religious puja signs on their forehead. Muslim sepoys were told to cut their beards. The sepoys were also expected to give up their turbans. In addition to these grievances, the mutiny was also said to have been instigated by Tipu's family who were living in the Palace in the Fort Vellore as East India Company's pensioners. However, when the time came to support the mutineers, Tipu's sons, unlike the Mughul Emperor Bahadur Shah Zafar in 1857, failed them and did not come out to support and lead them.

With the refusal of both the Hindu and Muslim sepoys to carry out the new instructions, the sepoys went on mutiny killing their officers in the Vellore Fort on 10 July 1806. Over two hundred British troops and officers were killed. The British rushed cavalry from Arcot and over 300 mutineers were killed. With further support from Madras now known as Chennai, the British were able to quell the mutiny.

Yet another mutiny was in Barrackpore in Bengal in November 1824 when the sepoys protested against the negligence in supplies, disrespect to their religious and cultural customs. This mutiny was also crushed with heavy casualties suffered by both sides.

As I began to look into the names of revolutionaries who rose against the foreign rule of India, names such as Sohan

Singh Bakhna, Bhagwan Singh, Har Dayal, Kartar Singh Saroba and others kept cropping up. Also in my mind's eye came names like Surya Sen, Ganesh Ghosh, Ambika Chakrobarty, Tripura Sen, Subodh Roy and many more. It is also worth remembering that Sardar Ajit Singh, uncle of Bhagat Singh was arrested by the British and sent to jail in far off Mandalay in Burma. He had led an agitation of the farmers against two new laws against the farmers. The agitation became popular as *Pagri Sambhal Jatta* calling upon the farmers to protect their lands and reputation.

The names and parties mentioned above are few and as I sat down to research and write this book, so many more came up which you as a reader will find in this book. As against such active nationalists, the Indian National Congress of which Allan Octavian Hume was the founder, in my humble view was more of a club of retiring civil servants and emerging Indian elite. It is interesting to note that Hume came to India in 1849 as a civil servant and was posted in Etawah and had seen and survived the Mutiny of 1857. He had to flee Etawah and take refuge at Agra Fort.

The main objective of Hume via the Indian National Congress was to achieve Indian Home Rule and avoid repetition of any uprising. His explanation on Home Rule meant that those Englishmen resident in India together with the emerging educated Indian elite should be responsible for running the country's Government rather than those who were sent from London. India would have thus become a dominion of the British Empire like some others. And they meant to achieve all this through negotiations with the British rulers. These negotiations were hardly leading anywhere. The attitude of the British rulers was not to trust Hume and his colleagues at the Indian National Congress.

It is interesting that in 1887, Hume made an unequivocal statement that he considered himself to be the native of India yet when the time came, he returned to England.

Failing to see the British or Londoners who those days came to rule India grant such a home rule, Hume himself decided to go back to England in 1890. Why did he do so, if he considered himself an Indian, or as he said, native of India?

Indian National Congress continued as it was and in course of time among those who became its president were three more retiring Englishmen as well. All this was to change altogether as Mohandas Karamchand Gandhi returned to India from South Africa. Bal Gangadhar Tilak introduced him to the Indian National Congress with a hope that he would use his experience in fighting apartheid in South Africa to help Congress achieve the objective of home rule. While Gandhi agreed with the objective he was convinced the approach then being made to achieve the goal was not going to lead to success.

As Gandhi moved into the Indian National Congress, he introduced non-cooperation and peaceful satyagraha as tools to push their demand for Dominion Status. This was not agreeable to many of the old timers including Mohammed Ali Jinnah. He felt that Gandhi's methods would cause Independent India serious problems. He felt the methods if used against the independent government in furtherance of any demands could lead to law and order issues among others.

This book aims to bring out a brief history, the sacrifices and fight of those countless freedom fighters who pushed ahead fearlessly for the nation right from the day Prithviraj Chauhan lost Delhi. In deciding on the subject of this book, I was influenced by the study of so many unreported struggles and sacrifices made in the cause. I was also influenced by the loot that I saw in Britain during my long stay there and wherever I travelled. I was told that in Britain there were two warehouses of V & A museum where crates of artifacts from India had not even been opened even as late as 1995.

I must thank my good friends Ralph De Souza of Goa and Harinder Maan of London who have been instrumental in convincing me to work on this subject. Ralph helped me with research on Goa. Harinder has done a lot of research for me at the British Library now housing papers of the India Office of the former Secretary of State for India. He convinced me through our long chats and with books that I had not heard of earlier. I hope this book will help in remembering the unsung heroes of India.

Prem Prakash
New Delhi
24 February 2025

Chapter 1

BHARAT: EARLY INDIA, ALEXANDER, ARRIVAL OF MUSLIMS

India, an ancient land with history dating back to five thousand and more years was known as Bharat. Elsewhere in the world, people were still moving around, searching for areas to settle down, whereas the residents of Bharat were already well ensconced in their homes. Earliest known movement into India was of Aryans. Even as the rishis penned the Vedas, a vedic civilisation flourished. Interestingly, in Kabul is a hill still known as *Rish Koh*, the mountain of rishis.

While historians contend that the epic *Mahabharata* is mythical, some recent excavations show it may have existed. The city of Delhi was then known as Indraprastha.

The earliest records of the well-settled powerful Indian empire was that of Chandragupta Maurya. However, Delhi was not recorded as the capital city. The Mauryan empire was set up following an attack on India by Alexander. It was based further north in areas which included Pakistan and Afghanistan.

Alexander's attack on India, then known as Bharat, was the first recorded one by any foreign power in 326 BC. Darius is said to have attacked Bharat earlier, but there is no record available about the area that he is supposed to have struck, save for an inscription.

Alexander infiltrated Bharat from the area now known as Afghanistan, marching ahead towards the heartland with success. He had reached river Jhelum where he fought what is known as the Battle of Hydaspes against King Porus, who lost his son in the conflagaration. Alexander had suffered such heavy casualties that at one stage it seemed that he was going to be defeated.

After the battle, Alexander came to an agreement with King Porus leaving him as head of his kingdom. At this stage, Alexander's troops refused to go further. They had come a long way, suffered heavy casualties in the battle with Porus and had heard of stronger rulers ahead, such as the Nanda dynasty. As Alexander decided to turn back, he left behind Greek governors to rule over various areas captured by him in North India.

Chandragupta carried out major battles against the Greek governors to throw them out of India and free the areas captured by Alexander. He eventually succeeded in overpowering all of them. His biggest battle was against Seleucus Nicator. Defeating him, he married his daughter. No one from Greece came to their rescue. The great warrior that he was, Chandragupta then proceeded with attacking other kingdoms to create a unified country of Bharat. There is, however, no record of his moving towards South India. The capital of the Mauryan empire was Patliputra near today's city of Patna.

Chandragupta's fight against Alexander's governors with guidance from his advisor Chanakya could well be said to have been the first fight for independence by throwing out a foreign occupant from India. Chanakya's treatise of statecraft is the earliest known document in the world on how to run a government. Chandragupta ran his state on those principles, which was followed by others of his dynasty.

Emperor Ashoka followed in Chandragupta's footsteps and spread the empire to cover most of India. Significantly, the emperors of India in those days never displayed their splendour, wealth or power. In fact, Chanakya's treatise on state influenced the emperors to be humble.

Emperor Ashoka after the huge battle of Kalinga, which saw thousands killed from each side, embraced Buddhism and spread the message of peace across the land of Bharat. He has left the record of his empire and messages on several inscriptions on rocks and pillars. These are found in most parts of India. There is an Ashoka Pillar at the Feroze Shah Kotla in Delhi. Interestingly these pillars came to light when a British officer found one as being used as a road roller.

Ashoka and those who followed him sent monks and emissaries to South East Asian countries, China and Japan to spread the message of peace by Buddha. Emperor Kanishka is said to have sent monks to China. As a result, most of these countries adopted Buddhism as a religion, the only exception being the tiny island of Bali which still has 95 per cent Hindu population.

Some other islands notably Sumatra have a sprinkling of Hindus living there. The world's biggest Hindu temple is in Sumatra. Islam came later in some of these countries with the end of the strong Hindu empire in India. Even though Indonesia is an Islamic country, its people have not given up their attachment to Hindu culture.

India continued to prosper with stability and peace established by the Mauryan empire. Following the collapse of dynastic families, India came to be ruled by various kings.

Muhammed Ghori attacked Punjab in 1186 AD. Delhi was ruled by Prithviraj Chauhan. His kingdom covered most parts of today's North India.

In the first battle against Ghori in 1191 AD, Prithviraj defeated him but instead of executing his enemy, he asked him to go back to his country, warning him not to dare to come back. However, Prithviraj was betrayed by one of the kingdoms ruled by Jaichand. Back then there was the problem of lack of unity among Hindu rulers. In the second battle of Tarain, Prithviraj was defeated and taken prisoner to Ghori where he was killed. His *samadhi* is still said to be there.

The defeat of Prithviraj brought the first Muslim ruler to Delhi. Qutubuddin Aibak was left behind to rule by Ghori who did not wish to stay back in India. Qutubuddin Aibak was Ghori's slave, who rose by the dint of his service in the ranks. The word spread not just in Ghor but surrounding countries of the amount of gold and other riches that Ghori had taken from India. India now became a target for all the countries of South Asia to loot. To Muslim rulers, Bharat was now known as Hindustan—land of the Hindus.

Following the success of Ghori, more invasions began into India, mostly for loot. Muslim invaders largely from Afghanistan, once a part of the land of Bharat, would invade, loot and go away. Many settled down making India their home. They hardly made any effort to convert the local population to Islam. History is also witness to the fact that when Afghanistan was a Hindu country, its kings had bravely defeated seven invasions by Islamic Turkic armies who would come to convert.

During my several visits to Afghanistan and meeting historians there, I learned that most of the conversions that happened in Hindu Afghanistan were voluntary, casteism being responsible for it. Attacked by the Arabs, at the end of each day's battle, the soldiers of the invading Muslim army would be seen sitting together and eating together from one plate. On this side Afghan soldiers would be sitting in different areas and having their food with their own caste groups. When the soldiers would return home as victors after defeating the invading Arabs, they would suffer caste discrimination again instead of being honoured for victory. It was this discrimination that led to many Afghan Hindus converting to Islam.

In later invasions when compromise would take place between the invading army and the defenders, the elder brother, *lala*, would remain Hindu while the rest of the family converted to Islam. Thus, the relations in Afghanistan in happier times between Muslims, Hindus and Sikhs were brotherly.

In 1526, the founder of the Mughal dynasty in India, Babur of Ferghana, decided to attack India for all its riches. He had heard that the Sultanate of Ibrahim Lodi in Delhi was crumbling. And that the country was very rich. Crossing Khyber Pass, Babur marched towards Delhi indulging in loot and mayhem on the way. He hardly met resistance in his march towards Delhi.

Ibrahim Lodi, hearing of Babur's march towards Delhi decided to stop him before he reached Delhi. Babur came face to face with the forces of Ibrahim Lodi at Panipat. Then followed what is known as the first Battle of Panipat between the two armies. Ibrahim Lodi had a much larger force than Babur. But Babur used better tactics and defeated Lodi who was killed during the battle. Victorious Babur marched to Delhi. Thus was established Mughal rule over Delhi and North India.

The last challenge to the establishment of Mughal rule came from Rajput King Rana Sanga who rightly considered Babur to be a foreign ruler as much as Ibrahim Lodi whose tribe came from Afghanistan. History is silent about why Rajput rulers had accepted the establishment of foreign rulers in Delhi from Qutubuddin Aibak onwards. The armies of Rana Sanga and Babur clashed at Khanwa on 17 March 1527.

Even as Rana Sanga had superior forces, he was betrayed by one of his own men, Silhadi, who disclosed the tactics of Rana Sanga to the invader. Babur, thus, succeeded in meeting this challenge to his drive for establishment of Mughal rule. Interestingly, both Prithiviraj Chauhan and Rana Sanga were betrayed by traitors.

During his march towards Delhi, Babur had adopted cruel methods against the civilian population. He used violence to force many to convert to Islam. Earlier Lodi had adopted torture and violence against Hindus to forcibly convert them. This is well recorded in the Sikh literature of the period.

Guru Nanak Dev witnessed the violence and killings by Babur and his army. He saw the plundering and burning of Lahore by Babur and his men. Women were raped and many taken away. He described the plight of people in the face of atrocities by Babur, on both Hindus and Muslims, on women and children, in four hymns in *Guru Granth Sahib*. When read in English, one of the hymns of Guru Nanak describes Babur as the 'messenger of death.'

The beginnings of how a rich and prosperous India began to suffer poverty in its villages, can be seen from the fall of Prithviraj Chauhan. Ghori after defeating Prithviraj not only took everything away from his treasury, but also looted the people in areas where he passed through, and many were killed. His army looted as much as they could. Later these rulers, by imposing heavy taxes on the farmers, not only reduced them to poverty but impacted upon their will to work hard on the land.

Babur too looted the treasury of Ibrahim Lodi and also the people of Delhi. Not satisfied with looting the people, Babur's army forcibly converted many to Islam. Babur then lay claim to all the land of the areas he had captured; he gave away farm lands to those who had given up their Hindu faith and accepted Islam. It is notable that from Guru Nanak Dev onwards, it was the Sikh gurus who resisted the atrocities of Mughal rulers and tried to advise them to be fair to the people.

Though Babur fought and won he did not want to stay in India. In *Baburnama* (book recording his achievements), he describes his dislike for the people of India and decided to go back asking his son Humayun to rule. Carrying the loot and slaves, he began his journey to Samarkand. When he reached Kabul, he found that both Samarkand and Ferghana had been captured by his enemies. He realised that he had no chance of being able to defeat them if he carried on his journey further.

In his victory over Ibrahim Lodi of Delhi, Babur had lost his own kingdom and was now stuck in Kabul. He decided to stay there. He lies buried in Kabul at *Bagh-e-Babu* (garden of Babur).

During one of my trips to Kabul, I visited this modest garden. There lay the man who had committed atrocities and torture on the people of India. He was the man responsible for establishing the Mughal dynasty over India. Babur's victory highlighted a major weakness of India—the country was ruled by one too many maharajahs who were usually at each other's throat. If they had faced the foreign aggressor unitedly, India could never have fallen. It began with Prithviraj Chauhan who fought Ghori on his own strength. The Mughal dynasty in India stayed for long, till it was ousted by the British.

Humayun, the son of Babur, followed him in December 1530. He was 22 years old when he assumed charge of Mughal territories in Agra. Humayun's reign again saw atrocities committed on the population. Humayun was challenged by Sher Shah Suri who defeated him in the battle of Kannauj in 1540. Humayun took refuge in Persia and fifteen years and later with support from the ruler of Persia, Shah Tahmasp, he was able to regain his territories. That established the Mughal rule now largely influenced by the Persian Court.

Later Humayun with the help of the Persian army was able to win back Kabul and Kandahar. Persian language was adopted by the Mughals and continued till the end of the Mughal Empire. Not just Persian language, but Persian art and culture too were adopted by the Mughals. Once in power again from June 1555, Humayun expanded the area under his control. The Old Fort (Purana Qila) of Delhi was his base. Fond as he was of reading, he built a library in the fort. It still exists there. Coming down, he fell on the steep stone steps. He could not recover from the injuries and died on 27 January 1556.

Akbar, the third Mughal ruler who was only 13 years old at the time of his succession, was campaigning in Kabul with his guardian Bairam Khan. Delhi had in the meanwhile been captured by Samrat Hem Chandra Vikramaditya from Rewari. He was popularly known as Hemu and was keen to throw the Mughals out of India. He had earlier also captured large areas of North India. So as to take back Delhi, Akbar marched towards the city with Bairam Khan. The two armies fought at Panipat and Bairam Khan succeeded in defeating

Hemu's forces. Delhi was now back in the hands of Mughal King Akbar.

To make the Mughal rule acceptable to the Hindus, Akbar adopted a secular approach in dealing with the people of India. Forced conversions were stopped. The Mughals were now making this land their home. Akbar began using many Hindus in the day-to-day administration of the city of Delhi. His court had many Hindus appointed to senior positions, much to the dislike of the mullahs.

To deal with the hostility that the Mughals were facing from Rajputs, Akbar approached the ruler of Jaipur for a hand of friendship. To consolidate that, he proposed to marry Princess Jodha Bai. Despite opposition from mullahs and other Muslim leaders in his court Akbar went ahead. Jodha Bai was now the Queen Empress of India. This precedent set by Akbar was followed by several other senior Muslim courtiers of Akbar.

Rajput rulers of most other Rajputana kingdoms did not accept the rule of Akbar. When fighting against the Mewar kingdom, Akbar described the war as a *jihad* to teach infidels a lesson. When Akbar attacked, the ruler of Mewar moved to Udaipur while he placed Chittor under the command of his trusted General Jaimal with a strong army and cavalry as also some artillery. Akbar's forces besieged Chittor fort, but could not make any headway in capturing the fort. The siege lasted for almost of two months. It was then that the Mughal forces reached near the walls of the fort. Mughal artillery made some breaches. Rajputs were repairing the breaches at night when Jaimal who was supervising the repairs was killed. The death of their commander Jaimal sent shock waves among the defenders.

That night, Rajput ladies inside the fort killed themselves

by self-immolation or a *jauhar* ceremony as it was known to protect their honour from Mughal Muslim forces. Mughals had suffered heavy casualties in the long drawn battle to capture Chittor on 23 February 1568. After capturing the fort, Akbar is said to have ordered a complete massacre of people inside the fort. Over 30,000 civilians were killed. Surviving women and children were taken as slaves. Akbar termed his victory as Islam finishing infidels. This victory and what followed remains a black spot on Akbar's claims of his government's secular policy.

Akbar did manage to destroy Chittor, but at a heavy loss of life for his army as also of those opposing him, the Mewar forces. He could not, however, secure the allegiance of the Mewar ruler despite his victory at Chittor. Udaipur remained opposed to him and independent of him, as also opposed to those Rajput kings who supported Akbar.

Akbar was succeeded by Saleem, his son from Jodha Bai who gave himself the title and name of Jehangir. He was in many ways a debauch who first fell for a courtesan and later married Mehr-un-Nissa giving her the title of Nur Jahan. She became extremely powerful and virtually ran the affairs of the State. Jehangir's rule is known for two major events, one, he granted permission to the East India Company to set up shop when Thomas Roe appeared in his court. This one favour given by Jehangir to Thomas Roe was to lead to colonial rule of the British over India. The British had failed to get any permission or make headway during Emperor Akbar's rule.

Thomas Roe's presentation to Jehangir had met with success when on being asked the strength of his king, Thomas Roe replied that his king was the lord of the seas. The Mughals had neglected creating a navy to defend the coast of India. Thus, whenever a trading ship would leave

Surat, on the West Coast of India, Portuguese naval ships would stop it mid-sea, collect a hefty charge and then allow it to proceed. The Portuguese were based in Goa close to Surat and had a strong navy and ground force including cavalry.

Feeling assured that he could get help from the English King in dealing with the Portuguese navy, while granting permission to English merchants to set shop in India, Jehangir in his letter to British King James I assured him that British merchants could take residence in whichever city of his empire they desired. They were assured full protection. Jehangir also allowed the merchants to bring in goods from their country.

With patronage of both the Mughal emperor and British king, the East India Company began to flourish. Why Mughal rulers allowed the company to raise its own army to protect its assets is a puzzle! In due course, this army kept expanding with the growth of trading in India. Following Jehangir, the Mughal Emperor Shah Jahan extended his patronage to the company and continued with the same policies.

Thomas Roe was awe struck by the grandeur of the Mughal court and the show of wealth there. Roe was also taken in by the quality of buildings that Mughals had built in Agra and the palace was described by him as a 'wonder of the world.'

He also writes in his memoirs about the Mughal king being an embodiment of absolute power but somehow wanting to show himself as benign and kind to his people. The Mughal king was always known as *Shah-en-shah*, a king of kings whose domains and provinces were run in his name by the imperial governors nominated by him. Further down in the administration were *jagirdars* and *zamindars* who lorded over the villagers reducing them to poverty while collecting taxes. Corruption was rampant in the administration.

The second major incident of Jehangir's rule was when he ordered the torture and killing of the fifth Sikh Guru Arjan Dev. It was the Sikh Gurus who were trying to protect the people from Mughal atrocities. Guru Arjan Dev was killed on a frivolous complaint by mullahs that the *Quran* was being quoted by the Sikh Guru. Most Hindu kings were loyal to the Mughal Emperor, something achieved by Akbar. Jehangir ordered the arrest and torture of Guru Arjan Dev without conducting his own inquiry but on baseless charges of him defaming Islam made by his court mullahs.

Jehangir was succeeded to the Mughal throne by Shah Jahan—King of the World. He built the Red Fort in Delhi on the banks of river Jumna. The huge fort with his palace inside was yet another show of grandeur. The king got built Juma Masjid, the world's greatest mosque in its time outside and away from the fort. The city of Delhi was renamed Shahjahanabad. A canal used to run through Chandni Chowk, the heart and high street of the city. Shah Jahan also built the Taj Mahal in Agra, one of the wonders of the world.

Aurangzeb came to power in 1658 after a coup against his father Shah Jahan whom he held in Agra Fort. Though he expanded the Mughal Empire, Aurangzeb was an extreme Islamist though he would say that he was only a devout Muslim. He imposed a tax, *jizya*, on the Hindus. They were exempted from the tax if they converted to Islam.

When requested by the ninth Sikh Guru Tegh Bahadur to stop his atrocities on Kashmiri Pundits, Aurangzeb ordered that the Sikh Guru and his senior disciples Bhai Mati Das, Bhai Sati Das and Bhai Dayala convert to Islam. On their refusal, the disciples were tortured in the most inhuman and merciless manner in front of the guru and then were executed.

Then came the turn of Guru Tegh Bahadur to be a martyr. Gurdwara Sis Ganj stands in Chandni Chowk, where the Guru Sahib was martyred. What used to be Mughal *kotwali* from where the then head of the Mughal police inflicted torture is also now part of the Gurdwara.

Guru Gobind Singh succeeded his father Guru Tegh Bahadur. His fight against the atrocities of Mughal rulers continued. Facing attack by Aurangzeb's forces, Guru Gobind Singh had to leave Anandpur Sahib. While retreating, he got separated from his two young sons Baba Fateh Singh, aged six, and Baba Zorawar Singh, aged nine. They were captured by Wazir Khan, the Mughal Governor of Sirhind. He asked them to convert to Islam. On their refusal to convert, Wazir Khan had them buried alive into a wall. Their two elder brothers Sahibzada Ajit Singh and Jujhar Singh lost their lives in the battle of Chamkaur against the Mughal army.

All these atrocities and the most horrible killing of Guru Tegh Bahadur and his close disciples by the Mughal Emperor Aurangzeb had shocked the people and made Mughal rule a hated one. With Aurangzeb continuing to force conversion of the populace to Islam, Guru Gobind Singh came to the conclusion that peaceful nonviolent negotiations with the emperor were not leading anywhere. He announced the birth of the order of Khalsa on Baisakhi day in 1699. The Khalsa was to be the most purified Sikh, one who could be a soldier when the situation demanded.

Wherever the Mughal soldiers would commit brutality, a Khalsa would emerge as a guerrilla fighter and inflict casualties upon the Mughal soldiers and disappear, causing panic and chaos among the Mughal army. Khalsas thus began taking a toll on the Mughal army. It had shaken the Mughal administration in Punjab and North India. Aurangzeb was away from Delhi fighting the Marathas in Western India.

In the course of time, with the successes of Khalsa, Sikh kingdoms known as *Misls* appeared in Punjab. Mughal might was being beaten. Then rose Maharaja Ranjit Singh whose investiture on 12 April 1801 at Lahore Fort of the Mughals saw the Mughal Empire on its last legs in Punjab and North.

Meanwhile, the East India Company was facing tough competition from the Dutch and Portuguese in other parts of Asia in the business of spices. The company decided to make India their strong base and set up the first factory to process spices at Surat. Taking note of the presence of the Portuguese in nearby Goa, the East India Company set up its next factory at Madras (today's Chennai).

Apart from spices, the other export from India was textiles. India's fine textiles were famous the world over. Exports of fine textiles from India, which were eagerly awaited by the British royalty and the Nobles made the company still more prosperous. The British King had also allowed the East India Company not only to maintain its own army, which had been also allowed by the Mughal emperor, but to issue its own coins. The British King also allowed the company in its charter to annex areas. The company had thus become a political entity. But the company avoided any dispute with the Mughal empire as it was powerful and strong till the end of Aurangzeb's rule.

The East India Company had established itself in Surat, but with the Portuguese so close in Goa, it decided to move towards South India. The company established its second factory in 1639 in Madras (Chennai), making it capable of exporting very fine textiles including silk from South India. Madras was a great centre of South India's finest silks and other textiles, sought the world over. Along with its trading post in Madras, the company also built Fort St George. The fort was like a self-contained city. Within the fort were residences of the British families, markets and offices. The fort was large and even today houses Tamil Nadu government's offices apart from the Assembly.

The company's business flourished in Madras. It expanded its operations to Calcutta (today's Kolkata) buying a large chunk of land on the banks of river Hooghly and building for itself a huge fort called Fort William, where the factory and residences were set up. The Mughal emperor took no objection. This fort is still in use, now by the Government of India. It houses the Indian Army's Eastern Command headquarters.

This fort is historic. Within it is the infamous tiny prison where during the Mutiny of 1857, over a hundred British prisoners were kept by the mutineers. Many of them died due to unbearable humidity and heat. It is known as the 'black hole' of Calcutta.

Towards the end of Aurangzeb's rule, the Mughal empire began to show signs of withering with the emperor staying away from Delhi for so long in his battles. There was no one in Delhi who could deal with the rebellious situation in Punjab and other parts. With a tax on non-Muslim population, the loyalty of people towards the Mughals vanished. Akbar's success in winning the local population's heart was gone. During this period, the East India Company remained aloof watching with glee the steady downfall of the Mughal Empire. The company itself was expanding all over India and in areas controlled by the Mughals taking full advantage of the corruption in the Mughal administration.

Aurangzeb died on 3 March 1707, aged eighty-eight. He will be remembered as a most unpopular Mughal king known for his brutality towards Hindus and forcibly trying to spread Islam in India. He also failed to nominate any successor to his throne. He had three sons and as had been usual among the Mughals, a war of succession followed among them. Aurangzeb, no doubt expanded his empire, but left it in utter chaos.

Chaos did follow after Aurangzeb's death. First his three sons started fighting each other to grab the Mughal throne. As this fighting continued, governors of provinces of the Mughal empire began to declare themselves independent of Delhi and nawabs of the province under them. No money collected as taxes was now reaching Delhi from these governors of the provinces. This resulted in weakening of the emperor in Delhi.

Finally, Aurangzeb's second son Muazzam succeeded and gave himself the title of Bahadur Shah. He tried immediately to fight and defeat all those who had declared themselves independent of the emperor's rule. Punjab was already under control of Sikhs led by Banda Bahadur. In his next move, Banda Bahadur started to march towards Delhi, slowly taking the areas on the way. Sikhs also brought an end to the Mughal rule over the holy city of Amritsar. In the fighting that followed, the Mughals were unable to defeat Banda Bahadur.

Bahadur Shah despite his all out efforts both by negotiations and fighting had failed to bring the Mughal empire back to its glory. He died in Lahore on 28 February 1712. He was succeeded by his son Jahandar Shah. But the Mughal empire was now as good as gone.

This period of chaos and confusion gave a free hand to the East India Company to expand its activities and strengthen its army. In negotiations with the governors and local kings, the company always seemed to have an upper hand in securing the facilities it wanted. This was due to the rising strength of its army. The rise of the East India Company as a strong political entity had begun.

Chapter 2

A STATE IN THE GUISE OF A MERCHANT

As predicted by him on his deathbed, Aurangzeb's death was followed by chaos in India. It was now too late for Aurangzeb to make amends for the wrongs done to his subjects during his rule, influenced by mullahs and maulvis in their urge to forcibly convert non-Muslims to Islam. The pernicious *jazia* or tax on being Hindu should never have been imposed by Aurangzeb in the first place, commentators say.

Throughout the period that Aurangzeb was fighting his battles around India, the East India Company remained aloof, only because it had received a thorough bashing by Aurangzeb, who had built a small navy to protect the Indian pilgrims. The company's naval vessels which had run into a confrontation with Aurangzeb's navy in Bengal were defeated. Aurangzeb ordered confiscation of the company assets and arrest of its men. Envoys sent by the company apologised to Aurangzeb and prostrated before him in his court. The emperor accepted the apology but imposed a heavy penalty on the company.

In his eighty-eight years long life, Aurangzeb spent most of his time as emperor, fighting, either other kingdoms around the country or his own Hindu subjects, pressurising them to convert to Islam. All the good work that emperor Akbar had done during his lifetime in trying to win the confidence of Hindu kings and the population was undone. By the time Aurangzeb realised the grave harm he had done to the Mughal Empire, it was too late to take any corrective action. The hatred created by him between Hindus and Muslims continued after his death.

He did not realise how his domains were slipping out as he remained away from the capital. He was fighting in Ahmednagar while in the north, Punjab was slipping out of the control of Mughals. In the west, the Marathas were a huge challenge to him. During his absence from Delhi, governors and nobles were working as though they were not answerable to the emperor. Corruption always present in the Mughal administration became worse, affecting state revenues.

Aurangzeb's successor Bahadur Shah failed to assert his authority on the provinces and nobles. The East India Company began to negotiate its expansion plans with the local Mughal governors, ignoring the emperor.

As the Mughal emperor weakened, it made India once again an attractive target for forces from the north. News had spread across Central Asia and Persia of the poor state of Mughal rule in India. Nadir Shah from Iran grabbed the opportunity to attack India and loot riches of the Mughals from Delhi. He started his march towards Punjab with a large force.

Crossing the river Indus, he faced the Mughal army led by Mohammed Shah at Karnal, some 80 miles from Delhi. In the battle that followed, the Mughal Army lost. Nadir Shah now moved to Delhi where the people resented the presence of his troops on the streets. Some clashes with Nadir Shah's men with local people were reported. This led to the Iranian invader ordering loot and massacre of the people of Delhi. In the long history of this great city, never before had such indiscriminate killing been seen.

In the face of such a brutal attack by the Persian ruler on unarmed civilian residents of Delhi, Muslims also started killing their women and children just as was being done by Hindus to save them from being abused by the soldiers of Nadir Shah. The streets of Delhi were covered with dead bodies and blood in the slaughter by Nadir Shah. The Mughal emperor Mohammed Shah was forced to beg for mercy from Nadir Shah for his people. He had to wait for at least two hours or more before Nadir Shah ordered an end to the mayhem in Delhi.

After looting the people of Delhi, Nadir Shah started emptying the rich treasury of the Mughal Empire, also grabbing as much as he could from the nobles of the Moghul Court. The famous Peacock throne of the Mughal emperors studded with diamonds and precious stones was taken away by Nadir Shah as part of the loot. This throne is displayed at the Tehran Museum of Royal Jewelry and Artifacts. Nadir Shah also collected the famous Koh-i-Noor diamond and all other crown jewels. He did not leave the nobles of the court alone. He collected all their riches and their jewellery.

The world's richest treasury had been emptied by Nadir Shah. The Koh-i-Noor diamond has had a long history of going into the hands of various emperors. Finally it reached the British in the 19th century from the Sikh Empire. They decided to cut the big diamond into two. The two piece Koh-i-Noor is mounted on the crowns of the British King and the Queen. It can be seen at the Tower of London along with other delicate and expensive jewellery collected from India.

Nadir Shah also annexed the Empire's territory on the

eastern side of the river Indus. The loss of these territories as also Kabul created serious problems for the defence of the country, with forward positions gone. The famed and powerful Mughal empire had now been weakened militarily with its riches gone. But the Mughal emperor, his family and the nobles had still managed to save a fair amount of their wealth that Nadir Shah could not find.

The army that the company had built by then without any control by the Mughals came very handy during these negotiations. The company was negotiating new agreements with the nobles and governors from a position of being equal if not stronger for the kind of army that the company had raised under English officers. This period following Aurangzeb's death saw the company as a strong new political entity, negotiating its expansion. Whenever it failed to get the desired terms, it would enforce those with the force of its army, annexing areas to bring them under its rule. This was the beginning of the colonisation of India by the East India Company.

As the company expanded its operations in India, it was now using the powers granted to it by King Charles II to mint its own money in areas that it controlled, beginning to administer the areas on civil and criminal issues. It was the first time that a company had emerged as a ruler in parts of India.

The company soon had 39 factories in India and this meant a still bigger army as each factory had its own unit. India's biggest earnings used to be from the export of fine cloth and silk that were much sought after by British Royalty and other nobles. Export of spices from India too was big. In return, India was getting gold and silver from abroad. The East India Company instead of exporting made efforts to import cloth from England but failed as it was not of comparable quality. However, that cloth began to be used for dressing up horses and elephants.

Interestingly, during the reign of Emperor Akbar, the English had failed to get permission to set shop in India. Portuguese Jesuits had great access to the emperor as he looked for a religion that would unite all his people and which he called *Deen-e-Ilahi* (Religion of the God). These Portuguese Jesuits, avoiding any conflict with Mughal rulers about Christianity, invariably managed to ensure that the English did not get the emperor's permission to do business in India. Akbar also had a Portuguese wife, named Maryam Zamani whose original name was Dona Maria Mascarenhas. Her sister Juliana was a doctor who looked after the ladies of the Mughal emperor's harem.

Lacking a fine administrative and management expertise led to the granting of such concessions by the Mughal rulers that proved very damaging to India and the Mughal rule in due course. The Mughal administration had no knowledge that the company had been authorised by its shareholders to wage war where necessary to protect its assets and was authorised by the British Crown to annex areas. The Mughal system of justice and administration all rested with one man, the emperor, though he had his ministers and other officials.

Away from the eyes of the Mughal rulers in Delhi, the company had begun to expand itself in South India starting from Madras. It did so when acquiring a three-mile-long piece of land along the coast from a local ruler Damodra Venkatadri Nayaka. Originally a fishing village, it had deep enough water for a port. The place was known as Madrasapatnam on the coast. The company built a large area like the structure Fort St George. It housed the company's factories, residences and offices apart from the quarters for its army.

The area is now a major part of the city of Chennai. The Tamil Nadu government has several of its offices there. Significantly, the first European power to set up its business and virtual colonies in India were the Portuguese and the French. They did not have to contend with the powerful Mughal army as they based themselves mainly in South India.

Madrasapattinam later known in abbreviated form as Madras was to become a major source of growth for the company. The areas around the huge Fort St George became a habitation also known as St George Town. This grew in due course to be the great city of Madras. The area owned by the company grew fast and by 1653, the British called it the Presidency of Madras. Today, Fort St George continues to be the most important part of the city of Chennai. It also houses the State's Assembly buildings.

It was from the Presidency of Madras that the East India Company began its expansion into other areas. First the company decided to move to Bengal and built a factory on the banks of river Hooghly in 1650. As they expanded in Bengal, the company administration there got similar powers to expand and do business as the Presidency of Fort St George. The company was avoiding any conflict with the Portuguese or the French, though the French had also moved towards Bengal to expand their business.

The company was doing extremely good business, exporting fine textiles, silks, spices from India to Britain and elsewhere. Those selling the goods to the company wanted payment in gold or silver, though the company had minted its own coins with these metals.

Mughal India was very rich and accounted for 25 per cent of the world's GDP during the time. India was rich even during the Hindu period as well. The company's staff too made big money for themselves or what came to be known as 'loot' in England from their posting in India and working for the company.

When the company extended its operations to Bengal, it first bought a huge chunk of land, as it had done in Madras. In Calcutta its choice fell on the banks of river Hooghly. In 1690, the company bought three villages, one of which was named *Kalikata*, from a local landlord Subarna Roy Choudhury. Both in Madras and in Calcutta, these areas did not belong to any Indian kingdom considering the laws and practices of the time. As in Madras, so in Calcutta, the company built another huge fort, Fort William.

The company began developing the city as a Presidency as in Madras. Fort William is now a landmark in present-day Kolkata housing the Indian Army. One can safely say that the East India Company had not only become a huge commercial success, but as Edmund Burke described it in the British Parliament, it was now *'a state in the guise of a merchant.'*

As the East India Company grew in its stature, the Mughal empire in Delhi was beginning to lose control of its provinces. At Fort St George rose a figure—Robert Clive—who was to later change the presence of the British in India into rulers of large provinces. He had no time for appreciation of the beauty of India, but only wanted to make a fortune for himself. His rise in Madras was phenomenal—from an accounts clerk to a military commander who led his troops to victories. Born in 1725, Clive's moment of glory came when he saved Fort St George from an attack by the Nawab of Carnatic (Karnataka) Saadatullah Khan. He came back to Madras after the battle as a hero. He had made a fortune on the side for himself by 'loot' in victory against the nawab.

Clive is considered to be the father of British rule in India for he recognised the fact that the company was like a state and needed to control territories. Clive's military capabilities were earning him stronger positions and great opportunities for loot wherever he fought. Treasury and personal holdings of each of the rulers, whether in Tanjore or Arcot were big in gold and jewellery and Clive helped himself to as much as he could gather. Indians like any other people around the globe love gold and jewellery—perhaps Indians far more. Thus, the riches of Clive became huge.

In 1756, Siraj ud-Daulah became the Nawab of Bengal following the death of his grandfather Nawab Alivardi Khan. He was determined to secure back the territories of Bengal particularly Calcutta taken by the British. He worked hard to raise a large army, well-trained and well-armed. Beginning his campaign to oust the British, Siraj ud-Daula's forces clashed with the company's army at Kasimbazar. Defeating the company, he moved ahead towards Calcutta. By the end of June he succeeded and captured Fort William in Calcutta. His objective had been achieved. What followed in dealing with the prisoners was cruelty. The British forces too had been cruel with prisoners in the past. In the terrible heat of the month of June, the British prisoners were herded into a small cell measuring 18 ft by 14 ft. (However, various other studies say that there were only 64 prisoners of which 23 survived.)

Most of them died of heat and lack of water. The nawab was now a prime target of the company.

By the end of 1756, the nawab carried his campaign further and attacked the company's holdings at Fort Budge Budge and took it over. Fighting back, Clive who was leading the company's forces started making overtures to the commanders of Siraj ud-Daula's army. In particular, he contacted Mir Jafar who was leading the large force of the nawab. He told him that if he helped the company destroy Siraj ud-Daula he would be made governor of Bengal, Bihar and Orissa. Mir Jafar was already conspiring with other members of the Court of the Nawab to depose him in a coup. So when an offer came from Clive, Mir Jafar decided to betray and stab his ruler in the back.

Clive had used one Umichand, a merchant in Bengal as the middle man-between the company and Mir Jafar. Clive is said to have agreed to the amount demanded by Umichand for himself and Mir Jafar. Going ahead to prove the company's seriousness, Clive gave him an agreement, duly signed, guaranteeing payment. When the time came, the agreement could not be enforced by Umichand. He was denied the amount to be paid. Clive had Umichand sign two copies, one of which did not say if he was to be paid anything.

In the famous battle of Plassey that followed in June 1757 after Clive had made sure Mir Jafar was going to betray the nawab, he marched with his forces towards Murshidabad, where the Mughal governors for Bengal were based. He had covered the journey partly by boats on Hooghly. The month of June in Bengal is not only a very hot month but one that receives heavy monsoon rains. In the midst of such weather, Clive marched with his small force of British and other European mercenary soldiers, plus 2,000 sepoys to the battlefield of Plassey. Nawab Siraj ud-Daula had a force estimated by some at over 50,000 soldiers apart from horse cavalry and the support of artillery. Clive hesitated as he and other commanders of the company forces discussed the hopeless situation they were in. But Clive was confident that Mir Jafar would betray the nawab as agreed.

It rained very heavily before the battle. The company

forces were able to protect their ammunition from getting wet and becoming dud. Clive had prepared well for the battle. The nawab's forces had failed to protect their ammunition because Mir Jafar didn't do so, perhaps on purpose. The battle started on 23 June. Nawab Siraj ud-Daula found that the gunpowder and other ammunition was dud, as it had not been protected from the rain. The Nawab's forces could do little in the absence of ammunition. They failed to put up a fight as the company's forces mounted an artillery attack. Nawab Siraj ud-Daula was shocked when he saw Mir Jafar leaving the battlefield in retreat. Facing this situation, Siraj ud-Daula's forces fled from the battle field resulting in a huge victory for Clive.

Siraj ud-Daula escaped from the battlefield of Plassey taking with him whatever wealth he could from his rich treasury. He was captured later by Mir Jafar and executed. This victory of Clive at Plassey had a far reaching impact in establishing the supremacy of the East India Company in India.

Clive entered Murshidabad and cleaned up the nawab's big treasury which was filled with gold, silver coins, jewellery and other artefacts. Here was one more of India's treasures being looted and taken away to enrich a person—Clive—who was comparatively a nobody in his own country. The loot is said to have been so big that even members of the company's committee were presented with enough gold from the loot.

In the Battle of Plassey, twenty-two sepoys were killed and some wounded. No British soldier was killed or injured. This battle became the most glorious point in Clive's career. The East India Company was now ruling over a large part of India. Clive was beginning to be recognised as one person whose actions signalled the start of British rule of India.

The result of the Battle of Plassey gave a huge shock to the Mughal Emperor in Delhi, who was already weak.

Mir Qasim, was installed as Governor of Bengal by the East India Company. Soon his relations with Clive and the company got sullied. He was unhappy with the ways of the company in collecting taxes from the farmers—a contract for which had been given to the company by the Mughal Emperor. He decided to rebel against the company taking help from Shuja ud-Daula of Avadh with permission from Mughal ruler Shah Alam II to fight the company's forces.

The armies of the three—Mir Qasim, Shuja ud-Daula and Shah Alam came face to face against the forces of the East India Company at Buxar (today's Baksar) on 23 October 1764. Buxar is located in Bihar by the South of river Ganga. The strength of the combined forces is said to have been over 35,000 men versus East India Company's 10,000 plus. However, the lack of coordination in the combined force of the Mughals led to their defeat by the East India Company. This defeat led to the signing of a Treaty at Allahabad on 16 August 1765 between the Mughal Emperor Shah Alam II and Clive on behalf of the East India Company.

The result of this treaty was far reaching. Mir Qasim, the Nawab of Bengal was gone as the province was ceded to the East India Company. Sovereignty of Bengal was also surrendered to the British. The East India Company which had started its operations in Bengal when it bought a chunk of land on the banks of river Hooghly was now the master of Bengal as a result of the Treaty of Allahabad. As the British Crown had authorised the company to annex territories, Bengal came to be ruled by the British.

As for the Mughal Emperor, he was required by the Treaty of Allahabad to pay five million rupees to the company to cover their losses in the battle suffered by the company. Delhi was restored to Shah Alam II. But he lost the right to collect taxes of a huge area, over a hundred thousand acres, that he was forced to concede as part of the treaty. One wonders if Shah Alam or his advisors applied their mind to what they were signing. This treaty resulted in a huge loss of revenue no doubt, but the fact also was that the company had captured this large area of India smartly without a fight. The Mughal Emperor had already lost Punjab and virtually all of North India. Shah Alam was now reduced to a 'Shahenshah' Emperor in name, only. He was restricted to Delhi and inside the Red Fort.

The Treaty of Allahabad had virtually finished the Mughal empire. With the defeats in the battles of Buxar and Plassey, the country lost civil control. The law and order rights were gone in the large areas that were said to be under the nawabs and the Mughal rulers. Chaos had broken out. There was no administration in sight. Travelling from one place to another, became dangerous with dacoits running riot. At this stage, the company was more interested in collecting taxes to enrich its coffers than spend anything on the protection of the people.

The company failed to create any system of its own to collect land revenue, the right to which it got on signing the Treaty of Allahabad. It was simple and easy to use the jagirdars and zamindars to do so. That was how the Mughals and nawabs collected taxes via these middle men. The burden of huge payment of taxes was to be borne by the farmers who had already been reduced to extreme poverty. Collection of taxes was done in a most cruel manner irrespective of the fact whether there was a good or bad harvest. With large numbers of farmers unable to pay, their lands were confiscated by the zamindars and jagirdars. India's agriculture suffered heavily with land owners reduced to landless labourers.

When Clive returned home, he was perhaps the richest man in Europe, considering the amount of gold, silver and very expensive royal jewellery that he carried back, in addition to the artefacts from rich Indian palaces. Clive bought a house in the most fashionable part of London's Berkeley Square.

This author in 1957 had the pleasure of staying a night in that house. Clive bought a huge country estate as well and wanted to enter the House of Parliament with the power of his money. Those members who were already there in Parliament did not welcome him. For them he was not a nobleman, but just a commoner.

In all this, India was the biggest loser. Its large population in the villages had already been reduced to poverty. The economy of India depended upon agriculture, textiles, silk and spice. The company instead of restricting itself to trading and doing business for which it came to India—the business of exporting spices and fine textiles—had used its army to fight and loot the captured areas. It was those earnings from exports which in the past had made India the richest country in the world. Many Indian merchants too were hand in glove with the company in misdeeds. With huge expenditure on the army and the fights that it had indulged in, the company's accounts showed losses, ever since it turned into a 'state.'

However, when any company staff returned home, he would be carrying back gold and jewellery apart from cash not earned but looted.

After the battle of Buxar, the East India Company emerged stronger than the hundreds of Maharajas and Nawabs ruling over tiny parts of India. The Mughal Emperor from Delhi could no longer control them. The company as a 'state' now began expanding its rule in India by various means. In the first instance it would seek recognition of its sovereignty by various small kings, in return promising to defend their territories, receiving annual payment from the king for such assurances.

The larger states like the Nizam of Hyderabad or Gwalior signed treaties which imposed the company's sovereignty over them while placing their forces at the company's disposal. British residents were based in the capitals of these big states to keep an eye on them.

In South India, the company received tough opposition from Mysore, which had become a huge obstacle in its expansion all over the South. It had to fight four wars against Mysore, the first one in 1766. Hyder Ali was then the ruler of the state and a great warrior. The Nizam of Hyderabad had joined the company in this war against Hyder Ali but withdrew almost half way as the going was tough. In the end, it was Hyder Ali who virtually dictated the terms of peace between Mysore and the East India Company in 1769 returning to status quo as was before the war.

The second war against Hyder Ali was launched in 1780. Hyder Ali had received support of the Marathas in this fight against the company. All was going well for Hyder Ali when the company forces were joined by more forces from Calcutta. It was a long drawn war. As the war proceeded, tragedy hit Mysore in the death of Hyder Ali in 1782.

Hyder Ali was succeeded by his son Tipu Sultan. Tipu carried the fight further but was not making a big push against the company. The long drawn war came to an end with the signing of a Peace treaty by Tipu at Mangalore in 1784. The company was now finding its reputation as a strong power in India being hit for its failure to bring Mysore on its knees. The Treaty of 1784 had made both sides equal friends.

In 1790, the third war against Mysore was started by Lord Cornwallis, the Governor General, totally ignoring the Mangalore Treaty which had made the two rivals, friends. Cornwallis started a campaign against Tipu. As the fights proceeded between the two sides, Cornwallis having carried out two campaigns was not able to make much headway. His forces, led by Gen Meadows, were forced by Tipu to retreat to Bangalore. Tipu had trained his army well and had made advances in technology. He was able to have at his disposal, rockets that were not available to the British forces. These rockets had been developed by the youth of Mysore. Tipu also had a good relationship with the French. He was said to have been in touch with Napoleon who was in Egypt at that time.

Finally, Cornwallis decided to march his forces to Mysore's capital Seringapatam (now known as Srirangapatna in Karnataka) by the end of February 1792. Lord Cornwallis had at his disposal, forces of the East India Company, British Army forces and the forces of his allies, the Marathas and Nizam of Hyderabad. While Gen Meadows of the East India Company had been forced to retreat to Bangalore, Cornwallis upon reaching Seringapatam was able to lay a siege of the Fort of Seringapatam. Tipu's forces were not able to break the siege. Tipu was compelled to sign a Treaty of Peace because of which he was forced to give his two sons as hostage to Cornwallis. Tipu's sons with senior staff and several ladies of the Palace were taken by the British and kept in the Palace of Fort Vellore. The terms of the Treaty were virtually all against Tipu. He was forced to give up half his territories to the British.

Tipu Sultan following the defeat at Seringapatam was taking steps to strengthen himself to meet any future challenge. Tipu was aware of the emerging global politics. He had succeeded in making friends with the French and was trying to contact Napoleon who had wanted to capture Egypt. Mysore was highly advanced in technology and was seeing an industrial revolution of the kind which Britain had not seen by then. A life-size mechanical toy in Tipu's court showing a British officer being mauled by a tiger making all movements and noises is today displayed at the Victoria and Albert museum in London.

Lord Cornwallis and the East India Company saw that the alliance that Tipu had made with the French was a serious threat to them. The British now started the fourth war against Mysore in 1798. Tipu had an army of some 35,000 men. The combined force of East India Company, Nizam of Hyderabad, and Marathas was well over 60,000. Mysore was attacked from all four sides to repeat something like the siege of Seringapatam. This decisive war ended with Tipu Sultan being killed on 4 May 1799. However, the British and their allied forces had suffered heavy casualties. In the face of attacks by rockets, the British felt they were losing. When the fighting was seen as going against Tipu, he is said to have been advised by his allies the French to leave the field and escape to *fight another day*. Tipu refused, preferring to die while leading his soldiers.

The British had won the war against Mysore and annexed much of the territory. The city of Mysore and some more areas were restored to the Wadiyar royal family who had been in power before Hyder Ali became the de facto ruler, though he was the commander of the forces of the Wadiyars. With Tipu's defeat, the Wadiyars ruled the Kingdom of Mysore, accepting the sovereignty of the British.

All of South India was now in British control directly or via local kings loyal to them. British victory in Mysore was used by them to scuttle India's industrial revolution. The later

British regimes did not encourage any scientific thinking or development. It is only in the 20th century and more so after Independence that Mysore and Bangalore have flourished with science. In Bengal too, the British regimes destroyed the fine textile industry. There were allegations of fingers of several Indian weavers being cut to stop them from being able to work or train future weavers in the art of making fine textiles. All this was done to promote whatever was being made in Britain and to use India as a market to sell that.

There were grievances all over India against this strange ruler who could not be identified as people could do of the Mughal emperor in Delhi. These were strange people from across the seas who came to India to trade and secured permission from the Mughal Emperor Jehangir to have their own force to protect their assets. With passage of time and with the power of their new weapons, the East India Company was now in control of a large part of India.

People of India as also the sepoys of the company were aware of how this trading company had outsmarted the Mughal Emperor into surrendering large parts of his Empire in lieu of tax collection. This had all happened because of the corruption of the Mughal governors and the decay of the Mughal dynasty that started following the death of Aurangzeb. One could even say that it was the corruption among the staff and administration of Mughul emperors and their governors in provinces which gave a British trading company, a free hand in collecting taxes and brought British rule over large parts of India.

By the middle of the nineteenth century, a major part of India was ruled by the British and the company. The five hundred plus small kingdoms spread around the country were either protectorates of the company or respected its sovereignty over them. The exception to this area was the vast empire of Maharaja Ranjit Singh who ruled from Lahore. The strength of Maharaja Ranjit Singh and his modern army which had many French officers was a challenge to the British. But the great Maharaja avoided any fight with the British.

Ranjit Singh's Punjab Empire in the north was a major and powerful independent part of India. His people were happy and prosperous. Ranjit Singh had avoided fighting the East India Company. On 25 April 1809, he succeeded in concluding a Treaty in Amritsar with the East India Company. It was signed by Charles Metcalfe on behalf of the East India Company. This treaty fixed the boundary of the two. It was not a defence treaty which the British wanted but defined the areas under control of the two powers with river Sutlej dividing them.

Maharaja Ranjit Singh continued to strengthen his army by making it disciplined. He had several great generals who had expanded his rule all over the North going up to Tibet. The Maharaja is said to have asked for the map of India to be shown to him. On seeing large parts all over the map coloured in red, he asked what the red colour was for. When told that the red colour reflected the areas under the rule of the English, Maharaja Ranjit Singh is said to have commented, 'One day all of this will become red.'

Chapter 3

THE CALLOUS EAST INDIA COMPANY

Following the weakening of Mughal rule in Delhi after Aurangzeb's death, many of the provincial *subedars* or governors declared themselves free of Delhi. Smaller kingdoms also rose in the sub-continent without allegiance to the once powerful Mughal rulers of Delhi. Their number rose to over 500, big and small. Apart from provincial subedars trying to assert themselves as local lords, the ruling Mughal family failed to give a powerful successor to Aurangzeb, as no one had been groomed to succeed him. The Mughal army, once a dreaded force, suffered in the absence of any warrior emperor or commander to lead it. A large part of the army was with Aurangzeb in the Deccan area where he died. His long absence from Delhi had caused the administration to suffer. The area of the empire with victories by Aurangzeb had become too spread out and vast to be controlled.

Aurangzeb was succeeded by Alamgir in Delhi who became a victim of palace intrigues in the absence of any clear rule of succession. He was soon assassinated. His son Shah Alam succeeded him. He managed to restore some order in his Delhi Court. Shah Alam, without much preparation or intelligence reports on the strength of his enemies, decided to recapture the areas that had rebelled. He moved towards Bengal. The governor there upon declaring himself to be the ruler of the province had strengthened himself with all the money he was obliged to send to Delhi. With a weakened army, local nobles not joining him, and lack of artillery, Shah Alam failed to recapture Bengal.

Although divested of all political and military power, the Mughal ruler in Delhi was still the Emperor of India. But his writ no longer ran all over the country. Nadir Shah had dealt a death knell to the Mughal Empire. The respect for the empire was now low in the eyes of the competing European powers in India—UK, France and Portugal. They knew as did other kingdoms and governors of Mughal provinces that Delhi now had neither the resources nor the power to be able to raise a strong army and regain its past glory.

The policing system of the Mughal administration suffered badly with weakened government and poor resources. Chaotic conditions prevailed. People were not safe. Travel became a dangerous affair with dacoits roaming freely. Those who had taken over parts of India's territory from the Mughals were not bothered about the welfare of the people.

The East India Company had now emerged as a powerful political entity or state in the garb of a trading company. The army controlled by the company was now the strongest in India. The company had emerged by the end of the eighteenth century as a major ruling power in India. It now ruled over areas that it had won by its power such as those in South and those that it had managed to grab from the Mughal Emperor by acquiring *divani* (tax collection) rights. But the question still remained: who was responsible for India's law and order?

The relationship of the East India Company with the British Crown was a puzzle from the very beginning. It was

Sir Thomas Roe, envoy of the British King representing England, who had appeared in the Court of Emperor Jehangir to seek trading rights for the British. What followed was a joint stock company, the East India Company. The British government had earlier given the right to the company to annex Indian territory when necessary. Several of the members of Parliament apart from members of the Royal family held shares in the company.

As the company began annexing or taking control of large areas such as Bengal, Bihar and Orissa, the role of the Governor General in Calcutta was to take complete control over all of British territory in India. Areas captured by the East India Company were considered British territories. It was thus the responsibility of the Governor General to maintain law and order and provide proper administration in such areas.

Anarchy and chaos spread all over the country. Law and order suffered. People of India became victims of a weak government in the country. Apart from attacks by local dacoits, the people were also looted by Nadir Shah's forces. In the North, the Sikh Khalsa was asserting itself in Punjab. The policies and fanaticism of Aurangzeb were gone, but the anger among the people persisted. Small Sikh kingdoms were beginning to emerge in the Punjab.

Apart from anarchy, retrograde practices like child marriage, particularly of young Hindu girls was becoming common. The parents wanted to protect their young daughters from being kidnapped and raped by Muslim troops or other marauders. This became a short cut for safety though there was no guarantee that marauding soldiers wouldn't kidnap or rape married women. Education became rare for both boys and girls, and virtually came to a stop, as traditional Hindu schools with a composite syllabus from ancient days were shut down. Tragically, great universities including Nalanda that also attracted students from abroad had been destroyed by the Muslim invaders. Hundreds of precious manuscripts and books were lost as the invaders set libraries on fire. In the Muslim schools known as *madrasas* run largely by the mosques or clerics, there was hardly any education as they mostly taught the Quran.

In such a situation, the Governor General based in Calcutta began to restore some public order in the areas that were now under the East India Company. It was a strange relationship between the company and the British Government. As the company began getting involved in the politics of India and capturing territories, it became the agent of British imperialism, ruling the territories for the British Government. It was only after the Mutiny of 1857 that the British Government took direct control of British India. However, the company, as can be expected of any commercial venture, was cautious in spending money on public order. Nevertheless, schools were opened in the territories controlled by the company. Law and order was ensured in those territories. But tragically, areas ruled by the Mughals or others continued to be chaotic.

The tax collection system established by the Mughals via jagirdars and zamindars had reduced the farmers to extreme poverty or landless labourers. With the collapse of the Mughals, both the zamindars and jagirdars, became rulers themselves to collect taxes. Control of the Mughal administration over these functionaries was gone. The land that had been deemed to be owned by the Mughal emperor was now with jagirdars and zamindars, the worst exploiters of the farmers, who were treated like slaves. The condition of the farmers was equally bad in areas where the Mughal Emperor handed over tax collection rights to the East India Company under what was known as *divani*, in a bid to get rid of jagirdars and zamindars. As for the emperor, he now got a fixed amount of money as pension in lieu of tax collected by the company. The emperor had no idea about how much tax had been collected by the company, which was now a big source of new revenue.

The East India Company instead of creating its own machinery to collect taxes, retained zamindars and jagirdars for the purpose. This resulted in a three-way loot of the poor farmers—by the zamindar, jagirdar and the East India Company. Unable to pay such taxes, most farmers lost their lands to the zamindars. This is how the zamindars became big landlords and owners of the land. And the farmers were turned into poor landless labourers.

This author was a witness to the terrible exploitation and treatment of the farmers by the zamindars. A few years before India's Independence, I was a young trainee in Bihar with a documentary film producer. We were staying with a zamindar. His house was no less than a palace. I saw the scene in the evening when a couple of hundred farmers after toiling for the day arrived at the huge courtyard of the zamindar. It was like that of cattle coming back after the day's grazing. They were housed in two large sheds that looked more like cattle sheds than even barracks for humans. There were no beds. They slept on the floor. They were served a frugal meal of rice and lentils. Next morning getting up early, they got ready, and were served a measly breakfast of gruel. Finishing that, these famished men and women went back to the fields to toil for the day. I was told many would die young.

If rains failed and drought hit the area, it would bring

famine-like conditions and it was the tillers of the soil who would suffer the most. Even a limited drought would leave the farmers in distress and death. Such a situation always gave an excuse to most zamindars to sack the farmers and tell them to find food where they could. The earliest recorded famine is of 1769 in Bengal. Monsoon rains failed. Land became parched. There was no way that any crop could have been grown. That also meant that the company was going to lose on its land revenues while it gave a guaranteed pension to the Emperor. It was now established beyond a shadow of doubt that the company by now was 'more of a state than a trading house.'

The archival records of the Bengal famine of 1769 show how all agricultural activity came to a standstill with the failure of rains. The ground became parched and hardened and could not be ploughed. There was no water. Rice crops need a lot of water as the fields need flooding. With stocks of grain held at home gone, the situation now turned into famine for the families who could not buy any food. Farmers were dying in the villages. They sold their cattle to raise money. Others were even selling their children to raise money and get some food. Those of the farmers who were healthy enough moved towards town and cities with their families to find work and food. The famine began to hit the poor in the towns and cities as well. They were not able to buy the grains at prices that had hit the roof.

The 1769 famine of Bengal was perhaps worse than that which hit Bengal in 1942-43. That famine was man-made, when Churchill the Prime Minister of the United Kingdom moved the grains away from Bengal for World War II. Over five million died in the famine forced by Churchill on Bengal.

Ironically, Churchill is honoured as a hero of World War

II, but for India he remains a villain and killer of over five million innocent Bengalis.

Records of the 1769 Bengal famine show officials had written to the company in Calcutta about the devastation that was taking place in the province. Streets of Murshidabad were said to be covered in many places with dying and dead bodies. This sight repeated itself in Calcutta when the famished and dying started arriving. Rains failed the following year as well.

By the middle of 1770, the whole of Bengal province was said to have been hit by famine. Failure of the monsoon is nothing new to India. In the ancient times or the pre-Mughal era, the rulers had a system of storage which could provide grains during periods of shortage. The rulers would also carry out public works to provide work and wages to the farmers in distress. But that was ancient India ruled by the wisdom outlined in Chanakya's *Arthashastra*. It all worked well and devastation was usually controlled. The rulers in the pre-Mughal era in most parts of India considered themselves responsible for their people's welfare, including looking after their wellbeing in times of need. This was neither done by the company in the areas it controlled, nor by the Mughal rulers who had lost administration of the territories that were now with the company, whose primary objective in India was to make money, and not to spend on public works.

The company was callous and least bothered about the havoc caused by the famine and misery it was inflicting on the people. Its major concern was about the loss of revenue to it. It was more worried that a huge loss of revenue from Bengal would hit the company's profitability. There were no crops and consequently no taxes were due from the farmers. The wellbeing of the taxpayer at a time like famine was of no concern to the company, which had failed to function as an efficient agent of the British government.

Then there is also the recorded cruelty of the company in several areas where it insisted on collecting land revenue irrespective of the condition of farmers. If the company had any iota of humanity, it would have considered providing relief to farmers and not levying taxes. The company in its role as a government of the area, since it represented the British Crown, had failed to provide seeds and other help to surviving farmers to enable them to till the land again.

It was classic confusion by the officials of the company: whether they were traders or merely tax collectors. They are said to have even used force in collecting taxes from the poor and dying who were in no position to pay. Then there were some officials of the company who enriched themselves at the cost of the misery of the famine-hit. Gold and jewellery from the famished families was taken away, showing the naked greed and callousness of company officials.

In the midst of this famine, chaos, misery and death, the company revenues had not suffered major losses or decrease. There were some among the company staff who also donned the role of grain dealers of those days and hoarders of food. They bought the rice at cheap or regular prices, hoarded it and sold it five to ten times the prices to the famine hit. These company servants were in India obviously to enrich themselves by any means and that is exactly what they were doing.

The year 1770 got over in misery but without much loss to the company and its shareholders in London. However, by 1771, stories and reports started reaching London about the way company staff had dealt with the famine. London began to be aware of the loot from India by the new 'white nawabs' or whom they used to call 'nabobs.' These 'white nawabs' wanted to enrich themselves so much that on their return to England they could settle down as rich country sires with palatial homes. That this was done in the most inhuman manner during a famine was of no concern to them. This kind of raw behaviour can only be termed as the biggest ever, most demonic loot of poor human beings recorded in mankind's history. What Nadir Shah had done in Delhi to the people of that city was, he had claimed, done in retaliation, because people of Delhi abhorred the behaviour of his troops. Nadir Shah killed and looted a prosperous city. But what the officials of the East India Company from London had done almost amounted to practising genocide—looting the famished and dying poor to become rich.

In London, it was now being openly suggested by the critics of the company in Parliament and outside that the British Government should directly take over Bengal as a colony and look after the people there. This was required as territories annexed or captured by the company became British. This did not happen quickly, as the company had distributed a hefty dividend to its shareholders in London. Many of the shareholders were members of Parliament or officials of the Government. They too became rich with hefty dividends received from the company.

Clive, a clerk in the company, had come under severe attack both in the British Parliament and outside for the manner in which he was alleged to have behaved with the ladies looting their jewellery in palaces and of denying Umichand his dues. The fact that he had returned as a very rich man from being just a clerk in the company did not go down well with British nobility. He had collected enough gold and expensive jewellery from the palaces after each victory. Among the many rare pieces was a rare jewelled flask.

It is estimated that this man who went to India as a clerk had a fortune of roughly over 300 million pounds in today's value when he returned to England. Clive was put on trial in Parliament to face the charges of misdemeanour, enriching himself through corruption. He denied the charges and got away with his crime.

He managed to survive charges of corruption—how only history knows—and believed he had not been treated well by the company or the British government for his achievements in India. However, he was not acceptable to the nobility of UK. He was treated by the Nobles of UK as a so-called low caste in India of those days would have been treated by those of high caste. He had his palatial house in London and all else that money could buy but no respect. He had failed to buy his entry into the power circle of Britain, and he lived the life of a dejected lonely man with his wife in the large mansion—45 Berkeley Square, London. Wallowing in self-pity, he committed suicide, though some say he died of an overdose of opium on 22 November 1774.

Clive was succeeded by Warren Hastings. Warren Hastings who arrived in a stronger position of a Governor General was responsible to the Crown in England. He was to manage the colonial India that had been created by the East India Company. It was a strange dual system of control that the British tried—leaving trade to the company and taking away control from the company of the territories won by it.

Hastings thus took control of British India and began to set up its administration. His immediate task was to review the law and order situation in the country. He directed the army and the police to deal with the dacoits ruthlessly and 'finish' them when necessary, so that people could travel freely. Then he began with reforms in tax collection, eliminating the role of nawabs from administration of the areas from where the tax was collected. With the administrative control now with the Governor General, law and order was restored in the areas from where the tax was collected.

After his victory over Nawab Siraj ud-Daula, Robert Clive had continued to retain Murshidabad as capital of Bengal. Warren Hastings declared Calcutta as capital of Bengal. By virtue of managing all of British India from Calcutta, the city became the de facto capital of India. The Mughal Emperor had hardly any role, being on pension from the company. Delhi had been the capital for as long as we know as it was a central point for Mughal rule in India. It was the Governor General in Calcutta who was administering the areas.

Warren Hastings, through his reforms laid what can be called the foundation of British rule in India. During my study of history at the University of Delhi, Hindu College, the history Prof Ganpat Rai showed a very high regard for Warren Hastings for the manner in which he tried to deal with the exploitation of farmers by zamindars. He abolished the powers under which the zamindars acted as judges and deprived the farmers of their lands. A court was established in every district of India with a district collector as the judge.

Later, Lord William Bentinck came to India and banned the horrible social evil of 'Sati' on 4 December 1829. Civil and criminal courts were already set up by Warren Hastings to deal with criminals. The powers of zamindars and jagirdars to dispense justice were removed. These powers had been used by zamindars and jagirdars to inflict extreme injustice on the poor farmers.

Warren Hastings himself was a very learned man and learned Bengali soon after his arrival and was soon speaking Bengali fluently. Steps were taken to set up a university in

Calcutta. This was going to be a huge step in bringing up educated Indians to take responsibilities of a modern state. He also helped set up what is today known as the Asiatic Society of Bengal under Sir William Jones. The first assignment he gave to the society was to translate the *Bhagavad Gita*. This society has flourished over the years and is today a storehouse of knowledge. It has a huge art collection. The library, with over a hundred thousand books, has a large number of Sanskrit books and manuscripts.

Warren Hastings, a literary person had read a lot of books on ancient India. He could also speak Urdu and knew Persian well. These two languages were of great help to him whenever negotiating with the Mughals or other nawabs. Unlike most other senior officials of the company or those who came from the Government in London, he had a high regard for India's culture. He studied the *Bhagavad Gita* himself and was greatly impressed by it.

Between Clive and Warren Hastings the foundations of British Raj in India was established. The credit, however, goes to Warren Hastings in well and truly laying the foundations of a Government, being the first Governor General of India. Warren Hastings impressed upon his officials to study Hindu and Muslim religious laws. Credit goes to Warren Hastings as being the one who truly brought about what came to be known as British India.

A major weakness of the British in India, as it had been elsewhere in the world, was racism. The British had been virtually begging the Mughal Emperor for permission to be able to set up its trading facility in India which had been denied by Akbar. It was his successor Jehangir who granted permission which brought the East India Company into India. Though very careful and respectful in dealing with

Indians, the English had a racist attitude. Warren Hastings was critical of the way company staff dealt with their Indian counterparts or even traders. There was an air of superiority among the company's English staff. This attitude came into conflict with Indian culture as Indians felt they were far more civilised than these guys from England whom most Indians considered as inferior.

They didn't have a bath every day and were thus considered dirty by Indians. It may not be wrong for me to say that racism was of two opposing kinds, as the British and Indians clashed with each other. Many a Hindu would wash their hands after shaking hands with an Englishman, signifying racism by Indians against the British.

The worst result of this clash of racism was to come later from the sepoys of the company who resented the better uniform and treatment that the English soldiers received when compared with theirs. Attitude of the British officers, too, was not accepted by the sepoys. There always was resentment among the sepoys, both Hindus and Muslims who were proud of their religious practices and other customs. India was rich and people were proud of their culture. It is only towards the final collapse of the Mughal Empire that the country faced poverty and a weak Mughal army.

By the middle of the nineteenth century and with the annexation of Punjab, the company's rule had spread all over India, barring small enclaves like Pondicherry and Goa under the French and Portuguese respectively. Over five hundred small and medium-sized kingdoms that existed around the country had been brought under control by accepting the sovereignty of the British Crown.

The company in return assured such small kingdoms their security and defence against any attack. The bigger ones like the Nizam of Hyderabad or the Scindias in Gwalior or the House of Jaipur Royals in Jaipur and several others became allies of the British with the presence of an English Resident in their capital.

The Governor General of India in Calcutta was now the real ruler of India. The Mughal Emperor in Delhi, a pensioner of the company had his jurisdiction over the Red Fort.

India was now a jewel in the crown of Britain.

Chapter 4

COMPANY RULE AMIDST UPRISINGS

The East India Company's rule over India had begun from Bengal, then expanded to the South and spread to more regions after the defeat of Tipu Sultan. The tragedy of these victories by a foreign power like the East India Company apart from the loss of freedom was racial discrimination. The rich people of India were not used to it though they knew of religious discrimination that the Mughal emperors like Aurangzeb practised.

To understand the racist attitude of the then British in India, we need to remember that Britan was a leading nation in slave trade from Africa. These unfortunate men and women from Africa who were brought to England were treated as commodities, owned by those who bought them. British traders were a major source of supplying African slaves to the United States.

This commodity, a black human being, was far more hard working than others and had his own culture and civilisation. A close study of the prosperity of the US then shows that it was totally dependent on the hard work of slaves who were not paid any wages but given just enough food to survive. Slaves had been bought for paltry sums and were expected to work twenty-four hours till dead. Women slaves suffered sexual exploitation as well. In America, the owners of slaves called them their property.

British prosperity in the Caribbean islands also came only from the hard work of slaves on sugar and tobacco plantations there. Both these products meant big money for those who owned these plantations.

Many among the British had the same racist attitude in India. This was strange because those among the British who were well read knew that they were dealing with highly developed, rich and proud people in India. It was a well-known fact, about which the British were very well aware, that Indian civilisation had its roots in prehistoric times.

Major cities of Britain that prospered from slave trade together with London included Liverpool, Bristol and Glasgow in Scotland. It is said that King James II had also invested in a company that was involved in slave trade. Some African slaves were even sold in India to the rich kings including the Mughals. The British traders brought them to India. In India, the descendants of such Africans have well integrated into Indian society. They live largely in Gujarat, Karnataka, and Hyderabad. Those brought by Portuguese can be seen in Goa and Mumbai.

Most were freed by the Mughal rulers or governor. One of them known as Malik Ambar who came from Ethiopia rose to be a rich noble in Ahmednagar. He raised an army of ex slaves. He got his daughter married to Sultan Murtaza Nizam II. There were few others who rose to high positions. Thus, unlike in America, the African slaves who were brought to India did well and were treated as human beings from day one.

With this background of slave trade and the use of

indentured labour from India, indulged in by the British, it may be easy to understand the racist attitude of most of the East India Company representatives in India. The riches of Britain came no doubt from all that they got from India, but also from this inhuman business of slave trade. In Britain, there were muffled voices against the slave trade and racist attitude, but obviously not strong enough to stop the inhuman business.

In 1792, Tipu Sultan, the ruler of Mysore with its ally France, lost his battle against the combined forces of the East India Company and its allies. The war had lasted three years till the British succeeded in the siege of Seringapatam. A treaty was signed under which Tipu had to surrender half his kingdom. Further, Tipu's two sons were taken as hostages by the company to ensure that he observed the conditions of the Treaty he had signed. The two sons were accompanied by some of their staff and ladies from the palace. They were all housed in the palace of Vellore fort.

Vellore fort also had a sizable presence of the company's army, both English and Indian sepoys. The sepoys seeing Tipu's sons and others from his family being brought as hostages were upset. They respected Tipu Sultan as ruler of Mysore and could not tolerate seeing his two sons and many others including ladies brought to Vellore virtually as prisoners. The sepoys in this fort were also said to be angry at the insults and racist attitude of their British officers that they were ready to rebel against their white officers.

The sepoys, both Hindus and Muslims, resented the quality and design of their uniform as compared to the uniform of the British soldiers. The first racist act of the British officers that upset and annoyed the Hindu sepoys was when they were ordered to remove what they called 'colourings from your foreheads.' This was no colouring, but a religious mark that was applied by the priest after prayers at the temple. Muslim soldiers were asked to shave their beards that many of them grew. They were also asked to cut time spent at *namaz* or prayers during the day. A devout Muslim is expected to offer namaz five times a day. The two orders were not acceptable to the sepoys.

With growing anger against the orders of the British officers, the sepoys in Vellore began to refuse such orders. The sepoys had been assured of support by Tipu's sons for such an action of rebellion. The soldiers were thus ready to go into mutiny and fight under the leadership of Tipu's young sons. Any uprising by the sepoys led by Tipu's sons would have made it look like a fight by Mysore against the East India Company.

It all started on a quiet note on 9 July 1806 when the sepoys gathered to join in celebrations of a wedding at the Vellore Palace. Then in a surprise attack late at night and in the early hours of the morning of 10 July 1806, the sepoys attacked the sleeping British troops stationed inside the Fort. Over 200 of these soldiers were all killed. The same fate was met by most of the officers of the sepoys. Tipu's sons at this crucial moment, when they were expected to lead the sepoys, refused to do so. Time was wasted as the sepoys waited for Tipu's sons to make a decision. Stuck now as the sepoys were inside Vellore fort, the British managed to send troops and artillery from nearby areas and crush the mutineers. Over 300 of them were killed. Those who escaped from the fort were traced and suffered death sentences. The manner of killing them was most cruel to say the least like blasting away the victim from canons. Some were hanged.

The Vellore uprising had no doubt been crushed by the

East India Company before it could spread further. This was the first mutiny of the sepoys. The word spread about it. The ruthless manner in which the mutineers were treated was also meant to show others as to what would happen to them if they thought of rebelling. The British then decided that Tipu's sons and other family members who were held in the Vellore Fort were responsible to some extent for the Sepoy Mutiny. After the mutiny had been crushed, all the members of Tipu's family held at Vellore fort were moved to Calcutta so as to be nowhere near South India.

As expected, an enquiry was held both in India and London by the East India Company over the reasons for the mutiny by the sepoys. The sepoys had been a loyal fighting arm of the East India Company. The enquiry did report back in London as also in Calcutta that due care had not been taken in understanding the feelings of the sepoys. They realised that interference in religious matters was a huge mistake. And that it was to be totally avoided in future. However, the report failed to recognise the racist factor that was responsible for the kind of orders that had been issued to the sepoys before the mutiny. That racism continued.

Vellore, in its time, was a very prosperous town and had a golden temple covered entirely with gold. It still exists. The staff of the company who could indulge in loot to enrich themselves did so even in this small town. The palace and many other areas of the fort have granite walls. The city prospered during the rule of Pallavas and Chola dynasties. That it offered enough loot to the East India Company clerks or officers of the army was seen by this author when staying in Bath in the UK at the Hotel Bath Spa on Sydney Road, in the outskirts of the city.

When walking to the city from the hotel, I noticed a road

sign for Vellore Lane. On my inquiry from the hotel staff I found that the huge luxurious building of the hotel with acres of grounds all around was the country home of a junior army officer of the East India Company. When he returned to England instead of going to the village where he came from, he had decided to settle down in Bath as a 'country sire.' He had with him all the cash, gold and other wealth that he had brought from India. The officer working for the company's army was based last in Vellore. He thus named the lane as Vellore Lane.

Barrackpore Mutiny

By the turn of the nineteenth century, the East India Company was ruling large parts of India barring the empire of Maharaja Ranjit Singh in Lahore. Demands were made in the British Parliament for the Crown to take over the territories in India for proper rule by the Governor General rather than leave those with a trading company. The welfare of the people in such areas was being neglected. In Delhi, the Mughal ruler continued to live on the pension given by the East India Company.

In 1830, the then Mughal ruler Akbar Shah decided to ask the East India Company to raise the amount of money and perks paid to him. His contention was that the company was collecting far bigger revenue under the 'diwani' granted to it. He had realised how unequal the agreement giving 'divani' right to the company had been to the Mughal ruler. He requested Ram Mohan Roy, reformist leader from Calcutta to go to London as his envoy conferring on him the title of Raja. He was to petition the company and the Crown to increase the amount of pension and perks paid to him to run his palace, the fort and other establishments. Such was the condition of the once most powerful dynasty in the world! Raja Ram Mohan Roy did not succeed in his efforts. While in England at Stapleton, Bristol he fell ill. He could not recover and died there on 27 September 1933. He was buried there.

In October of 1824, the East India Company was fighting a war in Burma that is known in history as the First Anglo-Burmese war. The company needed to send more troops as reinforcements into this war. Its strength was nearly a quarter million men (250,000) at that time in India. And by the year 1824 the army of the East India Company was the largest in India, and possibly in the world. Local maharajahs or nawabs could not match it.

To support the forces in the Anglo Burmese war, the company was required to send at least two regiments of its army. Without much thinking, the concerned officers decided to send two regiments of the Bengal Native Infantry. The sepoys of these regiments had just arrived in Barrackpore after marching for nearly a thousand miles from Mathura, where they had been on duty earlier. They had hardly taken any rest or gone on holiday when suddenly this order was received by them. The sepoys were now expected to march to Chittagong, a distance of some 300 miles from their base. They were naturally reluctant for yet another long march and to fight an enemy not known to them. They were angry that their officers had not considered their problems but simply insisted that the troops march to Chittagong.

The sepoys had also heard strange stories of Burmese magical feats, which had spread fear among them. They had heard that Burmese magical powers can make them weak and unable to fight. The sepoys were aware that the war in Burma had not gone well for the East India Company, which had lost with heavy casualties. They felt they were to be used now to retrieve the situation for the company.

As the final orders came for the sepoys to prepare for the march, reluctant as they were, the sepoys got angry when they were further told that there were no carriages available to carry their personal belongings. How could they carry those? They were also told to carry their own heavy weapons including their own ammunition. The personal belongings and other paraphernalia required by the troops when on the move was always carried by carriages pulled by bullocks.

The question they raised was why were no bullock carriages available? Nothing was explained and this became a major issue when the sepoys met their officers. The sepoys insisted that their officers arrange for carriages by taking up the issue with the higher ups. They bluntly told their officers only when the carriages are made available would they march to Chittagong.

The issue of providing bullock carriages was by then being seen as a case of the sepoys not being disciplined enough to accept orders. Several of the officers had earlier worked in other countries of the British Empire using slaves as fighting forces. The sepoys in Barrackpore were no slaves, but were free men in employment of the company as sepoys of the army. The company refused to meet the requests of the sepoys to be provided bullock carts in their march to Chittagong.

Instead they were finally told to carry whatever of their belongings they could manage and leave the rest behind.

Then came the proverbial last straw which made the sepoys rebellious. Hindu soldiers had already expressed their fear of crossing the sea which they had been told by priests to be against their religious beliefs. However, a study shows all this was meant to retain the learned men in India. The sepoys were using this plea to wriggle out of having to later on travel by boats. Hindu sepoys were also told to remove the religious markings on their foreheads. The turban of which the sepoys were so proud of was also to be changed with another head gear. Muslim sepoys were annoyed and angry when told to shave their beard. Many Muslims sport a beard as a religious belief. They too were as proud of the turban as headgear as were the Hindus.

Time was nearing for the march to begin. Bullock carts had not been provided. In the rising summer heat of Barrackpore, the temper of the sepoys was just as hot. They were ready to march but only when the carriages or carts arrived.

On 1 November, sepoys of the Bengal Native Infantry were ordered to be present at a parade after which the march was to begin. They all came, but without their knapsacks. When ordered to bring those, the sepoys refused—mutiny had begun with this refusal. The commanding officer got in touch with his seniors in Calcutta. The sepoys meanwhile remained on the parade ground in extreme heat. They stood there even at night maintaining discipline and telling their officers that they were ready to march as soon as bullock carts/carriages appeared. There is no explanation as to why the sepoys were kept standing in the parade ground even at night while awaiting instructions from Calcutta.

A senior officer came from Calcutta who asked the soldiers to lay down their arms and promised to consider their demands. The sepoys led by one Bindee Tewari refused to do that. Gen Paget from Calcutta took this position of the sepoys as an act of armed mutiny. He called for British troops including the Governor General's Bodyguards to handle the sepoys on the parade ground. On the morning of November 2, with all the European and loyal sepoys of other regiments surrounding them, the sepoys on the parade were given the last order to lay down arms in ten minutes.

But whether Gen Paget waited for exactly ten minutes or not is not known—he ordered cannons to be fired at them. Hundreds of the mutineers were killed instantly. Why were cannons used on disciplined sepoys who were standing? They could have been arrested and tried for indiscipline. Clearly Gen Paget had no value for the lives of the sepoys. He was perhaps another one of those British officers who used to lord over slaves. The final tally was over 400 killed in what can be called cold-blooded murder. Many of the sepoys drowned when they jumped into the river Hooghly to escape being killed.

Some newspapers in Calcutta that were published at the time carried the story of this mutiny on the front pages. A local Bengali newspaper *Hurakaru* which had official backing of the company reported only a hundred sepoys were killed. No one gave the figures of British officers or British soldiers killed in the mutiny. In the British Parliament again during the debate on this mutiny there was criticism of the British officers who had issued orders against the religious beliefs of the sepoys. Many of the members of Parliament voiced their concern for the way the situation was handled in Barrackpore. In Calcutta, the company and Governor General's office tried to keep silent about the mutiny. No reports were given about those having escaped when captured and killed instantly. Some were given sentences of 14 years in jail with hard labour. After a long hunt, Bindee Tewari, considered to be one of the leaders of the mutineers, was captured alive. He was hanged.

The mutiny had been crushed, but the anger among the sepoys of Barrackpore and Bengal regiments remained. The attitude of their British officers who refused to understand the genuine representations of their men was responsible for all this. This racist and inhuman attitude of the British officers, even by those settled in India, continued. That this attitude would result in a huge outburst later on could not be imagined by those indulging in such behaviour.

Maharaja Ranjit Singh's Empire

The rule of the East India Company had by the middle of the nineteenth century covered major parts of India barring Punjab that was ruled by Maharaja Ranjit Singh. He had a very strong Khalsa army, well-disciplined and trained by French and other Europeans whom he employed as officers. Practical person that he was, the Maharaja was aware of the size and strength of the company's army. He was also well aware of the presence of British troops. He followed a policy of 'guarded friendship' with the company by not attempting to expand his empire towards Delhi.

The British were also worried about North West India in the face of Napoleon having signed the Treaty of Tilsit in 1807 with Russia. Napoleon had advanced up to Egypt and the British suspected he could have his eyes on North West India. The East India Company wanted a defence treaty but was happy in signing the Treaty of Amritsar with Maharaja Ranjit Singh. This treaty defined the territories of the two signatories and fixed the border. That ensured for Ranjit Singh that the company won't interfere with him. He was not interested in Mughal Delhi which was de facto with the British.

The rule of Maharaja Ranjit Singh saw Punjab prosper. His attitude towards his people was secular and liberal; they were all treated equally. There were many Muslims and Hindus in senior command positions employed by him. A great warrior that he was, he had fought his first battle at the age of ten. By the age of seventeen he had foiled the Afghan invasion by Zaman Shah Durrani. He had lost an eye when he suffered from smallpox in his childhood. He had a number of wives; some records show twenty. He had eight sons but strangely he recognised only Kharak Singh and Duleeep Singh. During his victory in Afghanistan, he had gone to Ghazni and recovered the gates of Somnath temple from the tomb of Mahmud of Ghazni. He had his victory over Afghanistan parade in Kabul. Maharaja Ranjit Singh covered the holiest of Sikh shrines, Harmandir Sahib with gold. He also did that for Kashi Vishwanath Temple in Varanasi.

Maharaja Ranjit Singh passed away on 27 June 1839. His elder son Kharak Singh succeeded him on that day but he was deposed on 8 October 1839. Problems of succession started thereafter. Seeing the Punjab empire running into serious issues of succession, its army emerged as a strong entity though not taking over the empire. It left that to the successors to settle among themselves. Taking note of what was going on in Punjab, the British started strengthening their position on their side of the boundary across river Sutlej. Meanwhile the succession problems continued with no one emerging in the strong position of Maharaja Ranjit Singh. Maharani Chand Kaur proclaimed herself as ruler on 2 December 1840 only to be deposed on 18 January 1841. Sher Singh came back as Maharaja but was killed on 15 September 1843 when a minor Duleep Singh was proclaimed Maharaja with Maharani Jindan who had been a favourite of Ranjit Singh, acting as regent to the minor king.

Anglo-Sikh Wars

While Ranjit Singh's death resulted in chaos, his army under his loyal Sikh officers expanded rapidly to over seventy-five thousand men. It proclaimed that it followed Guru Gobind Singh's teachings, unconcerned with the goings on at the durbar. The British meanwhile set up a cantonment in Ferozepur only a few miles away from Sutlej, the boundary between Punjab and British-ruled India. The Sikh rulers in Lahore considered it as a violation of the Treaty of Amritsar. In December 1845, expecting an attack by the British, the Khalsa army without declaring war crossed Sutlej river to fight the British in their territory and stop their attack on Punjab. The first Anglo-Sikh War had thus been launched by the Khalsa army without any warning.

Severe battles followed at Ferozepur only around six miles inside the British ruled territory. Hard fought battles also took place at Mudki, Aliwal and Sobraon resulting in heavy human loss to both sides. The end result went in favour of the British who won the first Anglo-Sikh war by February 1846 and triumphantly entered Lahore, the capital of the Sikh Empire, under instructions from Governor General Lord Hardinge. However, the British didn't annexe Lahore.

Instead nearly half the territories of the Sikh Empire including Kashmir were annexed. Punjab also had to pay an indemnity of 1.5 million pounds. Duleep Singh remained the Maharaja, not with his mother Rani Jindan as regent, but under a Resident Henry Lawrence who was now based in Lahore.

As could be expected, the arrangement was resented by many Sikhs and the Khalsa army. They rallied around Mul Raj, former Governor of Multan. The uprising against the British now began from Multan when two British officials were murdered. Mul Raj had attracted a large number of Maharaja Ranjit Singh's family including Maharani Jindan. Mul Raj had also attracted many zamindars and jagirdars who had their own armies to support him. Mul Raj was now a leader of a very sizeable force. The battle of Multan seemed to be going the way of Mul Raj after the first three months of fighting at the end of April.

Surprised as the British were, they found it difficult to march reinforcements during the terrible hot months of May to the end of July, when rains also made it difficult to march. Once the rains subsided and the weather changed, the British marched towards Multan. Meanwhile Khalsa had given a call to fight for independence, their Maharaja Duleep Singh and their faith. With large British reinforcements, they were able to lay siege of Multan by the end of December 1848.

Early in January, the British forces managed to breach the wall of Multan and the forces entered the city. Bloody fighting took place almost from house to house ending only towards the end of January. The British forces and its men indulged in loot to collect as much as they could from Multan. The battle of Multan also known as battle of guns was fought well by the Sikh army of Mul Raj but was overpowered by a stronger force in the end.

Multan won, and the British forces fanned out to other small places of resistance in Punjab. Lord Dalhousie, the then Governor General, annexed Punjab in March 1849. The British were now in occupation of most of India. A trading company was now ruling over what was the richest country in the world, when Thomas Roe had sought trading rights from Emperor Jehangir.

To bring an end to the tragedy of Punjab, the British took Maharaja Duleep Singh together with several senior officials and his brave generals with their families to England. The assurance given was that they were all to be living where the young maharaja would be. Once in England, the young

Maharaja was separated from the rest who were all sent to different parts of the United Kingdom.

The young Maharaja was put in the care of Englishmen to be brought up as an English gentleman. That is another story. Tragically, Duleep Singh grew up to be one such English gentleman who loved the life of British nobility. However, as a young maharaja, he even worked as an ADC to Queen Victoria for some time.

By the time he realised what had been done to him and the great empire of Punjab, it was too late. There was no way he could fight the British for the manner in which they cheated his people. He died in France on 22 October 1893. His children took his body to England and had it buried next to his wife in Elveden. Whatever, the way the British took over Punjab speaks for itself. The Punjab army had lost the battles.

But can this justify the manner in which 15-year-old Duleep Singh was separated from his mother and from his accompanying entourage of senior Punjab officials and generals, which was totally against what had been agreed upon? The objective of bringing him up as an English gentleman, making him forget his religion and the fact that he was a maharaja of a proud powerful people, was achieved. All this goes to show the insensitivity and callousness of the British rulers.

Chapter 5

THE HEROIC 1857 MUTINEERS

There was anger all over India against this strange ruler who had no empathy with the people. These were strange people from across the seas who came to India to trade, and managed to secure permission to have their own forces to protect their assets. Then with the power of their new weapons and sepoys, they were now in control of almost the whole of India. With the remaining small and big maharajas or nawabs who had surrendered their sovereignty to the company, they had treaties. The tragedy that many Indians felt was that foreigners ruling over them were mere employees of a company against whom they could not go to the Mughal Emperor.

People of India as also the sepoys were aware of how this trading company had outsmarted the Mughal Emperor into surrendering large parts of his empire in lieu of tax collection on his behalf. All this was because of the corrupt or errant Mughal governors of provinces who failed to send the collected revenue to the centre in Delhi. It had all happened because of the corruption in the administration of the Mughal rulers, as mentioned by Thomas Roe when he travelled from Surat to Agra to present his credentials to Emperor Jehangir.

The once powerful Mughal army did not have a strong

warrior commander. There was no other powerful personality who could succeed the Mughal Emperor. All this made it easy for the East India Company to expand itself, strengthen its army further and emerge as a ruling entity. There was no one around to check what this company was doing. This tragic situation ultimately led to a British trading company ruling over India.

Never before in the history of mankind had a people been ruled by a trader.

In 1849, a young man from Balia, Mangal Pandey joined the Bengal regiment at Barrackpore. He, like other sepoys, suffered the racist attitude of his British officers. Mangal Pandey was a staunch Hindu, and being Brahmin, he believed himself to be superior in culture to his officers. It was sheer poverty that had compelled him to accept a position that would involve working under someone whom he considered to be inferior. The British had introduced new cartridges for the Enfield rifles that were to be used by the sepoys. Both the Muslim and Hindu sepoys considered using these new cartridges to be against their religion. The sepoys had to bite the cartridge before it could be used in the rifle. A word had gone around that the bullet that was to be bitten had the lard of cows and pigs.

The sepoys protested and told their officers that they were not going to use those bullets. Angry sepoys looked up to Mangal Pandey for leadership in this protest, despite the threat that he could be dismissed from service. Not to be deterred, Mangal Pandey refused to carry out the orders of his officers to bite the bullet to load it in the gun. There was yet another reason at Barrackpore for the sepoys to be angry. Copies of the *Bible* written in local language were distributed to them. Why? The sepoys suspected that they were to be converted to Christianity.

Pandey was at the guard room on 29 March 1857 when his refusal to bite the bullets was not accepted. He threatened to kill the English officers with a loaded musket in his hands. He called upon his colleagues to rise using the slogan *'Maro Firangi Ko'* (Kill the foreigners). Pandey attacked the British officers. This act of defiance, attacking the officers and calling upon other members of the regiment to join him led to his arrest. During his trial, Pandey declared that the act to rebel was his and called upon the foreigners to leave India. Pandey was sentenced to death and hanged on 8 April 1857.

Mangal Pandey from Balia was now a hero not just for the sepoys but for the people of India who heard his story of defiance. In recent times, movies have been made on his life and his brave act to defend his religion. Another soldier Jemadar Ishwari Prasad who had been ordered to arrest Mangal Pandey, but had refused to do so was also put on trial, sentenced to death and hanged on 21 April 1857. The British had imposed the death sentence as a norm for even a refusal to carry out an order. Was such a deathly sentence by the British intended to force loyalty?

Going a step further to teach the sepoys of Barrackpore a lesson, the British, in the days following the hanging of Mangal Pandey decided to disband the entire regiment to which he had belonged. The news of the hanging of Mangal Pandey and Ishwari Prasad plus disbanding of the 34th Bengal Infantry reached Meerut where the third Bengal Light Infantry was based. Hearing of the two brave martyrs, the sepoys based in Meerut rose in rebellion. Like others, these men were also against use of the new cartridges.

As all the sepoys rose in mutiny on 10 May 1857, shouting Mangal Pandey's slogan *'Maro Firangi Ko,'* they started attacking their English officers. This Sepoy Mutiny, indeed, was the beginning of India's first War of Independence, as rightly described by many historians.

Meerut was a strong British military base of the East India Company. Not just the third Bengal Infantry but several other sepoy regiments and English regiments as well, were based there. Several other batallions joined the rebellion. Many English officers were killed. The mutineers then began attacking other Europeans in Meerut irrespective of the fact that they were civilians and not army men. Several women and children were killed as well. Local criminals joined the sepoys in the attack on civil areas which was widespread. It also led to some looting as well. The mutineers managed to free all of the sepoys who had been arrested earlier and put behind bars for defying the orders to use the new bullets.

As night fell, the sepoys met to decide further action. They knew that they could be crushed by the large European contingents that were present in Meerut. Without fear of retaliation, the sepoys decided to march to Delhi that was just 40 miles from Meerut. They planned to call on the Mughal Emperor Bahadur Shah Zafar and seek his leadership and support. The sepoys arrived at the walled city of Delhi in the early hours of the morning and went straight to meet Bahadur Shah Zafar. He was reluctant, not knowing the strength and backing of the rebellious sepoys, who had entered the fort. It was after some hesitation that Bahadur Shah agreed to lead them. They proclaimed him Emperor of India.

What followed in Delhi was the killing of Englishmen, women and children by the sepoys. It has been claimed that this did not have the approval of Bahadur Shah. The sepoys were acting on their own. The British officers in Delhi managed to blow up the magazine where a large amount of ammunition was kept. This ammunition could thus not fall into the hands of the sepoys. Two sons of Bahadur Shah were made commanders of the mutineer army. But there was no discipline among the sepoys as they were used to British officers and Bahadur Shah's sons had no experience of commanding troops.

The sepoys in the initial stage after their arrival in the city indulged in loot. This made them unpopular with the people of Delhi. Delhi, now became the epicentre of this fight to throw the British out. 'Firangi ko Maro' slogan was heard everywhere as the killings and loot by the sepoys spread.

It was the news of the proclamation of Bahadur Shah as Emperor of India that created an atmosphere of rebellion all over North India barring large areas of Punjab. Sepoys were based in most areas of the North like Aligarh, Muzaffarnagar, Avadh, Roorkee, Etah, Mathura, Lucknow, Benares, Allahabad, and Kanpur. At each of these places, the English officers were killed.

The mutiny was now spreading as a move to throw the British out of the country. Soon the deprived Indian nobles like zamindars, talukdars and local chiefs also rose against the English. Most of these had been losers when the taxes began to be collected by the company for the Mughal government.

From Avadh, the mutiny spread to Bihar and Bengal. There was a strong presence of English forces in these areas. Did the people of India rise against the British? The answer is mixed. Aurangzeb's rule had left the local population in most areas against the Mughals. His successors were trying to undo the harm that had been done by Aurangzeb. As the mutiny spread, the sepoys had now been joined by some local rulers who had been dethroned by the British. They saw in this mutiny, a possibility of getting back their territories that had been annexed by the East India Company. Apart from the rulers of Avadh and Delhi, other notables who had joined the sepoy revolt were Rani of Jhansi, Nana Saheb of Kanpur and others.

Jhansi had been annexed by the East India Company after refusing to recognise the adoption of a son named Damodar Rao by her late husband Gangadhar Rao. After the death of her husband, Rani of Jhansi Laxmi Bai took charge of the state. The British Governor General Lord Dalhousie refused to recognise her as regent of the adopted son Damodar Rao. The strange law that the company had enforced was to only recognise one's own child. The Governor General ordered the annexation of the state of Jhansi. The Rani refused to accept this and joined the battle against the company. She was a great warrior herself.

A similar situation was faced by Nana Saheb who had been adopted by Peshwa Baji Rao, who was a pensioner of the company. Peshwa Baji Rao who had no son of his own had adopted Nana Saheb. He was a great gunner. After the death of Peshwa Baji Rao, Nana Saheb became the Peshwa and did some great work in developing the Peshwa kingdom.

Lord Dalhousie refused to recognise him as Baji Rao's successor. Nana Saheb refused to accept this order of Lord Dalhousie. The adoption was valid as per the Hindu customs whereas the denial to accept this was aimed at annexation of the Peshwa kingdom. Nana Saheb's rebellion and fight against the British was supported by the sepoys. He was helped by Hakim Azimullah who was a minister in the Peshwa kingdom and continued to be so when Nana Saheb succeeded. Tatya Tope, also a great gunner, was by his side with his troops.

The sepoys and their powerful, influential supporters continued their attack against the British. But the vast majority of people of India did not rise in support of the sepoys. A major reason for this was the fact of looting by the sepoys in several places including Delhi. British forces were putting up a stiff fight against the rebel sepoys and their supporters and steadily meeting success. The rebellious sepoys were running out of ammunition as time passed.

Rani Laxmi Bai of Jhansi was reputed to be a great young soldier. She was just twenty-two years old when she assumed charge of Jhansi. As regent and queen of Jhansi, having turned down the order of the British Governor General to hand over the state of Jhansi, she started strengthening the small army that she had. When mutineer sepoys heard of her decision, many headed for Jhansi to help her.

The British attacked her kingdom and were steadily making advances towards Jhansi by March of 1858. The company's forces led by General Rose managed to lay siege to the fort at Jhansi. The Rani had also been joined by forces of Tatya Tope. Overwhelmed by the company's forces, Rani Laxmi Bai refused to surrender. As the fort fell, she managed to escape from there with a small force of her palace guards. She headed towards Gwalior where she announced Nana Saheb as the Peshwa-ruler of Gwalior.

When Rani Laxmi Bai went into the battlefield with her forces to face the counter attack mounted by Gen Rose, a fierce battle followed. Rani's forces were facing defeat even as they put up a tough fight under the direct leadership of the Rani. Fighting bravely, the Rani was said to have been surrounded by British cavalry. She was hit and killed in the battle field. But her body could not fall in the hands of the British. It is said that it was taken to the nearby forest by her trusted guards and cremated as per her directions.

Nana Saheb

Nana Saheb, whose real name was Dhondu Pant, had been adopted by Maratha Peshwa Baji Rao. After the death of Baji Rao, Nana Saheb proclaimed himself to be the succeeding Peshwa. However, the British under Lord Dalhousie refused to recognise him as such under a controversial Doctrine of Lapse that the East India Company had adopted to annex states under their protection. The Doctrine of Lapse was cleverly introduced by the East India Company to annex any princely state if its ruler was incompetent or did not have a male heir.

With refusal of the company to recognise him, it stopped paying the pension that Baji Rao was entitled to and receiving from them. Nana Saheb had raised a sizeable force to defend his territory. This was known to the company but it had done nothing about it apart from refusing to recognise him or pay any pension. Nana Saheb decided to attack the British in Cawnpore (Kanpur). He met with success defeating the British forces that surrendered. After that, his forces murdered the surviving British soldiers and officers instead of taking them prisoners. He captured the British treasury as also the magazine where weapons and ammunition were stored.

Having pushed the British out of Cawnpore, Nana Saheb announced himself to be the Peshwa of Maratha confederacy. He then attacked the company's forces led by General Wheeler. He laid siege depriving British forces food and water. A large number of British civilians including women and children had taken refuge in an entrenchment with poor defence. They were protected by a small group of British troops and loyal sepoys. Fighting had continued for a week. Failing to defeat the besieged, both sides began negotiations. A compromise was arrived at under which the British were to be given a safe exit. Starting with women and children, the British were to be taken on boats on river Ganga to Allahabad. Nana Saheb is said to have assisted the British in providing carriages to take women and children to the boats. Then followed officers and men who were allowed to carry their weapons.

The manner in which the boats were placed in the river, posed problems in boarding them. And then all of a sudden the rebel sepoys of the company working under Tatya Tope attacked the boats and what followed was a massacre. The East India Company held Nana Saheb responsible for the massacre. It was however clear that Nana Saheb's trusted gunner Tatya Tope's men had done it, whether under his orders or as undisciplined mutineers is not known. A large number of British soldiers and officers were killed as were some women and children.

As was expected, a counter attack by the British came from a large contingent sent from Allahabad. Nana Saheb's forces were beaten in the battles that followed.

The British could not capture Nana Saheb who was said to have fled to Nepal where he died later. Nana Saheb's fight to restore the rule of Maratha Peshwa and throw the British out remains a major failed battle story of the Mutiny of 1857.

Tatya Tope

Tatya Tope who was also referred to as Tantia Tope was a general with Nana Saheb. He was an ace gunner who was feared by the British. He had forced the British to retreat from Cawnpore when they retook it. Tatya Tope was a great planner of strategy for each battle. His biggest problem was the indiscipline in the ranks of rebel sepoys he was using to fight the British. In Cawnpore, when these sepoys attacked the boats and indulged in looting and killing, they had let down Tatya Tope and Nana Saheb by dishonouring what had been agreed by them with the British.

Counter attacks by the English soldiers assisted by loyal sepoys were beginning to crush the mutiny. Rani of Jhansi had already been eliminated. Tatya Tope continued his brave fight against the British and moved towards Rajputana to get support of some Rajput kings. He met Raja Man Singh of Narwar hoping to get his support to fight the British.

But there was one warning by the British to the Raja that they would annex his kingdom, yet followed by an assurance to protect him and leave his kingdom in his hands as the British protectorate. Considering this situation, Raja Man Singh betrayed Tatya Tope and handed him over to the British, just as they had wanted. Tatya had not surrendered as demanded many a time earlier by the British, but fell in their hands after betrayal by one whom he considered to be a friend.

Tatya Tope was put on trial by the British. However, brave Tatya Tope during the trial declared that he was answerable for his acts only to the Peshwa, who was his master and not the British. He was hanged on 18 April 1859.

His brave exploits as a guerrilla fighter are recounted even today. His legacy as a great freedom fighter is still remembered in the country. Independent India had issued a commemorative postage stamp in his honour. There is a memorial park—Shahid Tatya Tope Smarak featuring a statue of Tatya Tope located at Shivpuri in Madhya Pradesh. Betrayed by Raja of Narwar, Tatya Tope is remembered as a great fighter for India's freedom.

Fall of Delhi

The mutiny by the British East India Company sepoys was failing not just because of strong retaliation by the British, but owing to lack of support by the people at large. At many places, the sepoys were to be blamed for this because they had indulged in looting of shops and homes. Where there was strong leadership like that of Rani of Jhansi, the people supported her, but with the defeat or killing of such a leader, the support would dissipate.

The people of the city of Delhi, angry as they were, because of some looting by the sepoys, still supported Bahadur Shah, the last Mughal emperor, a reluctant leader of the mutiny. Bahadur Shah was a poet king with his poetic title 'Zafar.'

He hardly had any experience of leading or directing an army. Further, he was 81 years old. He had been proclaimed as *'Shahenshah e Hindustan,'* Emperor of India by the mutineers, hoping to attract support from people of other areas, who wanted to restore him as the Emperor of the country. That was not to be.

The two princes who were made incharge of the army of sepoys too had no military experience. The forces from Delhi apart from approaching nearby areas had not moved to any other part of the country to assert their authority. The British realised that they had to recapture Delhi soon to demonstrate their power. This was a smart strategy as the proclamation of Bahadur Shah as Emperor of Hindustan was beginning to attract common people's support for the mutiny, which could turn it into a national revolt by Indians.

Punjab was peaceful and not many of the forces there had risen in mutiny. Three regiments of sepoys based in Jullundur rebelled and headed for Delhi. British officers were killed. There were smaller uprisings in Sialkot, Rawalpindi and Jhelum and some smaller places, but these were put down without much problem. Punjabis were also concerned about the welfare of their King Duleep Singh who was held by the British in England. In addition, with the proclamation of Bahadur Shah Zafar as Emperor of India, the Sikhs in Punjab had no desire to accept an islamic ruler. They had fought many battles against the Mughal rulers who were also responsible for killing two of their Gurus and finally the tenth Guru Gobind Singh had asked the Khalsa to fight them.

Western India too did not see any rebellion There was no rebellion in provinces and areas controlled by the British in Mysore or Travancore. The first Punjab troops moved from there and arrived in Karnal. In Delhi mutineers had been encouraged by the arrival of a large number of rebels, but none from Punjab. The mutineers in the city lacked a professional command. The Mughal princes had no military experience and thus drew little respect from the mutineers whom they were leading.

The British continued to strengthen their forces in the siege of Delhi. They were encamped at the ridge of Delhi in the North just about a couple of miles away from the city walls at Kashmere Gate. This is the area near today's University of Delhi campus. There is a memorial to the British troops there. Gurkha forces had also joined the Sikhs and other forces planning to make a major attack on the city. Delhi was a walled city protected by a very strong fort-like wall. The city was within the wall. The British were preparing for the assault keeping in mind that they had to break through the wall. The mutineers too had further strengthened the fortifications of the wall. The first planned assault on the city had to be called off as the British became aware of the heavy fortification.

In their fight for the Mughal Emperor, a fairly large number of retired or other Muslim soldiers and commoners calling themselves 'mujahadeen' also joined the mutineers in the city. The mutineers had attacked some of the British encampments around the city to push them away. It is said that in the case of an attack at the Hindu Rao area, the mutineers had almost succeeded but retreated in the face of a tough fight put up by the British and other supporting forces.

Those inside the city again tried to break this siege. The English outside were getting tired with the heat and rains. Monsoon rains in Delhi begin in end June and continue into September. The weather becomes humid, with too many mosquitoes around, raising fears of malaria. Many of the young British troops died of malaria. Their graves can be seen at the Nicholson cemetery outside Kashmere Gate.

The telegraph system had become operational from 1840. It helped the East India Company in its communications during the mutiny. The company was able to inform various centres of the developments and of how the sepoy mutiny was being tackled. In the prevailing situation in battle for Delhi, the strength of the besieging British forces was steadily increased. The company forces were aware of the defence and fortification of the city wall. Mutineers were making extra effort to break the siege and push back British forces. The object was not just to push the British back but to make it easy for other mutineers to enter the city.

The reinforcements from Punjab for the company came with the help of rulers of Patiala, Nabha and Jind. A major column marched towards Delhi under Brigadier Nicholson. They then began pounding the wall with heavy artillery barrage which was returned by the mutineers in equal strength.

Brigadier Nicholson then moved towards Kashmere Gate to make a breakthrough from there. Two of his officers undertook what can be called a suicide mission to attack the Gate. The mutineers were well placed on top of the wall over the Kashmere Gate. Despite heavy fire on them and on the supporting force, the two officers managed to place gunpowder charges on the gate and blew up a part of the Gate. The mutineers failed to kill the two who were on a suicide mission to open the gate.

The company forces charged through the gate, before the mutineers could take control or repair it. The British had suffered heavy casualties in achieving this success. This group was now inside the city and had taken their positions within the Church of St James just a few hundred steps away from the walls of the Kashmere Gate. Brigadier Nicholson moved into another part of the city with a small force towards Kabul Gate but was injured badly in the fire from the mutineers.

To attack the Red Fort and the palace from the river Jamuna side, the British succeeded in making a boat bridge. They attacked the Red Fort then known as Salimgarh fort. By now Bahadur Shah became aware of the British successes inside the city. Expecting an attack on the fort, he decided to move from the palace with his family to Humayun's tomb. The British now began moving into other parts of the city capturing Juma Masjid. The mutineers had already started leaving the city.

The company had suffered heavy loss of manpower both in officers and men in the victory of Delhi. The sad part is that after the company forces captured the city, they indulged in loot and murder in Muslim areas and at houses of the nobles. In several cases it had been led by the British officers. Bahadur Shah's two sons Mirza Sultan and Mirza Mughal who were commanding the mutineers were killed outside the walls of the fort. His grandson Mirza Abu Bakht was also killed there. The place is known by the name Khooni Darwaza—the bloody gate—because of these three killings there.

The British announced the capture of Delhi on 21 September 1857. This was to boost the morale of the company forces in other parts of the country where fighting was going on. Brigadier John Nicholson succumbed to his injuries. He was buried at the Nicholson cemetery near Kashmere Gate. The loot that followed the capture of the city virtually destroyed Delhi's aristocratic families. The loot that took place inside the palace left the ladies devoid of their jewellery and virtually rendered paupers. Properties of Mughal nobles were seized. Later these properties were auctioned mainly to a number of people that the company brought from Lahore. These people from Lahore were largely accommodated in houses at Katra Neel opposite Balli Maraan in Chandni Chowk. The beautiful city of Delhi, also known as Shahjahanabad was desolate, with many of its palatial houses known as 'havelis' destroyed.

Bahadur Shah was arrested from Humayun Tomb together with his family and other staff and brought to the Red Fort. The last Mughal Emperor was put on trial in the fort. He was charged with a conspiracy against the company and its rule. Most historians have regarded the charges as ridiculous. Bahadur Shah denied the charges. After a short trial, Bahadur Shah was sentenced to be exiled. He together with his Queen Zeenat Mahal and several of the staff were taken away from Delhi to the farthest corner of the subcontinent to Rangoon. Thus ended the Mughal rule, and the Mughal dynasty that had ruled over India.

The poet Emperor was now a prisoner of the British in Rangoon. Frustrated and broken-hearted for being so far away from Delhi, he died there on 7 November 1862. Before his death he had penned a ghazal (poem), a couplet which described his state of mind: *lagta nahin hae jee mera ujre dayar mei—do gaz zamin na milie kue yaar mei.* (I am sad and unhappy in this place—pity I could not get two yards of land for burial in my beloved place.)

The British Government took the administration of India away from the Company when it promulgated the Government of India Act 1858. All of the assets of the East India Company, together with its army were taken over by the Crown. An office of the Secretary of State for India was created in London to oversee the rule in India. Queen Victoria formally issued a proclamation on 1 November 1858 under which she was to take over India's administration, promising the people of India the same rights as were enjoyed by other subjects of hers. The Governor General in India Lord Canning became the first Viceroy of India, representing the British monarch. Unlike all the emperors and rulers of India preceding her, Victoria was not going to be living in India.

Hindustan or Bharat was now known as India as the British called it—a colony of the British Empire or as it came to be known as the jewel in the Crown of the British Empire.

Seth Ramji Das Gurwale

It was not just that Bahadur Shah Zafar was deposed and exiled to Rangoon. Those who helped him also suffered the wrath of the British. Seth Ramji Das Gurwale, who lived in Nai Sarak area of Delhi was a friend and banker of the Mughal Emperor. He, too, suffered a terrible end at the hands of the new rulers.

In the book, *Hindu College Delhi: A People's Movement* by Dr Kavita Sharma, former principal of the college and W D Mathur have reproduced two pages from *Ek Shatabdi* by Col Brij Behari Sharan. These detail the cruel end that Seth Ramji Das Gurwale met at the hands of the British. When the British began looking for collaborators, they found that the Seth had helped the last Mughal Emperor financially and also supplied him with provisions for his army. The help was crucial at a time when the royal treasury in the Red Fort was almost empty. Bahadur Shah Zafar may not have been able to carry on the fight against the British without help from his friend.

Seth Ramji Das Gurwale was arrested and was given the worst possible torture. The British officers unleashed on him, hounds and hunting dogs. Delhi's richest man and banker was mercilessly mauled and bitten almost to death before he was hanged in public opposite the Kotwali in Chandni Chowk.

In 1899, Seth Krishan Das Gurwale, the martyr banker's grandson established Delhi's Hindu College along with others. It opened its doors in Kinari Bazar in Chandni Chowk. The setting up of the college at that time was a nationalist move to provide high education to common Indians. The fire of nationalism lit by the supreme sacrifice of Seth Ramji Das Gurwale continued in the family. It should not come as a surprise to readers that during the fight for Independence, Hindu College produced many heroes, a fact stated by Dr Kavita Sharma.

Delhi's residents suffered immensely during the Mutiny. First, the sepoys of the East India Company looted and robbed them, and finally when the victorious British marched into the city, they, too indulged in looting as they went house to house under the pretext of looking for hidden mutineers. Many were killed. I consider them among Delhi's forgotten heroes.

Chapter 6

QUEEN VICTORIA AND THE COSY INDIAN NATIONAL CONGRESS

As the British government took over India from the Mughals at the end of the 1857 mutiny, the people of the country now regarded Queen Victoria as the ruler. However, unlike the Mughals or other rulers earlier, Queen Victoria did not reside in the capital of India but continued to live in her home, 'The Osborne House,' on the Isle of Wight. A viceroy represented the monarch as ruler of India or in London. He was based in Calcutta, because the East India Company ruled from there.

An interesting development took place as she became the monarch of India. The first coins that came out from the mint after she was proclaimed as ruler of India, carried her bust on one side, mentioning her title, Queen of England. It was only when pointed out by several of her Indian staff that she was the Empress of India, a position far superior than the queen of a small island country that the correction was done. The coins then began to mention her as Queen of England and Empress of India.

Queen Victoria had several Indians on her royal staff who it is said were never tired of telling the English staff that they were the staff of the empress. At the Osborne House, she also had a royal Indian style ornate Darbar Hall where she used to meet dignitaries and hold receptions. The Durbar Hall can still be seen by visitors to the Isle of Wight.

One of the first acts that the British administration undertook as rulers of India was to disarm the country. Not that common people of India carried any arms on them. Having just crushed the mutiny the government was aware that there were a lot of weapons around. Every weapon had not been surrendered or captured. A large number of mutineers had disappeared into their villages. Then there were these jagirdars, zamindars and other officials or nobility that kept armed persons to protect them and their properties. Even their underlings had access to the arms.

In order to bring peace to India and ensure complete law and order, the British administration achieved its objective in disarming India. As for the five hundred odd princely states ruled by the maharajas and nawabs, the British had them all answerable and knew what they had and where. These states had all accepted British sovereignty and surrendered many other powers including foreign policy. They retained internal administration. Thus, after the Mutiny of 1857 no resident of India could keep a weapon. Shops dealing in arms were allowed to sell some government approved rifles for *shikar* (hunting) or personal revolvers only after a license to own one was obtained from the authorities. All this was done to forestall any threat of an armed insurrection.

In this author's view, it was tragic that the Victoria government in India retained most of the employees of the East India Company. As was expected, the company's culture of loot and exploitation continued which was what the employees were addicted to. The city of Delhi lost its charm and glamour as it was no longer the capital of India. Also, the viceroy in Calcutta would not know much of goings on in North India. Then there was also the office of the Secretary of State for India in London to report on India matters. If you go to London, you must visit the India House building, far superior even to the foreign office of the British Government next to it. The majestic building of the Secretary of State and Durbar there were built by the Government of India and should have been rightly with India.

Queen Victoria in many ways began shedding her powers and letting elected leaders run the United Kingdom government. She virtually stopped wielding political power. After the death of her consort Prince Albert, she was spending more time at the royal residence Osborne House. During her long reign, she steadily turned the British monarchy into a symbolic one. The powers of Parliament and the House of Commons were such that the country became a democracy where the monarch was a titular head.

As Empress of India, though not based in India, she took keen interest in the developments that were taking place there. A visit to Osborne House where she spent many years of her life would show any visitor how she treated her relationship with India. In the Durbar Hall she would meet visitors and hold discussions in the durbar style of Indian monarchs. She had employed several Indian staff who were never tired of telling the English staff she was Empress of India. Maharaja Duleep Singh who was attached to her office as ADC was a favourite of Queen Victoria as also of her husband who drew a painting of his that can be seen at the Osborne House.

Peace was returning to India as the British hierarchy settled down after the mutiny. But deep down the people were unhappy as the new rulers carried on with their racist attitude towards the population. When visiting a British official, Indians were not offered a chair or expected to sit down. In her proclamation, the queen had assured the people of India that as her subjects, she would treat them at par with her British subjects. This unfortunately was not happening at the ground level in India. There seemed to be no way that people could convey this to the empress.

The British government started an enquiry to probe the reasons for the Mutiny of 1857. This uprising against the British had somehow remained confined to the sepoys and some Indian nobles and maharajas. While all kinds of reports were made available to the government, one civil servant who knew and had suffered during the mutiny at first hand was Alan Octavian Hume.

Hume had originally studied in London to be a doctor. When he found a job for himself in the Indian Civil Service, he was sent to the East India College at Haileybury in England to study for the job. After finishing his studies, he arrived in Calcutta in 1849 and was posted as magistrate at Etawah in the province of UP. He was appalled at the condition of the people and farmers of Etawah. During his early days of stay in Etawah, he took steps to improve the service to people and the farmers. He was also involved in some of the military actions. When the Sepoy mutiny happened in 1857, he felt he was safe in Etawah because of his popularity. Etawah was not far from Meerut where the mutiny began.

With the company sepoys now in mutiny at many places including those who were based in Etawah, Hume was protected by all of his Indian staff who remained loyal to him. When the sepoy mutiny gained more ground, his loyal Indian staff helped him to take refuge in Agra. He stayed there for six months. As the situation began to settle down, Hume moved back in January 1858 to Etawah to his job. To protect Etawah, he raised a small force of local troops.

Hume was convinced that the policies followed by the British officers in not understanding their men were responsible for the uprising. As soon as he came back to Etawah, he was welcomed by the local people. His term in Etawah was considered a singular success by the government because of his relations with the local people and his respect for their beliefs and religion.

Hume, during his stay in Etawah had brought about many reforms and executed development work. He started with the police department making it people friendly. He also set up a number of free primary schools for children. He conversed regularly with the locals to know their problems and issues. He involved the city's rich in the reforms. He was able to establish several scholarships for higher education for deserving students. He built a high school with his own money. This school is still in operation at Etawah and now has a college. He encouraged women's education and schools for girls were also set up. He advocated widow remarriage. To bring greater business to Etawah, he set up a proper commercial market that is still known as Humeganj.

With his great success in Etawah, he was able to advise the Governor General of India about steps that needed to be taken to ensure that there was no repeat of the uprising of 1857.

Lord Mayo, the Governor General appreciated the ideas for reforms that Hume was providing when he got transferred and was posted in the Central Government. Hume wanted modern practices in agriculture where poor yields from old systems meant poverty. He set up a model farm where farmers could see the improved methods of farming. He recommended to the Governor General the setting up of demonstrative farms in every district.

Inspite of the efforts of officials like Hume to improve the conditions of the farmers and introduce better agricultural practices, India suffered a terrible famine in 1876-78. This naturally led to anger with the death of around eight million people. However, exact figures were not available. The government was concerned, about the reaction of the people to this natural calamity. As far as the poor were concerned, nothing could be worse than what had already happened with their lives. Could there be another uprising?

Hume had his ups and downs while in government service because of his belief on what had led to the 1857 uprising. However, he was firm in his belief that there should be continuous dialogue with the people of India if any uprising or a situation of revolt was to be avoided. He had begun to approach several educated Indians and other Englishmen who had decided to stay in India to build an organisation that could continuously have dialogues with the government and convey people's concerns.

Indian National Congress

In 1883 after his retirement from government service, Hume wrote an open letter to the graduates of the Calcutta University to form a national political movement. This ultimately led to the formation of the Indian National Congress. He took the initiative and convened a meeting in Bombay where he invited carefully selected people—those who were considered loyal to the British. Hume reached out to Mr W C Bonnerjee to be the first President of the Indian National Congress. Mr Bonnerjee was in many ways more English than the English.

When the group met in Bombay (today's Mumbai), in the course of the meeting the group members ensured that in their speeches their loyalty to the British was not put in doubt. Not even one educated commoner was part of the meeting. Commoners were shunned even thereafter till Gandhi appeared on the scene. The Congress Party was more like a meeting club of gentlemen, an organisation that underwent a sea change in the course of time when Mohandas Karamchand Gandhi became better known.

Many in the British administration were not happy with the emergence of the Indian National Congress, even though it was never tired of expressing its loyalty to the British Crown.

As the son of a radical politician, Hume too had radical ideas and steadily expanded the base of the Congress. He wanted the Congress to focus on the issues of poverty, farmers' welfare and women's education. He felt that there was not enough support or action by the Congress leaders of the time on these issues. Even as he perhaps wanted to stay on in India, he felt he had achieved his life's mission in India with the birth of the Indian National Congress. He decided to return to England in 1894 and passed away in 1912.

Economic deprivation, periodic famines and disease were leading to dissatisfaction among the people of India. They were looking for an administration which could provide not just stability but deal with other issues of development expected of a government or a ruler. Education was meanwhile leading to the awakening of India from its long dark period that started with the rule of Aurangzeb. Early Muslim invaders too had done a lot of damage to the educational institutions. A great University at Nalanda had been burnt down with extremely precious manuscripts. It is said that it took more than a year to burn all the books at the University. The founding of the Indian National Congress had given some hope to the people to voice their concerns. People also became aware of their rights. As declared by Queen Victoria they expected to be treated at par with her other subjects including the British subjects.

Chapekar Brothers

Poona (now Pune) was hit by plague towards the end of 1896. It was around this time that London too had faced plague, though on a small scale, and consequently managed to contain it. The British had experience of dealing with plague as they had suffered the worst attack in 1666 when it spread all over Europe with nearly two-thirds of the population being wiped out.

In Pune, the government failed to contain the plague. Instead of dealing with the problem in an organised and humane manner, the government used force in removing those hit by the killer disease. Poona was also a military cantonment. To deal with the disease, a special Plague Committee was formed under W C Rand, an Indian Civil Service officer. He used British troops to enforce government instructions on the plague. These troops entered people's homes at many places to remove suspected plague victims. There were serious complaints of loot by the troops from these homes. There were complaints that in many cases, the troops had taken away idols from the temples at home. There were complaints also of molestation of women when they resisted robbery of their jewellery by these troops. In many cases, the troops entered people's homes, sometime past midnight.

This manner of dealing with the plague led to anger among the people of Poona. Congress leader Bal Gangadhar Tilak severely criticised the tyrannical manner in which Rand had gone about controlling the plague. But the administration ignored Tilak's criticism. This public anger hit the Chapekar family of Poona. The family's young sons were shocked and two of the brothers, Damodar and Balkrishna, decided to eliminate Rand for being responsible for the actions of his men and the English troops.

The two brothers decided to carry out their task on the occasion of Queen Victoria's Golden Jubilee celebrations on 22 June 1897. As Rand and his escort returned from the celebrations at the government house in their carriages, the brothers were waiting for them at their selected spot on Ganeshkhind road. The first to be shot was Lt Ayerst and then Rand. Ayerst died on the spot, while Rand succumbed to his injuries and died on 3 July 1897.

Both the brothers escaped after murdering Rand and Ayerst. Damodar was arrested when the Dravid brothers gave information to the police of his whereabouts. When put on trial, Damodar did not express any regret about his action. He told the court that his action was in response to the behaviour of European soldiers when entering the homes of people in Poona. He said these troops had broken idols, misbehaved with women, and mercilessly handled victims of plague. He declared that what he did was to take revenge. Damodar was sentenced to death and hanged on 22 April 1898.

Balkrishna who had disappeared after the shooting was found by the police, betrayed by a friend. The police arrested him, put him on trial and he too was sentenced to death. He was hanged on 18 April 1898. The Dravid brothers, the informers who were responsible for the arrest of Damodar were eliminated by the third Chapekar brother, Vasudeo. He was arrested. He also in the end faced the gallows on 8 May 1899. There is a small memorial to Chapekar brothers in Poona at Ganeshkhind Road. But it has no details as to what this memorial is about. This was the first act of violent reaction against the British since 1857. Tilak was arrested during the Rand episode. His political writings and speeches were beginning to raise political awareness.

Raja Ram Mohan Roy and the Renaissance

Opening of schools and providing education at higher levels was bringing about a new awakening in the country. It had started from Bengal where the East India Company had taken early action on education, setting up a university in Calcutta. This awakening of the people of India after a long dark period of Mughal rule and chaos that followed is better known in history as the Renaissance from Bengal. This impacted all aspects of life, not just religion. The first effort of the movement was to try and change the existing customs of the Hindu religion such as caste, cruelty and sati. The renaissance brought about a political awakening beyond the 1857 mutiny. People were learning the ideas of democracy and self-rule.

Ram Mohan Roy, later to be known as Raja Ram Mohan Roy after being conferred the title of Raja by the Mughal Emperor Shah Alam II, was the father of the renaissance movement. His movement started from Calcutta where he helped in the founding of the Presidency College in Calcutta together with some educationl institutions. Raja Ram Mohan Roy pushed for education of science among other subjects. In course of time, Bengal produced some notable scientists. He also campaigned for women's education. All this education was not just going to provide civil servants for the Raj, but was beginning to influence political thought. Educated Indians were able to deal with the British at par. Most British who came to India were not that well-educated. Education and studies of India's ancient literature brought a new sense of awakening and pride among the people.

Aurobindo Ghosh

The first Indian to be selected for the coveted Indian Civil Service, which was till then the exclusive preserve of

Englishmen, was Satyendra Nath Tagore from Bengal. Once inducted into service, he served his tenure in Bombay. There were others also who enthusiastically studied and appeared for ICS selection, which also meant study and training in England for the job. Among them was Aurobindo Ghosh coming from a highly anglicised family of Dr Krishna Dhun Ghosh. He lived the lifestyle of an Englishman at home. He wanted his son to be a perfect Englishman and be educated for the Civil Service. He took him to England and had him live with an English family during his studies there.

While in England away from his father, Aurobindo was getting influenced by nationalist thoughts. In England, he met a large number of Indians, many of them with nationalist thoughts or belonging to groups advocating India's freedom. This was something that his family had never thought or discussed. He cleared his exams for the ICS, but somehow decided not to go for it. Instead, he joined the civil service of Maharaja Sayajirao Gaekwad III of Baroda. Aurobindo was very happy with his work in Baroda for the maharaja. The maharaja, agreeing with his ideas, went on to provide funds to Aurobindo to open more schools. He also began carrying out social reforms. The two would agree on issues such as freedom of India from not approving the way English ruled in India.

While Aurobindo was in Baroda, his brother Barinder Ghosh known at home as Barin came to spend some time with him. The two brothers would talk for hours, as any two brothers would, but their talk was for creating centres for propagating and training for revolution in India. Barin was so taken with the idea of fighting for India's freedom that he took an oath holding the *Bhagavad Gita* in hand to work for and devote his life to the cause of freeing his country from the British.

Returning home, Barin spent his full time spreading ideas of freedom and setting up branches of Anushilan Samiti, something like today's gyms but also to train members in martial arts.

When the Delhi Durbar of 1911 took place, all the princes and maharajas and nawabs of technically sovereign areas were expected to be there in full regalia and bow before the King Emperor three times and then backtrack not showing their back to him. Sayajirao III was the only maharaja who defied the British suggestion. He was not dressed in his regalia, walked to the emperor, bowed once and turned and walked away.

Aurobindo now began taking interest in political writings and in one such writing, he criticised the Congress being run by a tiny elite who celebrated any small concession made to them. In his view, the Congress was a party of loyalists to the English. As Aurobindo was also writing speeches for Sayajirao III, in one such speech he compared the prosperity in England with the extreme poverty in India. Maharaja Sayajirao accepted the speech written by Aurobindo.

Aurobindo thought it was time to take leave from Maharaja Sayajirao and move back to Bengal from Baroda to get involved in the fight for freedom. His brother Barin Ghosh had been busy setting up branches of Anushilan Samiti. Barin and his colleagues had managed to learn bomb making. Barin had inspired many young people in Anushilan Samiti to take part in revolutionary action for freedom of the motherland.

Once back in Calcutta, Aurobindo set up a newspaper *Jugantor*. At the same time, he started writing for *Bande Matram*, Bipin Chandra Pal's newspaper. His articles were hard hitting and critical of the British administration.

Aurobindo was not content only with writing. He was concerned about the kind of education being imparted that could only prepare the young to work as clerks for the government. He busied himself to this cause of education and succeeded in setting up a national college as an alternative to missionary run institutions. The college has grown over the time into being today's Jadavpur University.

Bengal Partition

In 1905, Lord Curzon, Viceroy of India decided to partition Bengal for what he called better administration. This came instantly handy to Aurobindo and other revolutionaries to launch an agitation against such a plan. The partition would have made East Bengal Muslim-dominated and West Bengal, Hindu. To Aurobindo and other revolutionaries, this was clearly part of the British policy of divide and rule of the two communities.

The agitation against the division of Bengal received India-wide support and one great leader who rose from this agitation was Bipin Chandra Pal. He was to be later part of the all India trinity of Bal Gangadhar Tilak from Maharashtra, Lala Lajpat Rai from Punjab and Bipin Chandra Pal from Bengal. They were popularly known as Lal Bal Pal. Aurobindo supported the trio against the Indian National Congress. The trio of Lal Bal Pal were severely critical of the Indian National Congress of that time which they considered as a cosy club rather than a party fighting for India's independence.

The agitation against the partition of Bengal not only galvanised the people of Bengal to fight the administration but made an all India impact. During the agitation, the leaders propagated a swadeshi movement calling upon people not to buy British cloth or other British goods. The movement was not about propagating handmade cloth which appeared later with the charkha when Gandhi entered the scene of the freedom struggle and also adopted swadeshi in a different form.

People of Bengal at all levels, enthusiastically participated in the movement against the partition of Bengal. This shook the British rulers, who were not expecting this reaction. They expected at least the Muslims of Bengal may welcome it. Indians at that time were also inspired in their resolve by the news of a small Asian country Japan beating Russia in war. In the midst of all this, groups set up by Barin Ghosh were getting very active. Meanwhile, the British started going after Aurobindo Ghosh for his writings. They started questioning and harassing the staff of *Jugantor*, arresting some of them. All this was being done by the local district magistrate Douglas Kingsford. Barin Ghosh and his colleagues decided to make him a target and teach him a lesson.

The task of eliminating Kingsford was given to two—Prafulla Chaki and Khudiram Bose. After carefully watching movements of Kingsford, the two decided to act on 29 April 1908. As Kingsford together with his friend Fraser and their wives neared a spot where Khudiram and Prafulla were waiting in hiding, young Khudiram jumped on the first carriage and threw a bomb at it and ran away. Unfortunately, this carriage carried the wives of Kingsford and Fraser. Both died from the injuries they received from the bomb blast. Prafulla also ran away from the scene and later was intercepted by a police officer while travelling in a train to Calcutta. Before the police could arrest him at the next station, he took out his revolver and fired at them while running to escape. Before he could be overpowered, Prafulla turned the revolver on himself and died.

Khudiram who had managed to escape reached the railway station at Wani. Here two police constables managed to grab him before he even had a chance to pull out his revolver. Khudiram Bose, just 18 years old was put on trial and hanged on 11 August 1908.

He was the first young martyr in India's battle for independence from the British Raj which came into being with Queen Victoria's proclamation.

Khudiram Bose was just seven when his parents passed away. His older sisters looked after him. Khudiram was inspired with the nationalist thought from the very young age of twelve and by sixteen he was active in planting bombs at some of the police stations. He was thus considered to be the right choice by Barin in dealing with Kingsford.

The authorities now zeroed in on Barin Ghosh and his associates being responsible for attacks on Kingsford and Fraser. In a raid on his office, Barin Ghosh and a number of his associates were arrested before they could escape. Police also went in and arrested Aurobindo Ghosh. Meanwhile, members of the Anushilan Samiti in other places of Bengal carried out attacks on government premises in protest. They managed to track down the police man who had tried to arrest Prafulla and killed him.

The trial of Aurobindo Ghosh and others including his brother Barin began at Alipore in what came to be known as Emperor vs Aurobindo Ghosh. Barin Ghosh and his associate, Ullaskar Dutta, were sentenced to death, which later turned into life imprisonment while thirty-six others were given sentences varying in years. Aurobindo was acquitted. Barin and Ullaskar were sent to Andaman Cellular jail.

Aurobindo, on his release in 1909, was welcomed back as a national hero. He started a new newspaper *Karmayogin*, which was a huge success with his nationalist writings demanding complete freedom. In his view, the Indian National Congress was only seeking a small pie in the home rule. Aurobindo continued to be critical of the Congress and its policy of begging facilities from the British. His newspaper had an all-India appeal and soon had editions in other languages. Celebrities from India and abroad when visiting India were calling on him being the tallest Indian leader. Early in 1910, Aurobindo received information that the government was planning to arrest him again for his writings. On hearing the news—without waiting and without going home—he made his way to the Hooghly river with a couple of his colleagues.

On reaching Hooghly, they hired a boat and made their way to the French enclave of Chandernagore where the British had no jurisdiction. It was a very tiny enclave, not far from Calcutta. The British could not enforce any of their laws there. But as may be expected, the place was full of British spies and informers. Aurobindo decided that they should move onto the bigger French enclave of Pondicherry (today's Puducherry) in South India. He had planned to spend a few months there before making his way back. Once in Pondicherry, he decided to stay on there.

The fact is that by the time Aurobindo arrived in Pondicherry, he had already lit the flame of nationalism and demand for freedom in India. His brother Barin and the Anushilan Samiti had made great sacrifices. Barin was in Cellular jail at the same time as was Damodar Veer Savarkar. He managed to escape from there in 1915 and arrived in Puri. Escaping from Cellular jail was an impossible task in which Savarkar had failed.

Aurobindo had planned to spend only a few months in the French enclave. He had the time to peacefully take stock of all that had been done and plan for the future. He felt that, in an India that had accepted British rule after the failure of the Mutiny of 1857, he had been successful in lighting the flame demanding independence and exit of the foreign ruler. He believed that this cycle could not be turned back with the trinity of Lal Bal Pal carrying on their demand for India's self-reliance and independence. The people of India were now fully behind the movement for independence and swadeshi. He was convinced that the foreign ruler would have to go. Mangal Pandey and Bengal regiments of East India Company were responsible for leading the 1857 War of Independence.

Aurobindo had led Bengal to lead the ultimate fight for freedom of India.

In Pondicherry, he felt he had a different task to serve the people of India. He decided that he needed to make India aware of its rich heritage and shake it off from its complicity in accepting foreign values in the course of a long rule by foreign powers.

Many of India's educated and elite were accepting Western culture. To counter this, he decided to devote his time in Pondicherry to bring India back in touch with its own rich civilisation. This task he felt was not going to be easy. He wanted India to be aware of the fact that the word *Swaraj* comes from the Vedas.

Aurobindo made a thorough study of ancient Indian literature. To him Bharat was 'Mother Goddess.'

Chapter 7

AJIT SINGH, MADAN LAL DHINGRA, VEER SAVARKAR

The Punjab of 1901 was a different place. Hit by poverty, its people were unhappy with British rule. Punjab was blessed with five rivers and it was the number of those rivers that had given it the name of Punjab—land of five rivers. The British were steadily consolidating their rule over Punjab as they were doing in other parts of India. They had devised a system of administration whereby they could directly remain in touch with people on the ground. Punjab had been broken into a number of districts. Each district had a deputy commissioner as its top civil servant. The district was then broken down into tehsils ranging up to eight or nine depending upon the area of the district. Each tehsil had a *tehsildar* who was helped by a deputy known as *naib* tehsildar. The system apart from tax collection was expected to keep the administration informed of the developments in the villages.

The deputy commissioner was expected to travel through his district at least once a year going from village to village, spending a night there, and getting to know of the farmers' issues directly, and sort those out on the spot in the presence of the tehsildar, naib tehsildar and *patwari*. If the deputy commissioner was married, his wife usually travelled with him to be able to interact with village women to know of their condition and welfare. Civil servants of the British administration started their career from the base of the district. This helped them to get to know India and its people first hand. There were no vehicles in those early days of the second half of the nineteenth century. Either horses or horse carriages were used as conveyance. A tent party would go ahead and set up a tent for the travelling party of the deputy commissioner to have a durbar to meet the villagers and spend the night in a tent. While the deputy commissioner was in village 'A,' the tent party moved ahead to village 'B' and so on.

The big province of Punjab had a vast area of barren land particularly in East Punjab (today's Punjab and Haryana). The administration of Punjab worked out an ambitious plan whereby this barren and waste land could be developed into irrigable agricultural land. The plan was to move people from barren areas and offer them land in areas with canals. That was expected to change their life. This move as expected resulted in prosperous agricultural areas like Lyallpur emerging with its canals. As the scheme moved ahead and more barren land was made irrigable, areas like Montgomery and Sargodha came into being. This was the scene as the nineteenth century ended.

The farmers were a happy lot in the canal irrigated areas. They had worked very hard in developing the barren land to which they had come from East Punjab. This barren land had been promised free to those who moved there. Many of them were ex-servicemen from the army. Most of them had moved from East Punjab areas like Jullundur, Hoshiarpur and Amritsar. When they arrived, the only thing that existed was barren land and new canals for irrigation. The hard work of new settlers had made the barren areas not only fertile but a nice place to move, to live and work.

Pagdi Sambhal Jatta

At the turn of the century, the British government without warning promulgated a Colonisation Act under which it declared itself to be the owner of all the barren land. Suddenly the farmers who were given these barren lands when they arrived were reduced to landless farmers. The law even denied succession to the family after the death of the farmer—only the eldest son could inherit and if the eldest had died, the land would revert to the government. This was a strange anti-ownership law for the new settlers, who had arrived there in large numbers.

The new law, considered as extortionist, sparked anger among the farmers, many of them ex-servicemen. They had already been paying heavy irrigation charges to the government apart from the regular tax on their incomes. The farmers rejected the law most vehemently.

The farmers first approached the Congress party and its leader Lala Lajpat Rai to help them get their rights. But the Congress party simply refused to take up the farmers' cause, saying that the law had already been passed. Ajit Singh, uncle of Bhagat Singh, and his colleagues came on the scene, promising the farmers to lead their agitation and telling them that it would not be easy to have the law repealed. Lahore was now crowded with disenchanted farmers. There were large crowds of protestors at the rallies and demonstrations. The slogans in the rallies were not just for withdrawal of the 'black law,' but a demand that the English leave India.

Soon the agitation got a name when a newspaper, *Jhang Syal*, published a Punjabi song '*Pagdi Sambhal Jatta, Pagdi*

Sambhal Oye.' Pagdi means turban and it is a matter of honour for one to be wearing his turban. The song called upon the farmers to take care of their pagdi—in this case the pagdi being the land owned by the farmers. The British Indian Army had a large number of soldiers from Punjab. News soon reached them as to what was happening to their land, in most cases owned by their family. These soldiers started making representations to their officers. Some started attending the protest meetings to hear the speeches. The police and Punjabi soldiers refused to fire on the protestors.

The British then ordered the arrest of Lala Lajpat Rai, Ajit Singh and several of their colleagues. Many had already been arrested. Ajit Singh and Lala Lajpat Rai were sent to far away Mandalay jail in Burma. The author of this book once called on the mother of martyr Bhagat Singh. In the course of the talk, she told me that young Bhagat Singh used to tell her that when he would grow up, he would push the English out of India and bring uncle back home.

Soon after the arrest of Lala Lajpat Rai and Ajit Singh and their being sent to Mandalay jail, the Congress moved the government seeking release of Lala Lajpat Rai. It distanced itself from Ajit Singh and his actions and strongly denied any relationship between the two. Lala Lajpat Rai was released in November 1907. Realising that the *'Pagdi Sambhal Jatta'* agitation had reached the army, the British government withdrew the controversial law in toto. It was a great victory for Ajit Singh and his colleagues. He was also released from Mandalay jail. When he reached Punjab, he received an unprecedented welcome by massive crowds.

If the British were expecting Ajit Singh and his colleagues to go easy because their demand for withdrawal of the Colonisation Act had been accepted, they were in for a disappointment. Ajit turned his full attention to his Urdu newspaper *Peshwa* and to the Bharat Mata Society and Bharat Mata Book agency, which used to publish posters and pamphlets that were mass distributed. The government was alarmed by the impact of this literature. They wanted to shut down publication of literature of freedom fighters. Ajit came to know that the government was planning to arrest him and his colleagues. He rightly felt that he did not want to waste his time in jail. He decided to move away from India before the British could arrest him.

He, together with his colleagues Harkesh, Zia-ul-Haq and Amba Prasad managed to reach Tehran. For this escape from India, Ajit had changed his name to Mirza Hasan Khan. The British failed to arrest Mirza Hasan khan!

While in Iran, he asked his other colleagues to continue their activities in publishing. Ajit Singh left Iran and travelling through Turkey and other European countries, he finally reached Paris. Freedom fighters had a support base in Paris. He was in touch with organisations espousing the cause of Indian freedom in these countries. While in Paris, he received bad news that his colleague Amba Prasad was killed while fighting the British army alongside nationalists of Iran.

On reaching London, he met with Dr Veer Vinayak Damodar Savarkar, who was living in London at that time. He was popularly known as Veer Savarkar. The British looked upon Ajit Singh with great animosity because of his activities in the cause of India's freedom. To avoid arrest there that could result in his deportation to India, Ajit Singh moved to Switzerland and touched base with several revolutionary groups from other European countries operating there. He was able to meet Lenin and Trotsky, two tall Communist leaders.

Ajit Singh decided to move towards America and landed

in Brazil. He got in touch with the Gadar Party and its leaders in San Francisco. In 1932, he returned to Europe and in Italy, he founded the Friends of India Society. Italy was home to several other freedom fighters of India. They were able to get the use of the Rome Radio from the Mussolini government to broadcast programmes in Hindustani. He started broadcasts to India urging the listeners to rise against the British. At the end of World War II in Europe and the fall of Italy, Ajit Singh was arrested by the allies in December 1946. He was taken to different prisons in Italy and Germany, where he was tortured.

His health was deteriorating with all that was being done to him. When his colleagues in India became aware of his failing health, they urged Jawahar Lal Nehru, who was then head of the Interim government under Lord Wavell, to demand the release of Ajit Singh from the allies and bring him back to India. Ajit Singh was finally brought to London and handed over to the Indian High Commission.

Ajit Singh was very upset with the the Indian High Commission officials for they did not let him meet local Indians who wanted to felicitate and honour him. These officials were basically loyal employees of the British, yet to realise that India was heading towards freedom. Their attitude was very pro-British.

Ajit got a huge welcome when he finally arrived in India. Thousands of people were present when he reached Karachi, and it seemed as though the whole city had turned out to receive and cheer him. Meeting with friends and other people in Karachi, he then arrived in Delhi. Ajit Singh had a brief meeting with Nehru. Now that a government of Independent India was taking shape under Jawaharlal Nehru, he discussed and explained to him as to what should be the future of the country as dreamt by the freedom fighters. Remember he was a revolutionary and not a member of the Congress Party.

Ajit Singh left for Lahore on 9 April 1947 where he received a huge welcome by the people of Punjab. The son of Punjab was back on the eve of India's Independence. But he was a sad person even though the country was only weeks away from Independence. This was not the freedom they had fought for—the country was to be partitioned. He did not approve of this and had made known this to the leaders and people of India. In his message to the people of India, he reminded the youth that the nation needed social and political revolutions. There was a need to end ignorance, injustice, hunger and poverty in the country.

Ajit Singh was now in poor health and sad as he was moved from Lahore to Dalhousie, a small hill station to recuperate. The Communal riots had broken out on the verge of Partition. Millions of Hindus and Sikhs started to leave the areas that were to be part of Pakistan. Violence spread all over North India as also in Bengal. He felt sad and pained at what was going on. In Pondicherry, Aurobindo Ghosh who had lit the torch for the fight for Independence after the 1857 uprising was equally unhappy with this freedom that came with the partition of India. This was not the kind of freedom that the revolutionaries had fought for.

In Dalhousie, Ajit Singh did not bounce back to health. He felt helpless not being able to do anything when news came of the killings, rape and abduction of women as India neared its Independence Day. Ajit Singh mourned that the British had succeeded in their plan of dividing India and its people. A sad Ajit Singh, a great hero of India's fight for freedom passed away on the very day that India achieved Independence —15 August 1947.

Madan Lal Dhingra

Punjab towards the end of the nineteenth century was witnessing the emergence of many heroes who fought for India's Independence. The youth wanted to see the glory of the Punjab of Maharaja Ranjit Singh's days. Punjab unfortunately had a large number of collaborators serving the British. They were either rich businessmen or well-placed government employees. There were several highly anglicised families in the province as were in Bengal. Madan Lal Dhingra was one of the seven sons of a prosperous anglicised family in Amritsar. His father was the civil surgeon of the city and greatly appreciated the British rule over India. He wanted all his sons to study abroad. Sensitive as he was from a very young age, Madan Lal was shocked by the poverty that he saw as he moved about in the streets of the holy city of Amritsar or travelled with his parents. Why could the rulers not do something about it was a question that troubled his mind. The young boy never got any explanation from his parents or others.

As he grew up completing his school studies, he went to Lahore to study at the Government College. The streets of Lahore were full of beggars and that troubled him. Like all other young people, he had always heard in his childhood that India was '*sone kee chidiya*'—land of gold. He often wondered, 'why then poverty—what happened to India's wealth?' He would get the reply that it has all been looted and taken away by foreign invaders. In Lahore, he became fully aware of the Independence Movement notably of Lala Lajpat Rai. He realised the nationalist movement being carried on primarily was to seek home rule.

Young Madan Lal was greatly impressed by the 'Swadeshi' movement which called upon the people of India to use

Indian-made goods. Loyalists were against imports of cloth from Britain. Dhingra refused to accept the college principal's order to use woollen cloth imported from Britain for making the blazer. For not accepting this, he was expelled from the college. Like any father would be, his dad was upset on hearing of his son's expulsion. He asked his son to apologise to the principal and get the expulsion order revoked. Madan Lal defied his father and instead left home. He insisted on wearing clothes made from Swadeshi cloth.

Refusing to return home, he took up a petty job to earn whatever small money he could earn and carry on with his life independently. He had problems here too. He was working for a carriage firm at the foothills of Simla in Kalka. These carriages used to take British and other passengers to Simla. He was dismissed by the carriage company for indiscipline and soon joined as a labourer in a factory. He decided to move to Bombay for a better future. Here too, he could only find petty jobs. His mother and the rest of the family were extremely worried about his future. His elder brother Dr Bihari Lal got him to agree to go to London for further studies. He joined University College to study mechanical engineering.

Dhingra's stay in London was to change his life altogether. It was a different life here. He became aware of other Indians who were activists in the struggle for the Indian Independence movement. He met with Veer Savarkar and one Shyam Krishan Varma. Savarkar believed in revolution and not in home rule demanded by the Congress. In the friendship that Madan Lal developed with him, Savarkar became his hero. As Savarkar and he came to talk about India's struggle for freedom, Madan Lal heard of revolutionary ideas and use of violence to eject the British from India. As in India, Indians in the UK too were angry at the partition of Bengal in 1905 and were protesting about it. In London, Savarkar and several other students including Madan Lal Dhingra had come to the attention of the UK Secret Police.

Dhingra had started taking active part in the fight for India's freedom. He was under constant watch by the Secret Police. The head of the Secret Police was one Curzon Wyllie who was also a close friend of Dhingra's father. When Dhingra's father got reports of the activities of his son in London from his friend Wyllie, he decided to disown his son. He had that news of his disowning his son Madan Lal Dhingra published in the newspapers. Angry as he was at this turn of events, Madan Lal decided to get rid of Curzon Wyllie for he felt he was the cause of his problems with his father. Wyllie had no doubt told his father that his son was hobnobbing with the terrorists, as the freedom fighters were called by the British. To avenge what Wyllie had done to him, Dhingra got a revolver and started his practice at a shooting range on Tottenham Road in London.

The Indian National Association, a social organisation of Indians in London used to hold an annual 'At Home' function in London. On the evening of 1 July 1909, a large number of Indian and Englishmen were gathered at the Imperial Institute. Dhingra was also there. Attending the function was Curzon Wyllie with his wife. When Wyllie was leaving the hall with his wife, Dhingra fired at him almost point blank. Curzon Wyllie was killed. Dhingra was arrested on the spot by the police. Dhingra was calm and collected when the police arrested him. He had made no effort to escape from there. His friends including Savarkar were present when the killing took place.

Back home in India, his father having disowned him, his

family further distanced itself from him and refused to defend him. Gandhi wrote a strong article against the act of killing Curzon Wyllie. Gopal Krishan Gokhale while criticising his act said it had put India in disrepute. On the other hand, the revolutionaries were not bothered with such comments. A few days later, several members of the Indian community resident in London gathered in a meeting to pass a resolution of condemnation on the killing of Curzon Wyllie and declare their loyalty to the Crown.

When the time came for voting after speeches declaring loyalty had been made, the organisers expected unanimity when suddenly some one rose and shouted 'No!' This was Savarkar, a friend of Madan Lal Dhingra. He together with his friends was jostled, beaten and pushed out of the hall by these Indians loyal to the British.

Among others, people of Ireland praised and supported Dhingra for his act. Ireland too at that time was fighting for its independence and separation from the United Kingdom. There were posters and leaflets distributed not just in Ireland but in England clearly saying that Ireland honours Dhingra.

The trial of Madan Lal Dhingra began a few days later when the prosecution presented a lot of witnesses. Dhingra stayed quiet and refused to have an advocate for himself. He, however, got up to make a statement when the judge asked him if he had to say anything in his own defence. He read out:

'I do not want to say anything in defence of myself, but simply to prove the justice of my deed. As for myself, no English law court has got any authority to arrest and detain me in prison, or pass a sentence of death on me. This is the reason I did not have any counsel to defend me. And I maintain that if it is patriotic for an English man to fight against the Germans if they were to occupy this country, it is much more justifiable and patriotic in my case to fight against the English. I hold the English people responsible for the murder of 80 millions of Indians in the last fifty years, and they are also responsible for taking away Pounds 1,00,000,000 every year from India to this country. I also hold them responsible for the hanging and deportation of my patriotic countrymen, who did just the same as the English people here are advising their countrymen to do. And the Englishman who goes out to India and gets, say a Pounds 100.00 a month, that simply means he passes a sentence of death on a thousand of my poor countrymen, because these thousand people could easily live on this hundred pounds which the Englishman spends mostly on his frivolity and pleasures. Just as the Germans have no right to occupy this country, so the English people have no right to occupy India, and it is perfectly justifiable on our part to kill the Englishman who is polluting our sacred land. I am surprised at the terrible hypocrisy, the farce, and the mockery of the English people. They pose as the champions of oppressed humanity—the people of the Congo and the people of Russia—when there is terrible oppression and horrible atrocities committed by them in India; the killing of two millions of people every year and the outraging of our women? In case this country is occupied by Germans, and the Englishman, not bearing to see the German walking with the insolence of a conqueror in the streets of London, goes and kills one or two Germans, and that Englishman is held as a patriot by the people of this country, then certainly I am prepared to work for the emancipation of my motherland. Whatever else I have to say is in the paper before the Court. I make this statement, not because I wish to plead for mercy or anything of that kind. I wish that English people would sentence me to death, for in that case the vengeance of my countrymen will be all the more keen. I put forward this statement to show the justice of my cause to the outside world, and especially to our sympathisers in America and Germany.'

When told by the court after the statement as to why the court should not give judgement of death, Madan Lal replied confidently, 'I have told you over and over again that I do not acknowledge the authority of the Court, you can do whatever you like. You can pass a sentence of death on me. I do not care. You white people are all powerful now, but remember, we shall have our turn in the time to come, when we can do what we like.'

Madan Lal Dhingra was sentenced to death by hanging. No one from Dhingra's family went to see him in jail before his hanging, but Savarkar went there. He told him that his last wish was to be cremated according to Hindu rites. He also gave his final written message to the people of India which read as:

'I believe that a nation held in bondage with the help of foreign bayonets is in perpetual state of war. Since open battle is impossible for a disarmed race, I attacked by surprise; since guns were denied to me I drew forth my pistol and fired.

As a Hindu, I feel that a wrong done to my country is an insult to God. Poor in health and intellect, a son like myself has nothing to offer to the Mother but his own blood, and so I have sacrificed the same on her altar. Her cause is the cause of Shri Rama. Her service is the service of Sri Krishna. This war of independence will continue between India and England so long as the Hindu and the English races last (if the present unnatural relation does not end).

Vande Matram'

In the course of the trial a British poet Wilfrid Blunt wrote:
No Christian Martyr ever faced his judges more fearlessly or with greater dignity. If India could
Produce five hundred men, as resolutely without fear, she would achieve her freedom....'

Madan Lal Dhingra was hanged on the morning of 17 August 1909 at 9 am. He was only 24 when he embraced death. His wish to be cremated was denied and he was buried inside the jail. The British were concerned that his place of burial outside or cremation could become his memorial for Indians. A rabid anti-Indian British leader responsible for the death of five million Indians in a famine during World War II, Winston Churchill is said to have admired Dhingra's statement before the Court, '*being the finest ever made in the name of patriotism.*'

Long after Independence, it was in 1976 that his remains were brought back to Amritsar, his hometown, where a statue in his memory now stands. In 1992, a commemorative postage stamp was issued in his memory. Madan Lal Dhingra was the first Indian to be executed abroad in the fight for the country's freedom.

Veer Savarkar

With Madan Lal Dhingra gone, the British were now looking for his accomplices. Among others, they zeroed in on Veer Savarkar. Vinayak Damodar Savarkar popularly known as Veer Savarkar was born on 28 May 1883 in village Bhagur near Poona (today's Pune). He was born in a very orthodox Brahmin family; he was ahead of his time in refusing to accept the caste system and several other orthodox values. As a child, many of his friends were from lower castes and he would eat at their homes as well. Although a Brahmin, he was not a vegetarian and loved prawns. From school, itself, young Savarkar took keen interest in politics. Defying an edict of those days advising Hindus not to travel by sea or else you lose your caste, Savarkar had travelled to England for higher education. There, Savarkar took keen interest in a 'Free India Society' and another organisation known as 'India House.' Students would regularly meet here and discuss freedom for India. When Madan Lal Dhingra met Savarkar in the course of his studies, he was initiated into attending meetings at India House. Savarkar was already under observation of the British police. When he completed his studies in law, he was denied practice at the Bar. The reason given was that he had been charged for anti-British activities.

Savarkar had also met Gandhiji during his days at India House. He had bluntly told Gandhi that he did not agree with his methods of non-violence. Similarly, Savarkar and those working with him felt wronged, especially when Gandhiji rebuked them for their method which preached violence.

Veer Savarkar had undergone a traumatic period during the trial of Madan Lal Dhingra who had become a very close friend of his. His execution further shook him and he began to devote more time to freedom movement activities. Police cracked down on him and his associates after the execution of Dhingra. Savarkar had been staying at India House. The British Government ordered its closure, making Savarkar homeless. No one would rent out a room to him obviously under pressure from the British police.

Savarkar had also started working on what became a defining book on the Mutiny of 1857, which he clearly termed as the First War of Independence. The British became aware and tried their best to stop its publication. He managed to get the book published in Holland in 1909. He got it circulated in India and countries around the world. He wanted the world to know what had happened in India in 1857 and how the British were ruling over India. The translated versions of his book appeared in India soon despite restrictions by the British.

News from his family in India was not very encouraging for Veer Savarkar. Both his brothers had been arrested for anti-state activities, and one of them was sent to the horrible Cellular jail in Andaman islands. His family was in dire poverty and homeless. The British in England got a case filed against him in India on an incident that had happened in 1906.

Expecting that the British might arrest him, Savarkar whose health was not in good shape quietly made his way to Paris where he was looked after by Madam Bhikaji Cama. He stayed at her home and his health improved. He decided to return to London much against the advice of Bhikaji Cama and her group. The police were indeed waiting for him. He was arrested upon arrival and taken to Brixton prison.

If Savarkar had been tried in England, he would at best have got a few months in prison. Perhaps that is all that he was expecting when he decided to return to London against the advice of his colleagues in Paris. The warrant of his arrest from India issued in a 1906 case was manipulated in such a way that he was to be extradited to India from England. In India he would get a heavy sentence as per the colonial laws. The extradition orders passed, he was put on a steamer and sent towards India.

Faced with this new challenge, Savarkar in connivance with Bhikaji Cama and her associates decided to escape from the ship as it neared the French coast. He managed to get his body into the porthole of the toilet, slithered onto the sea and swam to the shore. He ran to the spot where he was to be picked up by Bhikaji Cama. Unfortunately, they were late and Savarkar was captured by the British from French soil. The British had no right to arrest him from the sovereign soil of France. This caused serious friction between France and Britain but the ship sailed away to India with Savarkar.

Savarkar's escape attempt had become global news. The British were under severe criticism, but they weren't bothered at all. Savarkar suffered the worst kind of torture on the ship from those escorting him back home. He was kept like an animal in a dark and dingy place. The ship arrived in Bombay on 22 September 1910 with a badly bruised and famished Savarkar.

The British wanted to muzzle Savarkar totally, and realising that they wouldn't be able to get a death sentence against him in England, they had intentionally not charged or tried him there. Soon after arrival in Bombay, he was taken to Yerwada jail in Poona.

Savarkar's trial before a special tribunal was a farce that the British authorities in India had specialised in. In a matter of three months ignoring the fact that his capture from French soil was subjudice in the Permanent Court of International Arbitration, he was sentenced to 50 years in jail with hard labour on 30 January 1911. He was to be transported to the notorious Cellular jail in Andaman Islands.

The world was shocked on hearing of this sentence. Savarkar had become known all over Europe and the rest of the world after they read the story of his escape and illegal capture by the British in Marseilles. He was being applauded by the people of Europe as a hero, a martyr and freedom fighter of India. The inhuman sentence given to Savarkar was reported by newspapers all over the world.

The Congress Party, which was no more than a club of the elitist Indians virtually disowned him. Surendra Nath Banerji and William Wedderburn, party president declared that they had nothing to do with Savarkar. Wedderburn was an Englishman who was among the founders of the party.

Veer Savarkar was savagely treated in jail in India before being sent to the Andamans. All his books, including the *Bhagavad Gita*, and his money were taken away from him. He was hardly given any food, other than dry *rotis* sometimes made of the hard cereal jowar. The only way he could eat the stuff was to gulp it down with water. Were the authorities trying a slow death for him?

Savarkar's appeal against the sentence was rejected. With handcuffs and shackles, Savarkar travelled to Madras by train. From Madras, he was put on board the steamer 'Maharaja' along with a large group of forty-odd criminals, all in a cage not large enough even for twenty persons. He was rarely taken to the deck for some fresh air.

Arriving in Port Blair, the authorities again deliberately put him with a Muslim prisoner knowing fully well that he was a practising Hindu. Even though he was a political prisoner, the jailor put him into solitary confinement. Savarkar was shocked to see how efforts were made to convert prisoners to Christianity in the Cellular jail. Many a criminal would gladly do so hoping to get better treatment in the jail or possible early release.

After spending over eleven years in the Cellular jail and suffering the worst of treatment, Savarkar decided to petition the government for his release. He felt that being in a jail like the one in the Andamans, he could hardly serve his nation in ways like social upliftment. During his days in the jail itself he had helped many prisoners in education. His first petition was rejected. However, he was transferred to a jail in India at Yerwada before his release. His brother who had also been imprisoned in the Cellular jail was also sent to Yerwada in January 1924.

Savarkar moved to Ratnagiri before moving to Nasik. He now decided to work on uniting the Hindus through Hindu Sangathan. Sadly, but true, his time was now spent on issues that hardly dealt with India's freedom. He was working on Hindutva. He passed away on 26 February 1966—unsung for his fight for freedom but maligned for his petitions for release and later for being a Hindu leader working for Hindutva.

Chapter 8

THE GHADAR MOVEMENT AND RASH BEHARI BOSE

Queen Victoria's Raj, in effect the British government, set up two twin offices, one in London and the other in Calcutta to rule in India. In the first office in London, it was the Secretary of State for India, who being part of the British government, was answerable to the British Parliament. The second office was of the Viceroy in India who was based in Calcutta. He was the one who looked after the day-to-day administration of India. The choice of Calcutta as the centre for Indian rule was a continuation of the work ethic and culture of the East India Company.

The Viceroy had a cabinet which consisted of some councillors and heads of various government departments like finance, law and order, among other departments. Then came the huge set up of governors, commissioners, deputy commissioners, police chiefs of provinces, judges, magistrates and so on. The British devised this system in a bid to administer the country from the districts upwards.

The weakness of the new administrative system lay in the fact that the East India Company culture still prevailed as most of the company employees had been absorbed in the first stage in the administration. It was as though the British government was now running East India Company minus its commercial activities.

On the ground, Queen Victoria's promise in her proclamation to treat all her subjects equally turned into a paper promise in India, as it didn't seem to matter to the administrators if royalty had let down the people.

Racism still persisted with impunity. Nothing describes this racist attitude better than Baden Powell, a British administrator who had worked in India. He wrote, '...I like my native servants, but as a rule *niggers* seem to be cringing villains....' He forgot that because of poverty, Indians may be working as his domestic helps, but they were proud of their culture and religion.

This attitude of superiority was a great hindrance to the British, who were living and working in India, to feel at home or develop sound relationships with the people whom they had colonised. There was deep anger among the people at large that they were ruled by a foreign country whose only interest was to loot India as was done by the East India Company preceding the rule of Queen Victoria. India's Empress was not living in India. That one fact alone conveyed to the ordinary Indian that she was not much interested in the welfare of her subjects.

Rash Behari Bose

Hardly known today, Rash Behari Bose is one of the early heroes of India's fight for freedom. He was born in village Subaldaha on 25 May 1866 in Burdwan district of West Bengal. His mother passed away when he was only three years old. He was brought up by his maternal aunt. His grandfather took care of his education. The early education was in the village school and later at the Dupleix College at Chandernagore, a French enclave not too far from Calcutta known today as Chanda Nagar. It was during his student days at the college that Rash Behari developed revolutionary ideas for the independence of India. His teacher at the college Charu Chand passed on radical and revolutionary ideas to Rash Behari and other students.

Rash Behari's grandfather wanted him to get on with life after education, which he did not complete. He started his career as a clerk, moved to other jobs, but his mind was always towards fighting for the country to throw the British out. He wanted the British Indian army to rebel again. He joined Aurobindo Ghosh and his people in their protest activities against the British. The strength of Rash Behari was his deep thinking, planning and being master of disguise.

During a meeting of the revolutionaries at Chandernagore, a plan was discussed to assassinate the Viceroy Lord Hardinge, who was to be taken in a Mughal style procession in Delhi in celebration of the city becoming the capital of India again. That was some fifteen months away on 23 December 1912. Thus, there was enough time to plan properly. The idea had come from another revolutionary Shreesh Ghosh, a dare devil himself.

When discussed among the gathered revolutionaries, most thought of the idea as impractical. But Rash Behari said that it was possible. He offered to lead it, but needed someone with him of solid honest commitment towards revolution. Rash Behari found one young man Basant Kumar Biswas from Chandernagore. He was a sixteen-year-old very handsome lad with a clean face.

Rash Behari was working at that time with Forest Research Institute in Dehradun. It was here that he and Basant Kumar did their rehearsals. They knew like everyone else that the viceroy and his wife would be riding an elephant and the procession would move slowly through Chandni Chowk, the heart of Delhi. This procession was to celebrate Delhi becoming the capital once again. The viceroy's procession was meant to show the power and splendour of the British in the style of processions that the Mughals used to have, marching to Red Fort.

Master of disguise that he was, Rash Behari decided that young Basant should dress in a sari and look like a girl, handsome as he was. Dressed like that he took Basant through Chandni Chowk and then chose a place near the clock tower, which was opposite to the town Hall, for Basant to be seated among the ladies. It was a high balcony and the elephant carrying the viceroy and his lady was expected to pass close to it. At the last moment Rash Behari changed the plan and took Basant to the street as a male. He had changed his original plan, concerned that the escape from the balcony could result in the arrest of Basant.

The procession in all its colour and splendour with bands playing was moving slowly through Chandni Chowk with the Viceroy waving to the crowds. As it came near where Rash Behari was standing with Basant at a different point, the bombs were successfully hurled atop the elephant where the viceroy and his lady were seated. Lord Hardinge was seriously injured. Another bomb fell on the crowd, resulting in the death of three persons and injuries to several others.

Rash Behari escaped from the spot and got back to Dehradun early the next morning. Basant managed to make his way to Lahore. The Viceroy was taken to the nearest doctor A C Sen, who treated him for his injuries. Rash Behari joined his duty in Dehradun as usual in the morning. Then he organised a meeting of the loyal citizens to condemn the attack on the Viceroy. Under such circumstances who could imagine that he was the mastermind of the attack. The authorities thus remained in the dark about those involved in the bomb throwing.

In Lahore, Basant Biswas got in touch with the revolutionaries there. He met Amir Chand, Avadh Behari and Bhai Balmukund and joined them in an attack on a British official and his team on 17 May 1913 in which a peon was killed. Amir Chand, Avadh Behari and Bhai Balmukund had disappeared after the attack. After an intense search, the three were arrested. Basant Biswas was still missing. He had managed to escape arrest in Lahore. Against the advice of Rash Behari, Basant decided to go to Bengal to his home where his father was critically ill as he may have been needed to perform his last rites in case of death. His father passed away. He reached Poragachha in Nadia without being detected to perform the last rites of his father. The police knew of the address and arrested Biswas on 26 February 1914.

A trial began in Delhi on 23 May 1914 and is known as Delhi-Lahore conspiracy case. Amir Chand, Avadh Behari and Bhai Balmukund were sentenced to death. Basant, because of his young age was given life imprisonment. The government appealed and Basant Biswas was also sentenced to death.

It was on 11 May 1915 that Basant Biswas was hanged to death in Ambala and became one of the youngest to embrace death in the fight for India's freedom.

In Dehradun, Rash Behari felt that it was time that he moved away from the town even though none of the four condemned to death had taken his name. He suspected that sooner or later the police may get him. In the first instance, he moved to Chandernagore. While there he felt that the British would be able to locate him as the town was crowded with British spies and informers. Rash Behari made contact with Sachin Sanyal, a sympathiser of the revolutionaries' work whom he had met earlier in Benares. Rash Behari felt he could carry on his activities from there and remain hidden from the police.

War clouds were hovering over Europe. Rash Behari Bose was confident that the British would have to depend upon the Indian Army to fight their war in Europe. He now thought of a huge plan to see if the British Indian Army men could be persuaded to repeat the Sepoy Mutiny of 1857 and be persuaded not to fight a war in Europe for the British.

Rash Behari was joined in this effort by a group of revolutionaries of the Ghadar movement from America, which had been set up by expatriate Indians—largely Sikhs from Punjab settled in and around San Francisco, United States—to throw out the British from India. Large number of Punjabis, Sikhs and Hindus were living in Canada as well, many of whom were also part of the Ghadar movement.

Ghadar Party leaders in America were confident that the British would depend upon the strength of the Indian army to fight the war in Europe. They concluded that this was the moment to repeat the 1857 uprising in India. Their members (membership is given around four thousand by some historians) decided to move back to Punjab to try and block recruitment to the Indian Army. All of them were sacrificing their comfortable living in the United States, moved as they were by the love of their motherland. They decided that they would approach members of the Sikh and Punjab regiments to rebel against the British. These regiments were the backbone of the British Indian Army.

The leaders of revolutionaries from the Ghadar movement were looking for a leader in India to guide them. They decided to approach Rash Behari to lead them. They were impressed with what they had heard of his revolutionary actions. The leaders of the Ghadar group from the United States, Vishnu Ganesh Pingle, Kartar Singh Saraba and Satyen Sen travelled to Benares to meet Rash Behari Bose. They met him and Sonu Sanyal and were favourably able to convey the mission for which the Ghadarites had come to India. Kartar Singh Saraba was impressed by Rash Behari during the discussions and convinced that he was the one who had the initiative, strength and understanding of the objective. Rash Behari was also impressed by the numbers of the revolutionaries who would be there to execute the task.

A bulk of the British Indian Army was recruited from Punjab with the British theory of martial races of India. Punjabis in general, but the Sikhs in particular were treated as a martial race. After meeting the Ghadarite, leaders, Rash Behari Bose decided to make his own assessment of the situation in Punjab. He asked Kartar Singh Saraba to move to Punjab. Vishnu Ganesh Pingle was assigned to Meerut in the United Provinces (UP). The families of the soldiers recruited from Punjab were against their men going to Europe and other destinations to fight the war. But it was poverty and lack of jobs which pushed the men to get recruited.

War had already started in Europe. Most of the Indian Army had been sent abroad to Europe and Mesopotamia and the Middle East to protect the Turkish empire. There were just about thirty thousand men left in India. The war in Europe at Flanders had run into a stalemate. That resulted in heavy Indian casualties. It meant that the British needed more recruits for the army and families of the men were opposing this. But the British resorted to a system of hiring contractors who were paid according to the numbers of men they brought for recruitment. Contractors were in turn using village tehsildars and patwaris, the two government officials who dealt with the farmers. They would threaten the poor farmers that they would file false cases to take away their lands, forcing them to send their young men for recruitment.

At Flanders, German artillery was causing heavy casualties among the Indian troops. The injured were taken to England for treatment in Brighton. Here in the hospitals they were treated by white nurses and many made friends with them. Racist British officers did not approve of this, but could do nothing about it. The soldiers in the hospitals were greatly encouraged when King George V and Queen Mary visited the hospital.

When the convalescent soldiers managed to visit the streets at night they found girls to spend time with. Many wrote back to friends to say that the 'girls in Brighton were no better than the girls back home in red light areas.' The Pavilion in Brighton that exists today is said to be where the hospital was for convalescing soldiers. The racist attitude of senior British officers is well described in what General Sir James Wilcocks had to say. He praised the men's valour, but regretted that they had to be treated by white nurses in Brighton. He did not approve of the liaison between Indian soldiers and local white girls.

Inspite of this bleak situation, the Ghadarite revolutionaries who had come from the United States dispersed themselves into the military cantonments to work on the men who were still there. Others went to the villages to get the families to influence their men to join the army.

A group of Ghadar party members were travelling by

tongas from Ferozepur to Moga led by Rehmat Ali Shah, when they were routinely accosted by the police near Mishriwala bridge. It led to an unnecessary argument with police abusing them and slapping one of them. Losing their cool, Jagat Singh and Ganda Singh, two of the Ghadarites retaliated, killing two of the policemen on the spot. Other policemen ran away from there. Meanwhile, the Ghadarites escaped from there. This incident alerted the Punjab government.

The police were on the hunt for all of the men who had escaped from Mishriwala bridge. Seven of them were hunted down and captured and put on trial in Ferozepur District Court on charges of sedition against the government and murder. The Sessions judge announced his judgement and sentenced them to death by hanging, including Rehmat Ali Shah who was only twenty-nine years old. Others who were also sentenced to death by hanging included Lal Singh, Jagat Singh and Jiwan Singh. They were all hanged at Montgomery Central jail on 25 March 1915.

Despite this setback, Rash Behari was very confident that with so many loyal committed revolutionaries working in Punjab, a revolution could be in the offing. He himself was moving across Punjab evading the police. It was decided that an uprising in the cantonments should take place on February 21. Everything seemed to be going well for action when on February 15, Rash Behari found a soldier Kirpal Singh in Lahore. He was from the British Indian Army and had joined to be part of action to be taken on February 21. His being in Lahore was against the instructions given to him by Rash Behari. He was supposed to be in Mian Mir cantonment but was roaming around in Lahore.

Shocked as he was, Rash Behari had a long chat with Kirpal Singh. It became clear to Rash Behari that the man had become a police informer and had already leaked out the plans of revolutionaries to the authorities, betraying not only Rash Behari Bose but also Kartar Singh Saraba and others. Rash Behari Bose had no option but to call off the planned insurrection.

Rash Behari and other revolutionaries found that based on information given by Kirpal Singh and maybe by some other moles as well, the British had already taken preemptive steps to meet the challenge. Disheartened at this failure and before he could be arrested, Rash Behari managed to leave for Benares under disguise.

Kirpal Singh, the traitor, had destroyed what could have been a major uprising since 1857 and with the preemptive steps taken by the British it was no longer possible to fight.

After returning to Benares, Rash Behari realised that he was not safe there with police looking for him all over India. He decided to move to Chandernagore as part of his plan to leave India. Master of disguise as he was, he gave himself a new name P N Tagore. He was able to get all his travel papers in his new name of disguise.

With his perfect disguise, Rash Behari managed to leave Calcutta for Japan on 12 May 1915.

Rash Behari Bose reached Kobe in Japan on 5 June 1915 and then moved to Tokyo. His first three years were spent in his efforts to protect himself from being extradited and convincing the Japanese government to support India's Independence movement. During these three years, he moved from one place to another as the British intelligence men were after him. In the face of all this, he decided to move out of Tokyo to Shinjuku, a suburb of Tokyo. Meanwhile, the Government of Japan turned down a request by the British government to extradite Rash Behari Bose.

His new hideout was with the family of Alzo Soma and Kotsuko Soma. He was welcomed by them with great affection. It was a delight for Rash Behari to find the Somas were very sympathetic towards India's freedom struggle.

From now on Rash Behari's struggle for independence was engineered from Japan. He met Dr Sun Yet-Sen, the great Chinese leader who too was in exile in Japan. His first political call from Japan was 'Asia for Asians.' This call not only won him the support of Japanese people but also from other parts of Asia like Indonesia, Malaysia, Singapore and other countries that were ruled by European powers. Rash Behari Bose was granted citizenship of Japan in 1923.

He had succeeded in his efforts to persuade the Government of Japan to support the Indian Independence movement. With his close relationship with the Japanese government, Rash Behari was permitted to establish *The Indian Independence League* in March 1942. He also began to raise the Indian National Army from among the Indian prisoners of war in Japan. Rash Behari was honoured by the Government of Japan with the 'Second Order of Merit of the Rising Sun.'

Age was now catching up with Rash Behari Bose, but he carried on his activities to fight for freedom of the motherland. It is he who is said to have written to Netaji Subhash Chandra Bose to come to Japan. Subhash Chandra Bose undertook a dangerous long journey of 39 days in a submarine to reach Japan, landing there in February 1943.

Rash Behari Bose met him and handed over charge of Indian Independence League and the nascent Indian National Army to Netaji Subhash Chandra Bose. Rash Behari Bose died in Tokyo on 21 January 1945. His daughter

Tetsu Higuchi brought his remains to independent India in 1959. There is a statue of Rash Behari Bose in the Memorial Park of Calcutta.

Vishnu Ganesh Pingle a Ghadarite, had met Rash Behari Bose in Benares earlier along with Kartar Singh Saraba and Satyen Sen. Pingle had been assigned to work in United Provinces starting from Meerut cantonment. However, he was also needed in Punjab in Amritsar. Pingle met Mula Singh who had come from Shanghai. Things had gone wrong in Punjab because of traitor Kirpal Singh who had given the British full information of the plans of revolutionaries and dates of proposed strikes.

Pingle was in Meerut when he was captured by the police in the cantonment on the night of 23 March 1915. He was busy trying to urge troops stationed there to join the rebels. Police also found bombs with Pingle.

Like his colleagues in Punjab, Pingle had lost his battle in Meerut. He was sent to Punjab where the police were looking for him and was put on trial in the Lahore conspiracy case.

Kartar Singh Saraba had also been arrested in Punjab, betrayed by Kirpal Singh. Kartar Singh Saraba was born on 24 May 1896 in Sarabha village near Ludhiana in Punjab. He was brought up by his grandfather after his father had passed away. After his initial education in the village, he studied in Ludhiana and then went to his uncle in Cuttack to complete his high school. Coming back to his village and after discussion with his family, he decided to move to the United States where a number of Sikhs were headed. He left for San Francisco by ship in July 1912. Instead of going to college, he started working in a factory.

He later came across one Sohan Singh Bhakna, founder of the Ghadar movement. When the Ghadar party was formed, Kartar Singh Saraba was its youngest founding member. Saraba started working on the *Gadar*, a paper of the party that was printed in Urdu, Hindi, Bengali, Gujarati and Pashto languages and copies sent all over India and to Indians in other countries as well. For Indians visiting San Francisco, the house where the Ghadar Party was formed still stands there as a memorial for visitors.

The well thought and ambitious plan to bring about a mutiny in the British Indian Army failed all because of a traitor. It is tragic but remains a fact that India has been plagued by traitors at some crucial moments whether in the defeat of Prithviraj Chauhan or the victory of Clive in the battle of Plassey. Kirpal Singh had foiled the well thought out plan for which hundreds had given up their cushy jobs and careers and come to India. It was just sheer good luck that Rash Behari Bose had spotted Kirpal Singh and become aware of what he had done.

The British Government was alarmed as it realised the dimensions of the uprising in the army that the freedom fighters had planned. For the first time the British realised that they must give importance to the families of the troops. Instructions were sent to the Governor of Punjab, Michael O'Dwyer, to act and take action against the members of the Ghadar Party who had landed in India. He had to explain how his intelligence had failed to spot this conspiracy.

The British had been ruling Punjab with an iron fist since the defeat of the Sikhs in the Anglo Sikh wars following the death of Maharaja Ranjit Singh. Michael O'Dwyer initiated action against suspected activists who were in Punjab. He issued blanket orders to check each and every one who had arrived from the US. Michael O'Dwyer ordered the arrest of anybody suspected to be a revolutionary or had arrived from the United States. Several innocent Punjabis returning from the US to meet their families were also arrested and harassed. The British were getting information on revolutionaries from two sources—one from their moles in the Independence movement and second, the elite of Punjab who had virtually become more British than the British. In a wild search for the Ghadarites, police were arresting every one who had returned from the US and putting them through rigorous questioning. Finally, some four hundred were detained. Police had managed to arrest leading members Kartar Singh Saraba, Vishnu Ganesh Pingle (brought from Meerut), Bhai Parmanand and Harnam Singh.

A huge trial now started by a Special Tribunal that was formed under the British Government's Defence of India Act of 1915. This trial was known as the Lahore Conspiracy case. The police had arrested over 300 revolutionaries, who were put on trial, but of these, 291 were charged as being the conspirators.

Lahore Conspiracy Case

A trial of 291 Independence movement heroes was now conducted in Lahore where a cruel, hater of Indians, governor Michael O'Dwyer, was playing a leading role. He was monitoring the progress of the trial of each of the conspirators. The case started on 26 April 1915. The authorities declared Rash Behari Bose and several others as absconders. All the 291 were charged with attempting to overthrow the government.

The trials moved with speed with Governor Michael O'Dwyer keeping a close watch. Out of 291 who were put on trial, forty-two were sentenced to death. These 42 included Kartar Singh Saraba, Vishnu Ganesh Pingle, Harnam Singh,

Jagat Singh, Surain Singh, Bakshish Singh and another hero also named Bakshish Singh. It was a travesty of law to sentence young Saraba to death. He could have been sent to reform home because of his age. But then, Saraba did not show any sign of remorse during his trial but was proud of his actions in the war against the British.

A total of 114 revolutionaries got life sentences and were sent off to the terrible Cellular prison of Andaman islands, which meant inhuman torture through the prison term. The rest of the convicts got sentences of varying degree but not life. A huge effort by the Ghadar movement from the United States to bring about an uprising of the British Indian Army and push the British out of India had failed because of a traitor.

Chapter 9

REVOLUTIONARIES HANGED
Gandhi Chose No-Revenge Policy

Unsung, unknown heroes, who were fighting for the freedom of their motherland India, had made it amply clear to the British by 1915 that they were not welcome in India. Michael O'Dwyer, governor of Punjab had resorted to extreme steps while conducting the trial of 291 Ghadarite convicts in Lahore. Men like O'Dwyer perhaps thought that they could rule India only by violent means. As the governor of his province, he was the appointing authority of judges whether English or Indian. He made sure that the revolutionaries get a 'teach them a lesson' sentence from the judges appointed by him.

But the heroic revolutionaries were not deterred by such actions and continued without fear, their fight for freedom of their motherland.

The war in Europe was not coming to an end. It had become clear to all sides that the stalemate between the warring countries was going to be a long one. The Indian Army was being used by the British as cannon fodder in this war. The soldiers from India were giving their best, but at the cost of heavy casualties. As the numbers of casualties rose, anger was rising that Punjabis were getting killed in a war of the British.

The return of Mohandas Karamchand Gandhi to India on 9 January 1915 was destined to change the role of the Indian National Congress from a pliable club of elitists to a body demanding independence. The revolutionaries were aghast when they found that the furthest that the Congress had gone was to demand Home Rule which would have still kept India under the sovereignty of the United Kingdom. The revolutionaries wanted complete independence at par with Britain and other nations of the world. Gandhi had also announced his support for the British in World War I in the hope that India would get self-rule after fighting the war.

Several freedom fighters from Bengal and other places in India were in Germany. They formed what came to be known as the Berlin Committee for Indian Independence. Led by Viren Chattopadhyay from Bengal, the committee had secured active support of the German government. This committee was also in touch with Rash Behari Bose in Tokyo to coordinate their actions. The Germans were keen to supply weapons to the revolutionaries in India. The committee in Berlin had printed pamphlets that were given to Indian soldiers fighting for the British.

The Ghadar Party in the United States had not given up its fight against the British despite what its members had suffered in Punjab. In the midst of the war, they thought of finding ways and means to attack Andaman Islands where several revolutionaries including Veer Savarkar and Barin Ghosh were imprisoned. It was an ambitious plan.

This task was given to several Ghadarites who were based in Siam (today's Thailand). But the Ghadarites in Siam failed as the ship bringing German weapons was searched by the Dutch authorities when it anchored enroute Siam. The Dutch seized the weapons found there. The Dutch also passed on this information to the British. The effort of the Ghadarites failed. But this did not in any manner come in the way of their resolve to fight for India's Independence. The determination of the Hindustan Ghadar Party keeping the torch of the fight for Independence alive was strengthened further.

Meanwhile, the British government was putting pressure on the government of the United States to take action against the Ghadar party in the US.

The British in order to win full loyalty of India's people and give them a feel that they were as much running their country's government, began to bring about some reforms in the administration. Minto Morley reforms announced in 1909 were meant to see some political participation of Indians in the government set-up of India. The British hoped to bring the moderate elements in the freedom movement into the government. The Indian Civil Service was opened to Indians. All this only had a very slight impact on the running of the government. The Congress too was not happy with the Minto Morley reforms.

The reforms introduced by the British did not in any manner placate the Ghadarite and other revolutionaries. Reforms or no reforms, the Ghadar party revolutionaries who were still around in Punjab and Bengal were continuing their efforts to attack the British in a bid to gain complete independence. There were killings of police and other British officers of the government at various places. The United States entered World War I in 1917. Already under pressure from the British government, the US authorities now moved to take action against the Ghadar Party. One of its members Taraknath Das was imprisoned for two years in America.

Taraknath Das

A professor of political science at Columbia University, Taraknath Das, a member of the Hindustan Ghadar Party, was a well-read revolutionary.

He had met Tolstoy and drawn inspiration from him for his cause for the freedom of India. Taraknath Das was from Bengal and had been associated with Bagha Jatin, a great revolutionary of Bengal. While in Bengal, he accompanied Bagha Jatin to Mohammadpur in Jessore. It was on that visit that he and three others decided to move to the United States for higher studies. The objective was not only to acquire higher education but to get knowledge about explosives and other revolutionary aspects. He was also seeking to create a favourable atmosphere among the people of the United States towards the cause of India's freedom.

Taraknath Das passed his M A examination from the University of California and later went in for his PhD on International Law. He became a teacher at the university with all these qualifications. He also earned an additional PhD degree in Political Science from Washington University. He visited Berlin in 1915 where he met Virendrenath Chattopadhay. He was informed about an Indo German Plan to help revolutionaries in India. Barkatullah, another great freedom fighter and Hardyal who were in Berlin also met Taraknath.

Taraknath Das married Mary Keating who had been his friend for a long time and was among the founding members of the National Association for the Advancement of Colored people. Readers must not forget that in the United States, black people of African origin have suffered extreme discrimination and exploitation. Their forefathers were brought as slaves to work in the US. With the work of the

National Association for the Advancement of the Colored People, the Afro Amreicans have come a long way in achieving some form of equality with the whites. One of them, Barack Obama rose to be the President of the United States.

Taraknath Das together with his wife established Taraknath Das Foundation to promote educational activities such as to help Indian students with money if they were working towards a graduate degree and needed help.

A large number of Indians, largely Sikhs from Punjab, had gone to the United States to help build the Western Pacific Railway in California. These immigrants were working side by side with indentured labour from China and Korea. Then there were a large number of immigrants also from Punjab who were working in agriculture and construction works. These agricultural labourers created a revolution of sorts when they obtained bumper rice crops. Taraknath Das worked among them to educate them and protect them legally from any exploitation. Being fully conversant with the local laws, he almost made it his life's mission to protect these illiterate compatriots and inspire them towards freedom of India. He founded Swadesh Sewak Home where they could go and seek help.

Taraknath Das was among those large number of revolutionaries who mourned the partition of India in 1947 after independence. He came back to India for a visit in 1952. It was a changed country that he had left 46 years ago. He founded Vivekananda Society in Calcutta on 9 September 1952. He also helped organise and presided over a public meeting to celebrate the 37th anniversary of Bagha Jatin's martyrdom and urged the people in general and youth in particular in Independent India to follow the values of Bagha Jatin. He returned to the United States where he died on 22 December 1958.

Events in Punjab were moving fast following the failure of the Ghadarite plan to bring an uprising in the Indian Army. People were angry with so many hangings. But the Governor Michael O'Dwyer would not stop for he had the support of the elite of Punjab that included Hindus, Sikhs and Muslims. Strangely, the Sikh elite even got the Chief Khalsa Diwan to condemn the Ghadarites.

It was sad to see that Gandhi ji who was planning his non-violent movement also asked for providing support to the British in World War I. He believed without any assurance or hint that the British would grant Home Rule to India at the end of the war.

The war in Europe was dragging. With mounting casualties, the British needed more recruits for the Indian Army. The men were fighting bravely. At home the Indian National Congress was supporting the war effort. The leaders felt that large scale Indian participation in the war would demonstrate to the British, India's fitness to manage its own affairs. Gandhiji speaking at a meeting declared: 'An empire has been defending India and of which India aspires to be equal partner is in great peril and it ill befits India to stand aloof at the hour of its destiny. India would be nowhere without Englishmen. If the British do not win, shall we go to the Germans?'

Gandhiji further argued that only by making the UK's position secure would India be in a position to make Englishmen listen to Indian demands. All this fitted with the fact that the Congress Party had made Home Rule or Dominion status within the British Empire as its goal.

The statements of Indian leaders in support of the war were causing a dilemma for the British government. It could not ignore the sacrifices made by Indian soldiers by the end of 1918. Over a million Indian soldiers participated in various theatres of that war, not just in France. The Indian government had spent a vast amount of money on the war effort which was a debt by the United Kingdom to India. Just because India was a colony, the amount owed by the British to India was written off. In this author's view, this was daylight robbery. And as for Indian leaders' demand for Home Rule nothing was conceded by the British declaring 'India was not ready for home rule yet.'

The British authorities in India whether with or without blessings of their masters in London were arming themselves with draconian powers to deal with the rising discontent. Living in Mughal style comfort with a number of servants at home, the British administration in India armed itself with two notorious laws known as the Rowlatt Acts. The police or authorities could enter any home to search for revolutionaries. Special Courts could be set up for speedy trials. The notorious Rowlatt Acts were passed even as three of the four members of the Imperial Legislative Council opposed them and resigned. The three were Mazhar Ul Haq, Madan Mohan Malaviya and Mohammed Ali Jinnah.

Public agitations against the bills started as the Indian population was no longer safe under these Acts. Leading the Indian National Congress, Gandhiji also opposed these Acts. He called for general strikes all over India and called upon the people to remain peaceful. The strikes on 30 March and 6 April faced police violence against the strikers at Ahmedabad and Delhi, where several people were killed in clashes by the unprovoked firing by the police. Gandhiji decided to go to Punjab where the agitation was at its height. But he was not allowed to reach his destination and was taken off the train in Delhi and sent back to Bombay.

Punjab governor Michael O'Dwyer known for his cruel methods of administration, was now resorting to heavy handedness in stopping even peaceful protests. He went so far as to try and close what were bodybuilding or exercise places known as *akhadas* like today's gyms. He charged that these places were training revolutionaries! These places in fact trained wrestlers and were popular among people who loved watching wrestling bouts. O'Dwyer was also alarmed with the fact of Hindu Muslim unity in this agitation. He ordered the arrest of the two Congress leaders of Amritsar Saifuddin Kitchlew and Dr Satyapal for no reason. People of Amritsar protested at their arrests.

O'Dwyer had also asked for military help and British military pickets were placed at several places. Among the persons who arrived in Amritsar was Brigadier General Reginald Dyer. He was the son of a brewer and had grown up in India with a superior attitude towards locals. He spoke Hindustani fluently and could thus interact with his troops easily. He had learnt to use brute military power. He was some kind of a sadist who liked using violence. Upon reaching Amritsar, he set up military pickets in the city. He wanted to bring peace in the city with a heavy hand and terrorise the residents with the presence of armed British troops.

A peaceful unarmed procession of people was marching towards the office of the deputy commissioner to petition for the release of the two arrested leaders. The procession was stopped at the railway bridge by the military picket there. The military men had no such authority to do so. They were a protective picket. The peaceful crowd was trying to explain to the military men that they were only going to the deputy commissioner's office to present their petition. More soldiers arrived and opened unprovoked fire at them killing four persons on the spot and injuring several others. The crowd ran back into the city where the news of the killings brought out many more people. As they reached the picket on their way to meet the deputy commissioner, the military men opened unprovoked fire again, killing 20 persons on the spot and injuring many others. The unprovoked firing reflected the kind of attitude the British had towards slaves from Africa and were now applying the same yardstick in India.

The incensed crowd then attacked in retaliation some of the British banks that had their branches in the area. These were Chartered Bank, The National Bank and the Alliance Bank. Their British managers were killed. Several of the British escaped with the help of 'sober' Indians. A formal meeting was then announced at the Jallianwala Bagh next day which was 13 April, the day of the Baisakhi festival in Punjab. It is a day sacred to all the Punjabis whether Hindus or Sikhs.

Jallianwala Bagh in Amritsar is located very close to the Golden Temple in a crowded area. It was used commonly for meetings and also for the people of the area to relax. The people first celebrated Baisakhi by praying at the Golden Temple, then headed for Jallianwala Bagh for the meeting. A small crowd of a few thousand people had gathered there to lodge their peaceful protest at the arrest of Amritsar's leaders. There were several women and children in the crowd as well.

Brigadier-General Dyer, the India-born Englishman was asked by the Punjab governor O'Dwyer to take action and deal with this protest. General Dyer was known for being a rabid, anti-Indian racist. He first verified as to how many were there at the meeting. Then taking his armoured cars and Gurkha troops, he marched towards the Jallianwala Bagh coming through narrow alleys. Finding the roads narrow for his armoured cars, he blocked the roads with orders to shoot even at those leaving from the Jallianwala Bagh.

As the general entered the ground, the first thing he did was to block the entrance so that the crowd could not escape. He then lined up his troops in firing position. The crowd got alarmed. And then without any warning, he ordered his troops to fire at the unarmed civilians gathered for the meeting.

With no warning given to those assembled to disperse, it was a straight genocidal attack on peaceful civilians. Several hundred men, women and children were killed. Several jumped into a well that was there in the ground to escape, but died of drowning. The well was full of dead bodies. Among those who escaped being killed was a young boy Udham Singh. He had seen his brother and sister killed there. He swore there to avenge the massacre of innocent unarmed people.

The government tried to play down this massacre saying only around 200 were killed and that too, they claimed happened in a stampede. But the figures were higher than a thousand who were killed largely by bullet shots. The injured were given no first aid to save them. Several were also killed by the pickets that Dyer had placed outside at the entrance and near the armoured cars. The massacre would have been much bigger if Dyer had succeeded in bringing his armoured cars fitted with machine guns.

The shameful part that followed this massacre was that several of the Punjabi elite supported both the governor O'Dwyer and General Dyer. They forgot that the government had earlier imposed a curfew so that no one could come to the aid of the injured and take them to hospitals. The Punjabi elite even made sure that Sardar Arur Singh, head of the Akal Takht at the Golden Temple invited General Dyer to the Golden Temple to receive an honour!

The general went to the Golden Temple and was presented with a *siropa*, a Sikh Honour. And as for the loyalist Punjabis, many of them were given some kind of honour by the British in the years that followed. Residents of the city were barred from walking to their business, work or home. They were made to crawl on their hands and knees on the road. There was even stripping and flogging of marriage parties. People were told that wherever they saw a British officer or policeman, they had to stop and salute the person. The British could not have treated the Punjabis more worse than this.

There were calls for Gandhiji and other Congress leaders to visit Punjab. Gandhiji was not allowed to enter Punjab. Finally, when Gandhiji did manage to arrive in Punjab, he found that the government had failed to act on its own report. He realised that horrible atrocities had been committed on the Punjabis. Gandhiji announced publicly that he was not interested in taking revenge against anybody. And advised the people to follow non-violent methods and not to cooperate with the government in any way. He advised Punjabis not to accept any British Honours and those who had received such honours to return it to the government. Gandhi hoped that the government would realise its mistakes.

But it was naïve on the part of Gandhiji to expect a colonial power to accept its mistakes against its 'subjects.'

What the British wanted to achieve by the Jallianwala Bagh massacre is perhaps not known, but the fact was that this terrible genocide inspired a wave of nationalism all over India and a hatred for the British. Sober elements in the British administration in India and in England realised the mistake. Both Michael O'Dwyer and General Dyer were sent back home. Both had to be provided security even back home to protect them from Indian revolutionaries in England. In its effort to win the goodwill of the people, a large number of patriots who were suffering in jails were released by the British. A few were even released from the Cellular jail at Andamans.

Udham Singh

One young boy who had watched the massacre at Jallianwala Bagh and had sworn to avenge that massacre was Udham Singh. He had not forgotten the commitment he had made to himself. As he was under watch in India for taking part in some of the activities of the Ghadar Party, he moved away to Kashmir. From there in his effort to get to his final destination, Udham Singh reached Germany and landed in London in 1934 declaring himself as a sports outfitter. He moved to Kent but was unable to find any employment. He started working as a peddler, even as he planned for the action for which he had come all the way. Jallianwala Bagh massacre, he believed was carried out at the orders of the governor of Punjab O'Dwyer.

Finding out where O'Dwyer lived, he began scouting around for ways and means to get there for his action. There was strong security around his home. An opportunity came his way when he heard that Michael O'Dwyer was to address a meeting of the East India Association and Central Asian Society on 13 March 1940. East India Association was an association of local resident Indians, including businessmen and others. On the given day, Udham Singh, well dressed like any other guest, a book in hand made his confident entry into the Caxton Hall of London where the meeting was being held.

Udham Singh sat through the meeting listening to the speech of O'Dwyer. He felt disgusted with the kind of praise that the office bearers of the East India Society showered on the former governor of Punjab, the man who sent Dyer to Jallianwala Bagh. As the meeting ended and several persons made their way to the stage to congratulate Michael O'Dwyer, Udham Singh also reached there with the book in his hand as though it was to be presented to him. Once face to face standing before each other, Udham Singh opened his book and took out the revolver hidden there. He then fired the first shot at his chest telling him in Punjabi that he had waited for long to do this. The bullet fired at his chest had gone through his heart that killed him instantly. He fired more, and among the others who were injured included Marques of Zetland, Baron Lamington. Udham Singh made no effort to escape and was arrested immediately.

After being charged with murder in April he was kept in the Brixton prison. In the prison, the police and jailor were surprised at his confidence in what he considered his achievement in fulfilling the vow he had taken at Jallianwala Bagh. It is said that he decided in prison to give himself the name of Ram Mohammed Singh Azad. The first three words denoted the great religions Hindu, Islam and Sikh. The last meant that he was free. When interrogated in the prison as to why he killed Michael O'Dwyer he categorically said that 'he deserved it.'

During the trial the British tried their best to deny the connection of the Jallianwala Bagh massacre with the assassination of O'Dwyer. It was proving uncomfortable for them. The prosecution even said that Udham Singh was not there when the massacre happened. V K Krishna Menon, among the Indian lawyers defending Udham Singh, clearly said that Udham Singh was there. The British public was unhappy with the Jallianwala massacre and those responsible for it. The Indian diaspora considered it as heroic that Udham Singh had dealt with one of the two guilty men responsible for the Jallianwala massacre.

During the trial, he told the judge and the jury that he did not recognise his court. 'I do not care about the death sentence. It means nothing at all,' he said. The judge tried to interrupt him, but he continued exposing the exploitation of India and its people by the British. He went on to call them dirty dogs who were exploiting their own workers and the poor people in England. The judge again tried to stop him, but he retorted that the judge had asked him to explain his stand and that is what he was just doing; so why was the judge trying to stop him. He closed his lengthy speech shouting the slogan 'Down with British Imperialism. Down with British dirty dogs.'

The judge sentenced him to death. Udham Singh was executed on 31 July 1940 at Pentonville prison in London.

In India, there was praise all over the country that someone like Udham Singh had avenged what O'Dwyer did to Punjab as its governor. In the Assembly of Punjab when the government moved a motion to condemn the 'assassination' of Udham Singh, the Congress led by Dewan Chaman Lal refused to vote for the motion. Even the London newspaper, *The Times*, called him a fighter for freedom. Sadly, Jawaharlal Nehru in March 1949 had condemned the act of Udham Singh as 'senseless.' However in 1962 on the occasion of his death anniversary, Nehru called him 'Shaheed-E-Azam.' In 1974, Udham Singh's remains were exhumed and brought back home where these were received by the Prime Minister of India Mrs Indira Gandhi alongwith the President of India and other senior leaders.

Udham Singh is still remembered and a museum in his name exists in Amritsar. His house in his village Sunam has been converted into a memorial for him. In 2018, a statue of his was unveiled at the entrance of Jallianwala Bagh by India's Defence Minister Rajnath Singh. He remains a great martyr for the cause of India's Independence.

Government of India Act, 1919

Declaring to Indian leaders after the War that India was not ready for Dominion Status, the British Parliament passed the Government of India Act of 1919. This Act sought to bring about limited participation of India's people in the government. It also divided Hindus and Muslims creating a separate electorate for each community. When presented in India, it was rejected by the Congress. Nevertheless, the Act was implemented and it sowed the seeds of division among Hindus and Muslims.

Rejecting the Government of India Act of 1919, the Congress Party led by Gandhiji started the non-cooperation agitation in 1920. Gandhiji seized the decision of the allies of World War I to break up the Ottoman empire. Gandhi also thought that it would win him support of the Muslims and launched the Khilafat movement. But this decision of Gandhi was not supported by several senior leaders of the Congress Party. Jinnah was among the leaders opposed to Gandhi's decision in supporting the Caliph of the Ottoman Empire. Ultimately Jinnah was proven right as the Caliph was overthrown by Kemal Ataturk. A tragic fallout of this Khilafat movement in India was witnessed in South India. Moplahs in the state of Kerala killed many Hindus taking them to be anti-Muslim because most of the landlords in the area were Hindus. The Moplahs wanted an independent kingdom of Malabar.

Gandhiji now started the non-cooperation movement to press for Home Rule. Again many in the Congress were not sure of the usefulness of the movement. Aurobindo Ghose was among the top revolutionaries who did not see any usefulness of the agitation. Others who did not approve included Bal Gangadhar Tilak, Bipin Chandra Pal, Mohammed Ali Jinnah and Annie Besant.

Later Jinnah resigned from the Congress, considering the movement as political anarchy. He further said that its impact on independent India would be negative. Gandhiji called for a boycott of British goods including clothing. There were large scale bonfires of foreign and in particular, British cloth. These bonfires all over the country were to exhort the people to stop imports and wear clothes made of hand spun cloth. It virtually became the uniform of all the Congress leaders.

The Prince of Wales landed in Bombay in 1921 on a visit. His arrival in Bombay was a tame affair because of Gandhi's non-cooperation movement. The welcoming crowd was made up of government officials and army men in civil dress. As many of those who were attending the welcome of the prince were going back, they ran into those protesting his visit. Riots followed and lasted for three days. His tour was marred by protests wherever he went. In the meanwhile, Gandhi's non-cooperation satyagraha was worrying the British as it had spread all over India. The British could not find any way of controlling it apart from arresting the demonstrators.

At the peak of the demonstration and non-cooperation movement, something happened in Bihar. At Chauri Chaura some policemen without any provocation, opened fire on a crowd and two persons were killed. Reacting, a large crowd went to demonstrate at the police station. Some among the crowd set fire to the police station and nine policemen were burnt alive. Without consulting other leaders, Gandhiji called off the non-cooperation movement. Most of the leaders were angry with this decision of Gandhiji. But for the

British it was God sent. The agitation died down. The British administration in India heaved a sigh of relief.

Jawaharlal Nehru who had returned from England had joined the Congress Party after a brief law practice. He was very active during the non-cooperation movement together with his father Moti Lal Nehru. Travelling through Eastern UP, he came face to face with India's poverty in small towns and the countryside. This was his first look at India that lived in poverty, robbed and deprived over the centuries by the Mughals, the East India Company, the French and the Portuguese as well. During the non-cooperation movement, he was addressing meetings at various places and large crowds would come to see this England-returned freedom fighter.

Describing the crowds, Nehru had written 'they were in rags, men and women but very excited and their eyes glistened and seemed to expect strange happenings which would, as if by a miracle, put an end to their long misery.' Nehru listened to their tales of misery and exploitation by the zamindars and jagirdars, who had usurped the land of the farmers under some plea or the other. Jagirdars and zamindars lived in extreme prosperity while those who tilled the land were in rags. Nehru's mind was made up during these interactions and meetings as to how Independent India was to restore India's agriculture and make its farmers proud.

The non-cooperation movement had really opened the eyes of the Congress leaders at the grassroot level to the misery and exploitation of India's poor. By contrast, the revolutionaries wanted to fight the British and push them out to get started with removing this poverty. Among those who considered this nonviolent movement as futile was none other than Aurobindo Ghose from Pondicherry and the Ghadarites who did not think much of it.

The British were able to deal with Gandhi's agitation from 1920 to 1922 without having to resort to the methods of O'Dwyer and Dyer. Unlike the fights that the revolutionaries would put up whenever they took action, the non-cooperation movement would die of its own in the face of equally determined inaction by the authorities. There were moments during the agitation that the government thought it could hurt the administration. Whatever be the government view and analysis of Gandhi's satyagraha, it had inspired the people of India who were now fully behind it. The expectation that the movement could lead to the British granting home rule was ill-founded.

With the massive backing that Gandhiji was getting, people had started calling him Mahatma, which is a highly respectable way of approaching a leader. Giving up western dress, he had adorned the humble Tamil farmer's dhoti. Mahatma Gandhi was now truly a mass leader of India. The British had to think fast and they decided to adopt a policy of 'divide and rule' which they were anyway following. Mohammed Ali Jinnah came very handy to the British. As a leader in the Congress Party, he had been opposed to the methods of Mahatma Gandhi to secure dominion status. The revolutionaries as opposed to both Jinnah and the Mahatma wanted complete independence and not to have anything like dominion status within the British Empire.

Jinnah raised a demand for a separate homeland for Muslims of India declaring that Hindus and Muslims needed two separate nations. This suddenly took India's political world by shock and surprise. India's political world suddenly stood divided with Congress demanding independence for India, and Jinnah demanding a separate country. Seeds had thus been sown successfully by the British and Jinnah not just for dividing India, but to foil the efforts of the revolutionaries and the Congress to seek independence for India as it was.

The British rulers and army officers continued to live a life of luxury for which Indians paid. Polo was the sport of the army officers. Enjoying the comfort of servants, cooks and gardeners was considered not a luxury but a necessity for them! These were the facilities they could not even dream of having in Britain.

Kakori Train Robbery

In 1925 the revolutionaries in UP led by Ram Prasad Bismil and Ashfaqullah Khan, considering the need for funds to buy arms, decided to raid a train from Saharanpur to Lucknow that used to carry bags of money to be deposited in the Lucknow Treasury. The funds were needed to bring a large consignment of pistols from Germany. Keshab Chatterji was to go there and do the job. The arms were purchased in Germany and brought towards India and handed over to Rajendra Lahiri in the Bay of Bengal.

On 9 August 1925, Bismil and Ashfaqullah Khan boarded the train near the guard's compartment as planned. At Kakori, a small rural railway station, the train was halted by pulling the emergency chain. All the passengers were advised by the revolutionaries to remain inside the train. Some members were placed outside the train to stop any retaliation. One of the passengers was unfortunately shot dead in the confusion. The trunk containing the money was taken out, the lock broken and money taken out.

The police got a solid lead when some of the stolen currency notes were found in circulation. This let to the arrests of Bismil, Ashfaqullah Khan, Rajendra Lahiri and Sachindra Nath Sanyal. Authorities tried their best through

Muslim officers to turn Ashfaqullah Khan into an approver, but failed. The revolutionaries tried to escape from their cells. Bismil had succeeded with two others, but found the boundary wall of the prison too high to climb.

While in jail, Bismil had composed the famous revolutionary song *'Mera rang de basanti chola'*. Finally in 1927 four of the revolutionaries—Ram Prasad Bismil, Ashfaqullah Khan, Thakur Rajendra Singh and Rajendra Lahiri—were sentenced to death. Others were sentenced to different terms of imprisonment. Four were given life sentences including Sachindra Sanyal and Jogesh Lahiri. A dozen more were given sentences ranging from five to fourteen years. The two, Banwari Lal and Indubhushan Mitra, who had turned approvers were released. These were traitors getting their colleagues killed.

There were widespread protests in public against these sentences with demands for their release. Elected members of the Legislative Council of UP passed a resolution requesting that at least capital punishment be turned into life sentence. Madan Mohan Malaviya met the viceroy to seek a reduction in sentences. But the adamant foreign government refused to consider. Bismil wrote his autobiography *The Revolutionary*, in the jail as he waited for his hanging.

Bismil was thirty when he was hanged on 18 December 1927, followed by the others. Ashfaqullah Khan carrying the *Quran* and Rajendra Singh and Lahiri clutching their copies of the *Bhagavad Gita* were hanged. Ashfaqullah Khan with the *Quran* tied around his neck declared before hanging that 'I tried to make India free.'

He smiled as he was hanged. The hanging and killing of the revolutionaries did not deter others from continuing the fight against the British. The revolutionary guerilla battle continued.

Chapter 10

BHAGAT SINGH HANGED

The Congress and Mahatma Gandhi were steadily carrying on their campaign of non-cooperation and negotiations with the British. But the campaign was not taking India forward in the goal of self-rule via dominion status under the British Empire. Meanwhile Ajit Singh and Rash Behari Bose were helping the revolutionaries back at home. Lala Lajpat Rai, a member of the Congress Party known as Lion of Punjab was carrying on his non-violent struggle in Punjab and establishing banks such as the Punjab National Bank that would be needed once India was free.

The sudden withdrawal of the non-cooperation movement by Mahatma Gandhi after the Chauri Chaura incident had disappointed not only many Congress leaders but also the revolutionaries who had been supporting it. In Punjab, Lala Lajpat Rai had launched National College as an alternative to the government run colleges. He had also laid the foundation of the Punjab National Bank so that India had its own banks and was not dependent upon British banks.

Ajit Singh's letters to his nephew Bhagat Singh were greatly inspiring him towards the fight for India's freedom. It was not long before he joined Sachindra Nath Sanyal when he was visiting Punjab to revive the Ghadar Party movement. This author, when producing a documentary on the life of Bhagat Singh interviewed his mother who recalled fondly how Bhagat Singh, even as a child would say that he wants to grow up fast so that he can bring back his uncle, Ajit Singh.

Salt Satyagraha

Meanwhile, Gandhiji's next agitation was against the salt tax. The British used to collect tax on the salt that was produced by drying the sea water. Salt is a necessity of life. The movement against the salt tax known as *satyagraha* attracted attention of the people of India at large. The revolutionaries also decided to support this non-violent satyagraha, which started on 12 March 1930. It was on that day that Gandhi began his march from his Sabarmati Ashram with his followers towards Dandi, at a distance of 240 miles on the Indian Coast.

His objective was to inspire the people enroute. As it happened several thousand joined the march as it made its way and reached its destination on 5 April 1930. After making salt at Dandi by evaporating sea water and defying the British, Gandhi and his followers continued the march along the coast of the country. Such a massive India-wide response by the people had never been seen before in the country.

Not just that, but as the police used violence against the protestors, the world took note of it. News reports, photographs and newsreels the world over were showing what was going on in India. Never before had India's Independence movement received such wide global coverage. The world suddenly became aware of India and what the British were doing there.

Gandhi and his followers continued their march towards the British owned salt works at Dharasana, where salt was produced to be sold at profit in the country. The British were now alarmed by the response that the people of India were giving to Gandhi and his salt satyagraha. The British, though concerned about the huge response of India's people to the salt satyagraha, had an army of informers and collaborators. Most of the rich and well-to-do of that time believed the British Raj to be good for India.

Salt was a subject that concerned every Indian. The poor and middle class did not approve of raising the tax. While ignoring all such protests, the British were also alarmed by the fact that the huge response could inspire violent revolutionaries also—the kind of young people who did not believe in Gandhi's nonviolence.

Gandhiji and his followers steadily continued their march towards Dharasana. However, before they could reach Dharasana, the British arrested him on the night of May 4. But that failed to end the satyagraha. Others marched towards Dharasana and were met with cruel treatment by the police. Subhash Chandra Bose records in his book, *The Indian Struggle*, how an English disciple of Mahatma Gandhi Miss Madeleine Slade, paid a visit to Bulsar in Gujarat to see with her own eyes how the satyagrahis had been treated by the police at Dharasana. She published her report in *Young India* of 12 June 1930. She found that the police had inflicted serious blows on the peaceful non-violent satyagrahis. She found evidence of:

1. Lathi blows on head, chest, stomach and joints.
2. Thrust with lathi in private parts and abdominal region.
3. Stripping of men naked before beating.
4. Tearing of loincloths and thrusting of stick into anus.
5. Pressing and squeezing of testicles till a man becomes unconscious.

6. Dragging of wounded men by leg and arms, often beating them.
7. Throwing of wounded men into thorn hedges or into salt water.
8. Riding of horses over men as they lie or sit on the ground.
9. Thrusting of pins and thorns into men's bodies, sometimes even when they are unconscious.
10. Beating of men after they have become unconscious, and other vile things too many to relate, besides foul language and blasphemy, calculated to hurt as much as possible the most sacred feelings of the satyagrahis.

Despite such cruelty as recorded by Miss Slade the satyagraha continued for nearly a year till the British were forced to release Gandhiji to have negotiations with Viceroy Lord Irwin. Over seventy thousand protestors had been arrested during the salt satyagraha.

It had dawned on the British, possibly with information from their intelligence, that the time had come to seek some kind of cooperation or accommodation for the rising political class of educated Indians who were drifting towards the Congress. But the negotiations with Viceroy Lord Irwin failed to get any favourable response to the demands of Gandhiji. This was something the revolutionaries had always maintained would happen. They did not believe in any negotiations with the British.

Though the salt satyagraha failed to take India anywhere closer to Independence, it had enthused the people of the country as never before. They had been made aware that they could fight together for freedom. The world watched all this.

Inspired by the movement in India, Martin Luther King Jr in the United States adopted nonviolence and non-cooperation during the civil rights movement against the laws in the United States that denied the Afro-American black citizens their rights. There was horrible discrimination against the blacks in America. In the United States the civil rights protestors were met not only by the state violence against them but also by several groups of whites notably the notorious Ku Klux Klan, who would kill the protestors or burn them alive. Hardly anything decisive was done by the US authorities to control the Ku Klux Klan.

The talks between Lord Irwin and Gandhiji were not making any positive impact. There were too many among the British officialdom who felt that they had already made enough concessions to the educated Indians. Many of them were not just clerks in the administration, but in political positions like running of municipalities. Further Minto-Morley reforms had opened enough positions for Indians to participate in the administration of India. Many in the British administration felt that far too many educated Indians were getting into positions of responsibility, thereby restricting the power of the British in those areas. These negative elements among the British would openly say that Indians were incapable of taking a balanced view. And that they were too overawed by their family and caste considerations.

Talks with Lord Irwin failed and were called off. Gandhiji continued with his salt satyagraha after his release. The satyagraha was now largely confined to Gujarat, where it continued for some time more.

Among those who were supporting Gandhi's nonviolent satyagraha was Ram Prasad Bismil. Though a revolutionary in his ideas, he was also a staunch Hindu and under the influence of the Arya Samaj. He would carry out even what was known as *shuddhi* ceremonies to reconvert back to Hindu religion those who drifted towards Christianity or Islam. Having drifted back towards revolutionary activities, he came in touch with Ashfaqullah Khan. Ram Prasad Bismil and Ashfaqullah Khan became very close friends and together planned the train robbery as described in a previous chapter.

The Salt Satyagraha and Kakori Conspiracy cases showed that the British were no longer having an easy time ruling the country. It was not their homeland. They had to keep more than full time watch on rebellions, agitations and revolutionary activities. Minto Morley reforms giving Indians a limited participation in the civil administration was working well as far as the British thought. But these were nowhere near the expectations of even Gandhiji or the Congress Party. As for the revolutionaries, they were dead set against any such compromise with the British.

With the Minto Morley reforms being in action for nearly a decade, it was time, the British felt, to assess the impact of those reforms and take the next step. To do so the British Government set up a commission under Sir John Simon. The commission had seven members, all of them British. Gandhiji and the Congress objected to the composition, as they wanted some Indian representation on the commission. The British view was that the Indian member on the commission could not be expected to be unbiased. And so, the Simon Commission came to be opposed both by the nonviolent Congress under Gandhiji as also by the revolutionaries. Punjab became the most active area in opposing the Simon Commision.

Bhagat Singh in the meanwhile had come of age, inspired as he was by the example of patriotism and service to the nation set by his uncle Ajit Singh. He had also studied at the National College. Bhagat Singh had already been arrested once when someone threw a bomb at the Ram Lila procession in October 1926. Several people were killed in that incident. The police looking for an alibi blamed this on the revolutionaries. Bhagat Singh was arrested. He was let off as there was no evidence of him committing the act. The revolutionaries were against hurting their own people in any such action. The police were keeping a watch on young Bhagat Singh since he had gone to Allahabad to work with the revolutionaries there after his education at Lala Lajpat Rai's National College.

Lala Lajpat Rai was a great leader of Punjab and senior to Gandhiji at the national level along with Bipin Chandra Pal and Bal Gangadhar Tilak. Revolutionaries and the people of Punjab loved him. He was among those forward thinking leaders, confident of achieving freedom. Leaders like him were simultaneously preparing the country for setting up economic and other financial institutions like banks and insurance companies and not be dependent upon the British. He was the founder of one of India's greatest banks—the Punjab National Bank. He had been earlier jailed and sent to Mandalay. In Punjab he was leading the agitation and protests against the Simon Commission. His protests were disciplined and nonviolent.

At Lahore where the Simon Commission was due to arrive, Lala Lajpat Rai was leading a large peaceful protest against the visit of the commission. The government in Punjab did not want the commission to face the demonstrators carrying black flags and banners saying 'Simon Go Back.' Police tried to push them back. Failing to do so, the police superintendent on location James Scot ordered a lathi charge. Targeting the leader Lala Lajpat Rai, he went for his head. If there arose the need for a lathi (baton) charge, the police had instructions not to hit people on their heads. Yet, an unconcerned Scot and another officer Saunders went for Lala Lajpat Rai's head. They were out to kill him it seemed. Severely injured in the head, Lala Lajpat Rai fell down unconscious bleeding profusely. This was a broad daylight murder by Scot and his men including Saunders.

Lala Lajpat Rai never recovered from the head injuries he received. This author believes that James Scot had achieved his objective. He wanted Lalaji dead. It was a headache for him as he had to keep a special watch on the activities of Lala Lajpat Rai to report to his seniors. Lala Lajpat Rai breathed his last on 17 November 1928. People all over India were shocked and could not believe such a thing could be done to the 'Lion of Punjab,' a leader of not just Punjab but the whole of India. There was no apology from the government or any other authority for this brutal act.

The Simon Commission went on as though nothing had happened. It is equally strange that Independent India has not sought a public apology from the British government for this murder and several others. But then there had been one too many killings of the revolutionaries over a long period of battle. But here was a nonviolent leader, who had been in the fight for freedom long before Gandhi appeared on the scene. Public all over India demanded revenge for the killing of the Lion of Punjab. Agitations for revenge were taking place all over India.

Bhagat Singh together with Chandrashekhar Azad, Sukhdev and Shivram Rajguru visited Lala Lajpat Rai's home, and swore to avenge his killing. Their target was Scot who had ordered the lathi charge and they wanted the British to know that violence by them would be suitably replied with violence. Sukhdev was given the charge of planning the details to ensure that the revolutionaries carried out the mission for which they had taken an oath. The first problem they faced was to get the right revolver for Bhagat Singh who was to fire and revolvers for others to give protective fire. The date fixed to eliminate Scot was 17 December 1928.

When the day arrived, the junior most member Jaigopal was to keep a lookout and advise others whether Scot had arrived and alert them when he was leaving the police station. The revolutionary group had made a plan for escape from the location of the shooting. On the given day, Scot did not come to the police station and had taken a day off. Jaigopal made a huge blunder when he advised others that Scot was leaving the police station on his motorcycle. But that was Assistant Superintendent of Police John Saunders, who too had participated in the killing of Lala Lajpat Rai.

Based on the information passed on by Jaigopal, they swung into action but Bhagat Singh immediately realised that a mistake had been made in not getting the right man, Scot. But he found that Rajguru had already readied his revolver and had begun shooting. Bhagat Singh also fired a few bullets as Saunders fell dead. They were able to get away and the only person who gave them a chase was a police constable Chanan Singh. Both repeatedly requested him to go back but he refused to do so. Ultimately, Rajguru shot him as he was the only eye witness to the happening. Revolutionaries had made a safe escape and managed to reach the house of Durga Devi. They now needed to have a safe exit from Lahore.

The police in Lahore were going house to house in search of those who had killed Saunders. But the revolutionaries managed a safe exit. It was decided that Bhagat Singh would dress up as a young civil service officer with Durga Bhabhi well dressed in tow and Rajguru would dress up as their servant carrying the young son. In the evening, Lahore railway station was crowded with cops when they walked in with confidence towards the first class compartment. Rajguru went to the servants' side. Dressed in perfect European clothes including an overcoat with felt hat and with assumed names of Ranji and Sujata, they looked completely authentic. Chandrasekhar Azad was also on the same train, part of a group of pilgrims going to Mathura.

Bhagat Singh and others had made a successful exit from Lahore. Durga Devi was reunited with her family having played a superb role both in the planning and escape from Lahore of the young freedom fighters. It was a pity that Scot had escaped unhurt because of one mistake in recognition.

Bhagat Singh apart from being greatly influenced by his uncle Ajit Singh also had admiration for the October Revolution in Russia which brought an end to the rule of the Czar in that country. He was concerned about the rights of labour in India. He felt that most British companies working in India were exploiting the Indian workers. In the midst of all this, the British government had planned to introduce a new law in the Legislative Assembly—Trade Disputes Bill that would have barred trade unions from going on strike. The other bill introduced was titled Public Safety Act. It gave powers to the government to detain anybody without trial.

The introduction of two bills agitated the minds of Bhagat Singh and his colleagues. They had in the meanwhile moved to Agra to escape too much attention from the police in Punjab. In Agra, they had been joined by others. Once the date for the introduction of the bills, April 8, was known, it was decided by the revolutionaries that they would make their opposition to the bills loud and clear without hurting any one. The task again fell into the hands of Bhagat Singh.

He was to be accompanied by Batukeshwar Dutt.

Even as all this was being discussed and planned, Azad and some others did not like Bhagat Singh leading it. It could expose him to the possible link with Saunders' killing. On the fateful day the duo reached the Assembly where they received two passes from a member of the Assembly to enter the public galleries. They were carrying with them a loud firecracker which the police later described as a bomb.

Once in the gallery and taking a vantage point, when the moment came the so-called bomb was thrown into the well of the newly constructed Legislative Assembly building. Sitting among the members below were Motilal Nehru, Mohammed Ali Jinnah and other well known Indian figures. As the crackers burst the two shouted the slogan of of *Inquilab Zindabad* and *Long live the Revolution,* a reference to the October Revolution of Russia. This slogan later became the war cry of India's Independence. The two were arrested on the spot and did not offer any resistance. They were taken to the Parliament Street Police station that is still in existence.

The act of throwing the so-called bomb in the well of the Legislative Assembly had not hurt anybody. Any honest court trial at best could have carried a sentence of a few years—even that being harsh. The government wanted to find out if there was any hand of the two caught in Delhi in the murder of Saunders. To the credit of the forensic team, they were able to establish that the gunpowder used in the Legislative Assembly bomb was the same as was used in the bullets that killed Saunders. With that established, the police soon reached the person in Lahore who had prepared the crude bomb as also the bullets. This led to the police now knowing the names of all those who were involved in the conspiracy and killing of Saunders.

The police began to prepare the case and worked on getting one if not two approvers out of the group that was involved in Saunders' killing. It was not before long that the police had two approvers. One was Jaigopal who had mistakenly declared Saunders as Scot. The second was Hans Raj Vohra. A third, whose testimony was only about the establishment of Hindustan Socialist Republican Party, was P N Ghosh. From time immemorial, as I have written elsewhere, India has never lacked in providing its enemies from within—collaborators and traitors. No surprises here if the two, Vohra and Jaigopal, members of the original group that planned to avenge the killing of Lala Lajpat Rai turned against their colleagues. Life did become difficult for the two and their families in Lahore. They faced virtual social boycott not only by the neighbours, but by but people at large.

In the face of all the information doled out to the police on a platter, Bhagat Singh and his colleagues knew that trying to defend themselves would be futile. Thus, they decided to challenge the court and the government for it to file a case against them. The proceedings started with Bhagat Singh and his colleagues telling the court in clear words that they did not recognise the trial or the court. They shouted slogans as they arrived and then began a long statement to tell the court that it had no jurisdiction to try them as they were a foreign ruling power, while what they had done was to defend their own country. The two nations are at what could be called a war. They were fighting against the foreign power occupying India. The court tried its best to stop them from speaking, but it did not work. The court was adjourned for the day, but the same routine followed the next day.

The prisoners now complained of the appalling conditions in the jail. They declared that they were political prisoners and not criminals. As the British had killed so many Indians including the Lion of Punjab Lala Lajpat Rai, they had every right to avenge that horrible killing by the British officers. They also complained that criminals of British origin were treated far better in the same jail.

The trial failed to make a start. It was being reported every day in the newspapers all over India. Gandhiji and the Congress had distanced themselves from the case. In fact, Gandhi had no sympathy for violence. The result was that not only Gandhiji, but the Congress too became very unpopular in Punjab and most other parts of India. Failing to get the trial started, the two British judges on the bench, Judge Coldstream and Judge Hilton, asked the police to use force to stop the contempt of court. However, the Indian judge on the tribunal, Aga Haider refused to support them and issued a statement. Police used force and dragged the revolutionaries from the court. With the presence of the press and reports being made almost ball by ball, the trial united the people of India in support of the revolutionaries.

Following this, the accused refused to participate in the trial. The judges then carried on the trial in the absence of the accused. The massive reporting of the trial not just by the domestic press but worldwide was causing the British extreme embarrassment. Even so they decided to move the trial to be carried from inside the jail. Moving the trial into the jail did not help as the newspapers were still getting reports of what was going on. The revolutionaries had not been given facilities and were still under fetters. They now decided to go on a hunger strike.

The hunger strike changed the situation altogether. Most newspapers now began to publish the day-to-day health situation of the strikers. The trial was reported abroad as was the hunger strike leading to global protests by Indian diaspora. Police tried to force feed them, but that also did not work as the accused resisted such efforts. The happenings in Lahore jail and the hunger strike reports reached British Parliament as the hunger strike crossed day fifty and health of the four strikers became precarious. There was serious discussion in British Parliament.

Finally, as day sixty-three arrived the British accepted the demands of the prisoners. Freedom fighters were to be recognised as political prisoners. Immediately their fetters were removed, proper facilities of newspapers, books, and food were to be provided. Bhagat Singh, Rajguru and Sukhdev broke their fast. But, Jatin Das despite efforts by Bhagat Singh refused to break the fast, saying, 'I am too close to death', and passed away soon after. Netaji Subhash Chandra Bose arrived from Calcutta to take his body.

As the body of Jatin Das arrived in Calcutta, it seemed the whole of Bengal had descended upon the city to join the funeral procession. The population of the city was just two million, but it had never seen the kind of crowd that waited for the body to arrive. The Calcutta police and the British administration were shaken and did not in any manner interfere with the procession. Bengal bid its farewell to its son Jatin Das on the banks of the river Hooghly.

The Conspiracy Case as the trial was known reached its culmination in jail. On 7 October 1930, the court announced its judgement. Bhagat Singh, Rajguru and Sukhdev were given death sentences by hanging. Two were released for lack of evidence but eight others were given varying jail terms. Now began the long wait and agitation all over India to try and get the British not to hang the three sentenced to death.

The manner in which the trial proceedings had been reported had made both Mahatma Gandhi and the Congress

Party extremely unpopular. Gandhiji had refused to issue an appeal for clemency. He refused to come under pressure from public opinion. There are some suggestions by historians that when he met the viceroy he did raise the issue, but not in a manner as to push for it.

It was an agonising wait for the people of India as they prayed for the sentences to be commuted. The Indian National Congress was holding its session in Lahore at the end of 1930. To try and regain some relevance and support among the people, Jawaharlal Nehru when raising the Congress flag on the banks of river Ravi declared that the fight for Independence was now for *Purna Swaraj,* complete Independence. This is what the revolutionaries had demanded all along. After ignoring it for so long, the Congress had been made to change its objective from dominion status for India to complete independence.

The date of hanging for Bhagat Singh, Rajguru and Sukhdev was set for 24 March 1931. Afraid that the date of hanging and cremation could shake all of India, the British decided again to break the law. Unannounced and illegally, they advanced the date of hanging by one day and the three were hanged on 23 March. The three had walked to the gallows singing glory to Mother India, and before being hanged, embraced each other, and then with slogans of glory to Mother India, the three breathed their last.

Neither the families of those hanged nor the people knew of this hanging. The bodies were smuggled out of the jail at night and taken to the banks of river Ravi and burnt—not cremated according to religious rites. It is said the villagers nearby cremated the half burnt bodies later. There was a huge backlash against the government and against the Congress and Mahatma Gandhi.

The three revolutionaries had moved into the annals of history in India's fight for freedom.

In their struggle and death they had made it easy for future freedom fighters who were to be jailed to be recognised as political prisoners entitled to all incumbent facilities.

The freedom fighters following the supreme sacrifice of Bhagat Singh and his colleague were no longer to be called terrorists and sentenced as such. The facilities for political prisoners were such that many prisoners wrote books during their jail terms. For Mahatma Gandhi, Aga Khan's Palace in Poona was used as a jail after he gave the 1942 call for 'Do or Die.'

March 23 is observed in India as Martyrs day–*Shaheed Diwas*. A Martyr's Memorial has been raised at the spot where Bhagat Singh, Rajguru and Sukhdev were cremated at Hussainiwala near the India-Pakistan border.

With passage of so much time, the fact is Bhagat Singh and his colleagues still remain a source of inspiration for the youth of India. Theirs was the supreme sacrifice that hastened the freedom of India. It was just sixteen years later in 1947, including the years of World War II, that India gained Independence.

Chapter 11

INDIAN REPUBLICAN ARMY ATTACKS THE BRITISH RAJ

The end of the 1930s decade found the popularity of Congress and Mahatma Gandhi at an all-time low. When Gandhi travelled from Gujarat to Karachi to attend the Congress session in 1931, his train was stoned by crowds enroute. The revolutionaries in Bengal undeterred by the events in Punjab continued their attacks on the British. In the farthest corner of East India in Manipur, Rani Gaidinliu born in 1915 was against the rule of the British in India. As a young person, she was highly religious and believed in the traditional *Heraka* (monotheistic) faith. Within the Heraka faith she came to be recognised as the incarnation of Goddess Cherachamdinliu. She wanted to get the British out of Manipur and surrounding Naga areas.

She led a violent armed struggle against the British in 1932 at a young age of seventeen. She was, as was usual for the British to do, declared to be a terrorist. Young Gaidinliu was leading the fight against the British from the front herself and keeping them on the run. Her luck soon ran out and she was arrested in 1932.

In the trial that followed, Rani Gaidinliu was sentenced to life imprisonment. Considering her young minor age, she could have been sent for a while to a reform home. Usually, prisoners with life sentences were released within twelve to fourteen years in age. Yet she was not released but kept in jail for life term. Jawaharlal Nehru met her in jail in 1937. He addressed her as 'Rani' and, thereafter, she came to be known popularly as Rani Gaidinliu.

Rani Gaidinliu was released only after India's Independence in 1947. Suffering torture and humiliation in jail, this great woman freedom fighter started to work in Manipur to better the lives of the people of Nagaland as also in the tiny state of Manipur. A staunch believer in traditional Heraka and Naga religious practices, she resisted the conversion of her people to Christianity. As a result, several Baptist leaders considered her to be anti-Christian. She was opposed to the secession of Nagaland from India as sought by the insurgents of Naga National Council. Continuing to work for the betterment of her people, she died in 1993 at the age of 78.

Fakir of Ipi and Khan Abdul Ghaffar Khan

Fakir of Ipi (a village located near Mirali in north Waziristan), whose real name was Mirzali Khan Wazir, was a tribal leader in Waziristan. He was a sworn enemy of the British Empire. Martial people as they are in NWFP (North West Frontier Province), Fakir had behind him a strong and well-armed group of his own tribe. The British had suffered heavy casualties fighting the Fakir's tribe in the inhospitable mountains.

As a devout Muslim, he visited Mecca for the Haj pilgrimage and came to be known as Haji Mirzali, throughout the NWFP (now Pakhtunkhwa in Pakistan). He later shifted his guerilla activities to Gurwek, a remote village also in the north of Waziristan. He would use his base in Gurwek and escape to Afghanistan to carry out his further attacks on the

British or British Indian forces. His demand was that the British go back to their home in England.

On 14 April 1936, Fakir along with other tribes declared a jihad against the British. This followed because a number of decisions announced by the British were considered by the tribes to be anti-Pushtun and anti-Islam. This decision of jihad helped him raise an armed force which some say was over 10,000. His men carried out road blockades, attacked British outposts and ambushed British troops. However, he too was suffering big losses, because the British had superiority of air power behind them. They would attack his men on the ground from airplanes.

The British also dropped petrol bombs to burn the crops and make his people suffer economically. The British would also attack the herds of cattle grazing on the ground. This would cause heavy economic loss to the tribal families, but they bore all that in the fight.

As World War II came to a close, India was heading towards Independence. Fakir alongwith Khan Abdul Ghaffar Khan, the Frontier Gandhi refused to accept creation of Pakistan and demanded an independent state of Pashtunistan. This meant the start of another struggle as the British refused to concede this. Afghanistan supported this demand for Pashtunistan hoping to see the Pashtun areas unified. They also expected that the areas of Afghanistan annexed by Maharaja Ranjit Singh after his victory over that country and not returned by the British after the fall of the Sikh Empire, could come back to the state of Pashtunistan if not to Afghanistan.

The fight for Pashtunistan has been a long one since 1947. During this struggle, the Frontier Gandhi, Khan Abdul Ghaffar Khan spent fourteen years of his life in jails of Pakistan apart from the years he had spent in British jails during

India's fight for freedom. Fakir of Ipi died on 16 April 1960. The Frontier Gandhi continued his fight for Pashtunistan.

The life stories of most of the revolutionaries saw tragic ends when they were hanged or spent time in jails. The tragic story of Khan Abdul Ghaffar Khan was one of serious let down by the Indian National Congress. Coming from the martial areas of North West Frontier Province, the great Khan, like Bhagat Singh, was also impressed by the 1917 revolution in Russia. His followers wore red shirts and were popularly known as 'red shirts.' He met Mahatma Gandhi in 1919 and joined the movement against the Rowlatt Act.

He was greatly impressed by the nonviolent struggle of Mahatma Gandhi. He, therefore, started preaching the nonviolence methods of Mahatma Gandhi to the great 'Pathans' of NWFP. Khan Abdul Ghaffar Khan in course of time came to be known as Frontier Gandhi. His followers wearing red shirts were known as *khudai khidmatgars*—servants of God.

Feeling badly let down and shocked by the Congress Party that agreed to partition of the country without showing him the courtesy of consultation, he felt betrayed. He felt let down when India under Jawaharlal Nehru, a friend of his, refused to support his demand for Pashtunistan. One can perhaps understand British refusal but why did the Congress Party and Nehru have to agree with the British and deny the Frontier Gandhi a legitimate demand for Pashtunistan?

It was conveniently forgotten by the British and the Congress that the areas forming NWFP were annexed by Maharaja Ranjit Singh. The British later created the new province of NWFP of Pashtun speaking people. In the face of this refusal by the British, Khan Abdul Ghaffar Khan announced a boycott of the referendum for the Frontier

Province to decide whether it wanted to be part of India or Pakistan. Despite a huge campaign by the Muslim League for people to participate in the referendum, more than 50 per cent of the people of the province abstained from voting in the referendum. Those who voted gave Muslim League only a majority of 0.5 per cent. If the call for boycott had not been given, it now emerged the electorate would have voted to remain part of India.

Now that he was a citizen of Pakistan, the Frontier Gandhi announced his allegiance to Pakistan. Mohammed Ali Jinnah and his Muslim League had hated the Frontier Gandhi throughout India's fight for Independence. Jinnah hated all those Muslim leaders who were part of the Indian National Congress. With Pakistan's new administration under Jinnah's Muslim League being dead set against him, the great Frontier Gandhi, saw his life in Pakistan being spent more in the jails of that country or in exile.

In spite of the sufferings that Khan Abdul Ghaffar Khan went through, his faith in the nonviolence of Gandhi was steadfast. I had the honour of interviewing him in Jalalabad early in 1980 when Hafizullah Amin, President of Afghanistan was assassinated and Soviet troops arrived there at the invitation of his successor Babrak Karmal. Hafizullah Amin had been very cruel to the people of Kabul and Afghanistan. Several thousand had been jailed or killed. The Soviets also suspected Amin to be joining hands with the Americans. This is what had led to his assassination.

The Frontier Gandhi, analysing for me what was happening in Afghanistan, clearly said that the solution to the problems of the people of Afghanistan lay only in nonviolence the way Gandhi taught. War and fighting was not going to bring any resolution to the crisis or the poverty suffered by the people of Afghanistan.

When he visited India for the first time since Independence in October 1969, he received a huge public welcome at Delhi's Palam airport (now Indira Gandhi International Airport). I covered his arrival. Dressed simply in hand spun clothes of salwar and kameez, he carried his personal belongings over his shoulder. Many Hindu Pathans who had immigrated to India after partition were there at the airport wearing red shirts to give him a warm welcome. During his short stay in India, he travelled to some parts of the country and made his opinion known that he was disappointed with poverty still being there and leaders leading a life of comfort as rulers.

In 1987, Independent India decided to honour one who had been a great fighter for the country's independence and its unity—Khan Abdul Ghaffar Khan. He accepted the country's highest civilian honour Bharat Ratna conferred by the President of India. He was the first non-Indian to receive it, though the people of India to this day consider him as one of them and have great respect for him. He died in Peshawar on 20 January 1988. He had desired to be buried in Jalalabad.

The fighting in Afghanistan between Soviet troops and Mujahadeen supported and financed by the United States, Pakistan and Saudi Arabia was at its peak in 1988. One day ceasefire was declared by both sides. This made it possible to bring his body from Peshawar in a huge procession by the Red Shirts, his followers. I was present in Jalalabad when the cortege arrived with a vast crowd of his followers shouting slogans that he lives forever. People also shouted slogans remembering him as Bacha Khan.

President Najibullah of Afghanistan was present to receive the body and give it a State burial. India sent a strong delegation of its leaders led by the Vice President of India Dr

Shankar Dayal Sharma, together with a delegation of cabinet ministers and other leaders, who arrived from Delhi to pay their last respects.

The Frontier Gandhi was buried with full State honours by the Afghan government. A number of his followers were killed when Islamic extremists fighting in Afghanistan exploded a number of bombs as the burial ceremony of the body was in progress. Several buses that brought the followers of Frontier Gandhi from Peshawar were turned into twisted metal after being burnt down. Scores of people were injured.

Revolutionaries in Bengal continue their fight

Revolutionaries in Bengal decided to form what they called the Indian Republican Army. About this time the struggle for freedom from Britain was going on in Ireland as well. There the Irish Republican army had achieved a fair amount of success against the British rulers in its fight to oust them.

In Bengal Surya Sen, popularly known as 'Master Da' because he was a teacher by profession, worked out a great plan to create a revolution in the East starting from Chittagong. Towards that end, the Indian Republican Army planned its first major action for Chittagong from where they proposed to collect arms and ammunition. The plan of action proposed by Surya Sen had other revolutionaries behind him, including Charu Bikash Dutta belonging to Chittagong, Anurup Sen assistant headmaster at Bora High School in 24-Parganas, and Nagen Sen, a former soldier of the 49th Bengal Regiment. There was another revolutionary Ambika Chakrabarty. They had participated actively early on in Gandhiji's non-cooperation movement. Though Surya Sen backed the non-cooperation movement, he believed in violent action if the British had to be forced to leave without any compromise. As soon as Gandhi's non-cooperation movement died, Surya Sen began violent actions against the British.

According to journalist author Uma Mukherjee, in her book, *Two Great Revolutionaries*, Surya Sen had an ambitious plan to capture Chittagong just as the Irish freedom fighters had captured Dublin and declared the birth of a free Irish Republic. Several Irish freedom fighters were brutally killed by the British soldiers during the fighting with the Irish Republican Army. Surya Sen was keen to achieve something similar by capturing Chittagong. He believed that no foreign ruler would give up its rule in the face of a nonviolent struggle. The British could play around with nonviolent agitation and let it be. Surya Sen now decided that an odd assassination of British officials would not lead to the capture of Chittagong. He needed to do more than that. His first problem was to get weapons.

On 18 April 1930, Surya Sen and his large group of revolutionaries went into action. The first action they took was to cut off all the communication lines of Chittagong including telephone lines of the British rulers. Railway lines too were removed at several points to stop or delay the arrival of reinforcements for the British. Then the main armoury of the British Forces was set on fire. Rifles and small arms with whatever available ammunition were removed from there. Police Lines of Chittagong too were now in the possession of the attacking party of revolutionaries. The flag of Free India was raised in Chittagong amidst slogans of *Vande Mataram*. Thus, says Uma Mukherjee, was formed the first Independent Revolutionary Republic with Surya Sen elected as its president. Proclamation was made by Surya Sen for extending the struggle and inspiring the rest of the country.

In a ploy to run down the idea of independent Chittagong, the British authorities projected it as a raid on Chittagong Armoury. The newspapers reported it as such. For Surya Sen and his large group of revolutionaries, this was the first big step forward. But they had to put off their plan to stage a march of the revolutionary army in Chittagong, and retreat into the hills and jungles. The British had succeeded in gathering a strong force to fight and eject the revolutionary army from Chitttagong. The revolutionaries were now on the defensive as the British forces and police were chasing them. The British forces next attacked the revolutionaries in the Jalalabad hills. The revolutionary army under the leadership of Surya Sen fought well, giving a great account of itself in fighting against a trained army.

The calm manner in which Surya Sen and Lok Nath Bal led the defence of their positions had resulted in a large number of casualties suffered by the British forces. Surya Sen made sure that no one opened fire on the British force moving forward to attack them. Their rifles could not shoot long range. They allowed the enemy to come within their firing range and then opened fire from all sides. It resulted in the attacking force making a hasty retreat as it lost many soldiers, killed or injured. British forces retreated back to Chittagong fearing that the city may fall to the revolutionaries.

Surya Sen and others continued to give more trouble to the government forces in the years that followed. Surya Sen was at large now virtually all over Bengal and carried out attacks on the British officials at a time and place of his choosing. Several senior police officers including Inspector General Lowman of Dacca were killed. The British administration was nearly paralysed. Surya Sen or Master Da always took steps to protect his group.

Then a tragedy was to hit the revolutionaries. Netra Sen who claimed to be a part of the revolutionaries, became a police informer when he learnt where Surya Sen was and informed the British of his location. Surya Sen was arrested at Goirala on 16 February 1933. He was executed on 2 January 1934. His death was a huge loss of leadership. But the revolutionaries did not abandon their fight, but continued with the battle against the British.

Yet another great revolutionary of Bengal Dinesh Gupta planned a daring attack against the British officials. His immediate target was the infamous Inspector General of Bengal Police N S Simpson, whose instructions to the Bengal police were to torture and ill treat the prisoners in jail. For his planned action against Simpson, Dinesh Gupta was joined by two other revolutionaries, Benoy Basu and Badal Gupta.

On 8 December 1930, three revolutionaries Dinesh Gupta, Benoy Basu, and Badal dressed smartly in European clothes entered the Secretariat of the Government of Bengal, Writers Building in Dalhousie Square of Calcutta. Their immediate target was no doubt the infamous Inspector General of Police Simpson.

After successfully entering the highly secured building, the trio went straight for Simpson and shot him dead. Then, a gun fight ensued between the revolutionaries and the police stationed in the secretariat. Some other senior British officers including Nelson and Prentice suffered critical injuries. Fighting continued in the corridors of the building and is known as the Battle of the Verandahs.

As could be expected, soon the revolutionaries ran out of ammunition and to avoid arrest Dinesh and Benoy Basu shot themselves with the last of their bullets. Badal Gupta is said to have taken potassium cyanide and died instantly.

Dinesh survived the near fatal injury in his attempt to commit suicide. In the trial that followed he was convicted and sentenced to death by the British judge R Galick. Dinesh Gupta was hanged in Alipur Central jail on 7 July 1931. Yet another revolutionary had been martyred.

The three young revolutionaries became part of folklore. People of Bengal gave them a huge farewell. After the independence of India, the name of the Dalhousie Square was changed to Benoy-Badal-Dinesh Bagh or as taxi drivers in Kolkata say BBD Bagh. A statue of the three martyrs stands in front of the Writers Building.

A historical movie film *8/12 Binay Badal Dinesh* was produced and released in 2022.

Revenge for Dinesh Gupta's hanging was not late in coming. Judge Galik was shot dead by a young revolutionary Kanailal Bhattacharjee on 27 July 1931. Kanailal was in turn shot by a guard of the judge. Young Kanailal had carried out the killing of judge Galick under an assumed name of Bimal Dasgupta.

The District Magistrate of Midnapore, Peddie had been shot earlier and it was suspected that Bimal Dasgupta was the one who had shot him. He was already a fugitive. When asked to recognise the body of her son, Kanailal'smother Katyoni Devi denied the body being of her son. It was her effort to protect her son.

Surya Sen, Maste Da, had inspired a large number of young people in colleges to fight for the country. Among them was a young lady Kalpana Datta from Chittagong College. She got herself involved in incidents where the police could not suspect a lady to be doing such revolutionary or what the British called terrorist activities. She was sent off to Calcutta to procure sulphuric acid and nitrite acid. These were required to produce bombs and other explosives. She managed to carry out the job assigned to her admirably well and with great intelligence. In Calcutta she was joined by another lady student Pritilata Waddedar who was inspiring the cause of the freedom battle at her college. The two young ladies had a tough task in liaising with other revolutionaries, particularly those behind the bars, and figuring out how to help them with weapons, if required.weapons if required.

The authorities, however, became aware that something was going on in the jails.

A thorough search of Chittagong jail found several daggers, explosive materials and a revolver that had been stolen from the Chittagong Armoury. During this time on 16 September 1931 two under trial prisoners were brutally murdered inside Hijli jail. There was anger and indignation in Bengal for the cruel and inhuman manner in which authorities had conducted their search and attacked the inmates of Hijli jail. Hearing of this, Netaji Subhash Chandra Bose arrived in Hijli to collect the bodies of the prisoners who had been killed. There was a huge funeral procession in Calcutta as the two bodies were taken for cremation.

In September 1932, Pritilata was assigned the task of attacking the European Club in Pahartali, eight kilometers away from Chittagong. Dressed as a male and leader of seven revolutionaries, she managed to reach Pahartali. Several Englishmen were killed and wounded as a result of the surprise attack by Pritilata and her companions. She allowed her companions to leave after what had been a very successful action by her. Why did she not seek a safe refuge and leave the place as she allowed her companions to do?

Perhaps she realised that the authorities will be after her. Instead of being captured by the police, she committed suicide at a little distance from the club by consuming pottasium cyanide. In a note to the women of India found on her person, she urged women to never feel that they are weak and to join in the fight for freedom.

The young revolutionaries in Bengal, though disheartened with the death and killing of their leaders, did not give up the fight. They were in particular going for traitors and police informers. They were able to find the location of Netra Sen who was responsible for the arrest and later hanging of Surya Sen. The task of sorting out Netra Sen was given to Khoka Nandy and Kiran Sen. The two were fully briefed and trained to use not just revolvers, but their plan in this case was to cut off Netra Sen's head.

On 9 January 1934, just three days before Surya Sen was executed, Khoka Nandy and Kiran Sen, surveying the location where Netra Sen was staying, reached there in the evening. Netra Sen was comfortably having his evening meal in the verandah of his house in Goirala, facing a small garden. The two revolutionaries hiding behind a bush in the garden suddenly appeared from there taking him by surprise.

Before Netra Sen could even react seeing the two of them, his neck was struck with a sword like weapon (*gainda*) and in the next split second, the head fell on the *thali* (metal dish) from which he was having his meal. The news of this action pleased the revolutionaries no end. For Surya Sen who was at that moment awaiting his execution three days away, it was a satisfying feeling before dying to learn that members of his Indian Republican Army were active.

Not much has been written about the activities of the Indian Republican Army after the death of Surya Sen. But the fact is that this fighting arm of the revolutionaries continued to be active even after the death of Surya Sen Tarakeswar

Dastidar who was a companion of Surya Sen was looking after the Indian Republican Army, while Master Da was in jail. But soon Tarakeswar was also arrested after an encounter with the police. Tarakeswar was also hanged on the day Surya Sen died. The president of the Indian Republican Army was now Binod Datta.

The period following the death of Surya Sen—from 1935 onwards—was very crucial not only for India, but for the world. There was the rise of Hitler in Germany, who was threatening a war in Europe. The British government was keen on avoiding it and was later seen doing its best to accommodate Hitler's demands. In India, Congress and Mahatma Gandhi had run out of ideas for their nonviolent non-cooperation movement, though talks between the Congress and the British as also other parties were continuing.

The fight against the British was actively carried on by those whom the British called terrorists—the revolutionaries. A British Intelligence officer John Hunt in his book, *Life is Meeting,* records that it was his task to catch Binod Datta, the commander of the Indian Republican Army. But despite exchange of fire on occasions, Binod Datta would disappear. He refers to Datta as an 'elusive and legendary character.'

Several other British officers together with Indian police in spite of all their operations had failed to capture Binod Datta, who had nurtured the Indian Republican Army and kept it active with new recruits.

India's fight for freedom had seen people from all kinds of backgrounds participate in what they considered a sacred cause. Important players in this fight for freedom were revolutionaries who would start young. One such great revolutionary was Manabendra Nath Roy whose family were Hindu 'pujaris' or priests. He was born in Arbelia in Bengal and studied at Harinavi Anglo Sanskrit School. Roy had been influenced earlier on by Swami Vivekananda.

It was the partition of Bengal in 1905 that had seen Roy become active in the agitation. As the agitation continued, young Roy was convinced that the only way to get the British out of India was by violence.

During World War I, the plan of nationalists including Roy was to get German help and throw out the British. It failed. Disappointed, Roy who was in Indonesia left for Japan, hoping to get Japanese support. He met famed Dr Sun Yat Sen, the Chinese leader who, however, also could not come to his help and advised him to work it out with the Japanese. Bad luck seemed to be chasing Roy and he had to leave for Korea from Japan. Roy, now decided to move to San Francisco from where the Ghadar Party was operating. It was from here that his career as a great Communist leader was to begin. He met a young lady Evelyn Leonara, and the two inclined towards revolutionary thought, fell in love and married.

In New York both husband and wife were spending a lot of time at the Public Library studying Communism and Marxist thought. Roy was already well influenced by Vivekananda's message of serving the poor. To escape British spies who had been following him from San Francisco and now in New York, he and Evelyn decided to move to Mexico. In Mexico, he came in touch with Mikhail Borodin of the Comintern—Communist International—in Moscow. Roy had come to the notice of Mexico's President Venustiano Carranza who was appreciative of his work for the newspaper *El Pueblo*. Roy founded the Communist Party of Mexico, the first Communist Party outside of Moscow. In 1920, Roy and Evelyn were invited to attend the Communist International Meet held in Moscow during the summer of 1920. Roy had almost moved to the centrestage of communism.

Roy was asked by Lenin to prepare India for a revolution. Was Roy playing into the hands of the Russians? Roy did not agree with that. He was in Tashkent as part of the Soviet Party to set up political training schools and also to train revolutionaries into bomb making. In India, Mahatma Gandhi's nonviolent non-cooperation agitation was attracting mass following.

In October 1920, Roy founded the Communist Party of India and started getting in touch with his revolutionary friends in India. Several revolutionaries at that moment in India were in two minds, whether to follow Gandhi's nonviolence or stick to revolutionary methods, not necessarily Communist.

In Moscow Lenin passed away on 21 January 1924. Stalin was now all powerful. With Roy's main supporter Lenin gone, he was now running into a difference of opinion with Stalin, who was not the one who would tolerate any difference of opinion. Realising the changed situation in which he could be purged or even be killed, Roy managed to escape the wrath of Stalin by leaving Moscow for medical treatment to Berlin in December 1929 and returning to India next year.

As he arrived in India and the British came to know of it, Roy was arrested in Bombay on a warrant issued against him in 1924. His trial was not held in public, but in the jail in Kanpur. After a prolonged trial he was sentenced to 12 years jail in January 1932. He went into appeal at the Allahabad High Court. Though his appeal was rejected, the sentence was reduced to half, six years.

However, terrible conditions in the dark dingy cells played havoc with his health. He had suffered lasting damage to his organs. But he continued to write and call upon the youth to participate in the fight for Independence. He was released in 1936 and moved to Dehradun. Stalin was chasing him there as well and wanted to have him killed.

The revolutionaries were keeping up the pressure on the British rulers. The British were continuing with their efforts to follow up on the Simon Commission to put some kind of political participation in India's affairs into the hands of educated Indians. British Parliament passed an Act towards that end, known as Government of India Act of 1935.

The first action under the Act was to separate Burma from India with effect from 1 April 1937. Provincial assemblies were created in large provinces of Bombay, Madras, Bengal, Bihar, Assam and United Provinces out of a total of 11 provinces that existed then. There was no such thing as an adult franchise, but selective franchise, and the total number was close to thirty-five million voters for all of India. The problem that Britain was facing was to bring into their net the tiny states ruled by the maharajas and nawabs otherwise known as princes.

The promulgation of the Government of India Act of 1935 left the British bureaucracy most unhappy. There was fear of a check on them by the elected Indian leaders on the kind of loot that the British had been indulging in. In the provinces even though limited powers were given to the elected representatives, the financial control still lay in British bureaucratic hands.

The Government of India Act of 1935, though a big advance in some ways, still failed to bring India anywhere close to dominion status. The British had succeeded in dividing Hindus and Muslims with Jinnah playing into their hands. The British had cleverly retained in the Act, powers under which they could at any time take control of any elected provincial government just as the viceroy could at the Centre.

The British pushed ahead with the provincial elections in 1937. Elections were held in eleven provinces as required under the Government of India Act of 1935. Jawaharlal Nehru led the election campaign for the Congress while Jinnah did it for the Muslim League, and a local leader Sir Sikandar Hayat Khan of the local Punjab Unionist Party did in his province.

It is interesting to study the election campaigns of that year. Nehru had totally downplayed Jinnah's call for communal divide between the Muslims and Hindus. However, the Congress could win only 28 of the 482 Muslim seats. Jinnah could get just about a hundred of the Muslim seats. The remaining Muslim seats went to local regional groups.

The elections were held in provinces of Madras, Central Provinces, Bihar, Assam, Bengal, Orissa, United Province, Bombay Presidency, Sind, Punjab and North West Frontier Province (NWFP). Even though the electorate was, one could well say, of British supporters, the Congress managed to sweep the polls in seven states. In Bengal, it emerged as the largest single party. In Punjab, Sind and Assam other groups led the way. Jinnah's Muslim League failed to win any province, though it was confident of winning all the reserved Muslim seats. The results came as a shock to the British as well as to Jinnah.

The end of the elections in 1937, saw Jinnah being irrelevant even though he claimed the right to represent Muslims of India. Muslims in the provinces, where they were in large numbers, preferred their local leaders rather than any one from Jinnah's Muslim League.

Congress had won seats throughout India, whereas Muslim League could not win even in provinces like Punjab with Muslim majority population. The fact is that the Muslims of India never accepted Jinnah as their leader. It was the British policy of divide and rule that propped him up as a leader of the Muslims.

Chapter 12

QUIT INDIA - 1942, NETAJI ESCAPES AND TAKES OVER INDIAN NATIONAL ARMY

As the 1937 elections in Indian provinces, although half-baked, saw the emergence of the Indian National Congress as the dominant political party in India, the British government sought the party's support in the fluid scenario in Europe. The rise of Hitler and Nazi Germany's support to the Indian revolutionaries was worrisome to the British. But the British were aware that Jawahar Lal Nehru, in charge of foreign affairs in the Congress, was against fascism and Hitler's dictatorship. However, Congress wanted Independence first before supporting the British in Europe. Several revolutionaries were already in Europe in the countries opposed to the British. Chempakaraman Pillai from Trivandrum was one of them based in Europe since 1914.

Just before the outbreak of World War I, Chempakaraman Pillai had arrived in Zurich, Switzerland for studies. As the war broke out in 1914, Pillai formed an international committee for Indian Independence with its headquarters in Zurich. Another student from Travancore, A Raman Pillai was studying in Germany and worked on the International Committee for Indian Independence. Around this time a number of Indian expatriates in Germany formed a similar committee in Berlin. Among those in the Committee were Maulvi Barkatullah, Chandrakant Chakravarty, Bhupendranath Dutta, Heramba Lal Gupta and a few others. Later in October, Chempakaraman Pillai moved from Zurich to Berlin and got the two committees to merge. Lala Har Dayal, another famous freedom fighter, was persuaded to join the group. They began to help the Germans in gathering intelligence from the Indians on army soldiers taken as prisoners of war.

Pillai, together with some friends was later to coordinate a daring attack by a German warship *SMS Emden*, when it entered Madras harbour and attacked the facilities there. Task executed, it managed to slip out of Madras harbour and onto the high seas before the British could realise what had happened. This attack did considerable damage to the facilities at the Madras port.

Pillai is also credited with coining the Indian greeting of 'Jai Hind.' This was adopted by Netaji Subhash Chandra Bose later on and is used in India to this day.

Many actions and events have somehow been lost to badly recorded history of the freedom movement post the 1857 Mutiny. The fact is that the British no doubt did get breathing time after the 1857 mutiny, but hardly any. Freedom fighters like Pillai operating from Switzerland were making life difficult for the British administration.

Again, not known or taught in India as part of India's fight for freedom is the fact that Raja Mahendra Pratap had set up a provisional Government of India in Kabul on 1 December 1915 during World War I. Maulana Barkatullah was the Prime Minister of that Provisional Indian Government.

Pillai from Berlin was the foreign minister. However, the defeat of the Germans in that war led to the withdrawal of this government from Kabul. During World War II, the Germans made much use of the propaganda machine of the revolutionaries in Kabul.

In Berlin, Pillai met Laxmi Bai from Manipur whom he married in 1931. Tragedy hit them and they ended up with a very short married life. Someone was suspected of having given slow poison to Pillai. He was flown to Italy for treatment, but could not survive. Laxmi Bai later took his ashes to Madras where these were ceremoniously immersed at Kanyakumai—Pillai's native place, as desired by him. His memorial statue stands in Madras, today's Chennai.

Rise of Hitler in Europe

In 1937, the rise of Hitler in Germany to absolute power was causing rising fears of war. Hitler was playing heavily on the highly nationalistic sentiments of Germans to restore Germany to its glory and undo the Treaty of Versailles signed by Germany at the end of World War I. Thus, in March 1936 he marched into demilitarised Rhineland. The Germans cheered him on, even though some of his Generals were more circumspect and suggested that he exercise caution.

The British Government in London was making all out efforts to stop Hitler from taking such actions as would lead to an all out war in Europe. But they were aware that it may not happen and thus wanted support of the Indian National Congress in the war effort. British Prime Minister Neville Chamberlain, both on his own behalf and speaking for the French, was accepting as many of Hitler's demands for territories in Europe to buy peace and avoid war. In October 1938, Czechoslovakia had been made to surrender its border regions and the defences there to Germany as a result of the Munich Agreement to which both Britain and France were parties.

Britain and France were hoping for peace at the cost of other European countries. However, Hitler was using all such agreements to get whatever he could without fighting and then go all out to fight for something he had made clear to his generals at the end of 1937.

Soon after his territorial gains in Czechoslovakia, Hitler turned on what he had planned. He attacked Poland on 1 September 1939. He moved rapidly before Britain and France could declare war on Germany. As for India's revolutionaries, they were in the least bothered about Hitler's fascism or dictatorship. They wanted his help in ejecting the British from India.

In India, the British had already started heavy recruitment in the Indian Army. They were confident of support of the Indian National Congress in fighting Hitler's facism. Announcing to the world that the Indian National Congress was opposed to the policies of Hitler, they declared that they could actively get involved against him in the war only as a sovereign independent country.

India was administered by the British with the Viceroy Lord Linlithgow being the head of the Government of India. Using his position, in 1939, he declared India at war against Germany. Congress challenged his declaration, saying that he should not have done that without consulting elected governments of the provinces. He responded by telling the Congress Party that no such provision to consult provincial governments existed in the Government of India Act of 1935.

The British now started making all out efforts to secure other political support in India primarily that of the

Communists and the Muslim League. The response of the people of India was in no way lacking in support to the British as far as recruitment to the army was concerned largely due to unemployment and poverty. There were long queues of volunteers offering their services in the Indian Army. The Congress Party could not stop this.

Hitler had captured France. British troops had to retreat and withdraw from France suffering heavy casualties. The British Army was in shambles after its withdrawal from France and needed virtual rebuilding after their defeat there. The United States of America had not come to the aid of Britain or Europe as of 1940. As for India's revolutionaries in Europe, several of them were in touch with Nazi Germany and Mussolini's Italy. Ajit Singh soon started using Radio Rome to make special broadcasts to India giving news of the war and determination of the revolutionaries to throw the British out of India.

Though opposed to facism and dictatorship, Nehru's view was not to take advantage of the problems being faced by Britain. Mahatma Gandhi's views too were not totally opposed to Britain in this situation, though he still wanted freedom first. However, Subhash Chandra Bose and his supporters were absolutely clear and had no sympathy for the colonial power and sought its defeat.

Rash Behari Bose in Japan was assisting and helping the Japanese in trying to create revolt among the forces of the British Indian Army. Men like him were not concerned about German Nazism or Japan's imperialism. They were focussed on getting rid of the British from India.

The Communist Party of India was looking at the Soviet Union for direction of its policies. So long as Germans and Soviets were not fighting, the Communists in India were opposed to the British. However, as soon as the Soviet Union and Germany went to war, the Communists in India were now with the British. They forgot all about India's Independence.

Japan was making fast advances in the Far East particularly in China. Indians have had a strange emotional liking for China. In the immediate instance, Jawaharlal Nehru decided to visit China and see the situation first hand. Field Marshal Chiang Kai Shek was the President of China. Though not taking part in the war, the Congress decided to send a large Medical Mission headed by Dr Kotnis to help the Chinese injured in the war. During his visit to China, Nehru was not able to visit North West China where Mao Tse Tung was supreme.

Americans were also putting pressure on Britain to accede to India's demand for Independence to fight against Germany and other Axis powers as an independent nation. But the British Prime Minister Winston Churchill continued to ignore such appeals from President Roosevelt of the United States.

The war in Europe was causing huge damage to Britain and its allies. The British were continuously assuring Mahatma Gandhi and the leadership of the Indian National Congress that India would be given independence soon after the war ended. To push their point, the government in London headed by a rabid anti-Indian Prime Minister Winston Churchill decided to send a senior cabinet minister Sir Stafford Cripps to assure the Indian leadership of this.

Sir Stafford Cripps, a liberal leader from Britain, arriving in India on 11 March 1942 was busy meeting Indian leaders across the political spectrum with that objective. This author was a school boy at that time, but my father was covering the Cripps visit very closely. I would hear the stories of Cripps

Mission from my father. The Cripps Mission lasted till the end of April 1942 making efforts to win over the Congress leaders. However, his efforts to bring closer the two warring political parties of India, the Congress and the Muslim League, could make no headway.

With the bulk of the Congress leadership being against facism and Nazism, the Congress leadership was still not favouring Sir Stafford Cripps' proposals. The Congress analysed Cripps' proposals as placating Jinnah and the Muslim League. Aurobindo Ghosh from Pondicherry was keen on Indian leaders accommodating Cripps. He issued an appeal to the Congress leaders on this issue. Aurobindo considered Hitler's ideology of Nazism as worse than colonialism.

Sir Stafford Cripps failed in the assignment given to him by the wartime British Government to get Indian political leadership to openly oppose Hitler's Germany. With his mission failing, Sir Stafford Cripps decided to return to London.

Just as the British were making these overtures, the Japanese were making advances in Asia and had captured Burma. The United States of America too had entered the war after Japan's attack on Pearl Harbour. To defend India from the advancing Japanese, a large number of US troops had landed in India. In Eastern India, towards Assam and Burma's border, a series of air strips and bases were being built by the Americans including roads for war. The Japanese had made air raids in the East including on Calcutta, which had created panic among the populace.

While the Congress and its allies were all out for helping the allies and fighting the Germans, Japanese and Italians (the Axis powers), the revolutionaries had different ideas. Rash Behari Bose in Japan was helping the Japanese in influencing the POWs taken by the Japanese from the Indian Army. He was raising an Indian National Army from among the Indian POWs. Ajit Singh was in Italy and broadcasting to India from Radio Rome.

A large section of the Congress led by Subhash Chandra Bose was totally opposed to the idea of helping a tottering colonial power. The British had suffered a terrible defeat at Dunkirk and had withdrawn their soldiers with great difficulty. In Calcutta, the British had charged Netaji with sedition and wanted to get rid of him. However, he announced that he would go on fast unto death. This was not the way that the British wanted him to die having seen almost the whole of Bengal turning up for the funeral of Jatin Das when he died in Lahore during the fast unto death with Bhagat Singh and colleagues. Subhash Chandra Bose was placed under house arrest as the British did not want him to die in their jail.

For the outside world and the British, he was on fast and thus during the period had grown a beard. Meanwhile Netaji had got Pathan clothes made for himself and was obviously preparing for some plan. Past midnight of January 16-17, when the policemen guarding the house had dozed off, a car drove up at the rear entrance of the house and Subhash Chandra Bose now dressed as Maulvi Ziauddin, a Muslim religious person and accompanied by his nephew Sisir Kumar Bose began his journey. They left Calcutta unnoticed and reached Gomoh some 210 miles away. They were hiding during the day and travelling at night. From Gomoh they boarded a train going to Delhi from where on January 19, he boarded Frontier Mail to Peshawar. In Peshawar he was met by Mr Bhagat Ram who was to now execute the next part of the plan.

In Calcutta, everything continued in the Bose house as normally as though Subhash Chandra Bose was there. Food would go to his room, be eaten by whoever but empty plates would come out for police or its informers to note. Then came 26 January 1941 when he was to appear in court. Where was he? Police and authorities in Calcutta were shocked at his sudden disappearance. The viceroy was naturally furious at his disappearance. In Bengal and Calcutta, the police and government authorities could offer no explanation. They had no idea where Bose was at that moment.

From Peshawar, Bhagat Ram, the Communist leader of the Frontier Province, now as Rehmat Khan and Netaji as a deaf and mute pilgrim left for Khyber by car and after a certain distance the journey started through the tribal territory on foot, escorted and protected by two armed men. They spent the night in a tribal village. The next night, they spent in a mosque at Adda Sharif.

Exhausted, they were by now deep inside Afghanistan on their way to Kabul. There was no longer any fear of being questioned for passport and other documents by any wayside authority. They could not find a car for their onward journey, but managed to ride an open lorry to reach Kabul's Lahore Gate as two virtually frozen bodies. Bhagat Ram found some wood planks which were burnt to warm their bodies.

Now began the final effort to reach Europe. Bhagat Ram was hoping to use his communist contacts at the Soviet Embassy. That did not seem to work. Netaji suggested that he go to the Italian Embassy. It was like 'open sesame.' The Italians welcomed him with open arms, more after knowing about Subhash Chandra Bose. But the problem was still there because journeys to Rome or Berlin could only be via Moscow. And the promised passports were still not in hand.

The journey from Kabul to the border of the Soviet Union itself is not easy. This author has done it in this day and time of wide mountain roads, efficient cars and all other facilities being available. The journey is one of the toughest in the world. Once the police in Calcutta became aware of the missing Bose, they began searching for him in Afghanistan. Afghan police had also begun their enquiries. The lorry driver who had brought them to Kabul became greedy for more money to be given to him to protect their secrecy. This forced Bhagat Ram and Bose to take refuge with an Indian, Uttam Chand, who welcomed them warmly.

It was only on 18 March that a passport arrived for Subhash Chandra Bose with a new name Orlando Mazzotta. Yet another tough journey for Bose began; going over Hindu Kush, the holy city of Mazar-i-Sharif. Then it was crossing river Oxus in rickety ferries. There was Samarkand to see on the way and the city of Bukhara. Finally reaching Moscow by train from the border, Bose was able to take a flight to Berlin on 28 March 1941. A journey that began on the night of January 16-17 concluded finally on 28 March. Revolutionaries working from abroad now had a towering leader with them. He was the kind of man that Rash Behari Bose had been waiting for.

With Bose in Germany, it became all the more urgent for the British to win the support of the Indian National Congress. After Nehru's visit to China, Chiang Kai Shek is said to have written to Roosevelt that if the British failed to come to some agreement with the Indian leaders, there was every possibility that they would not resist the Japanese when and if the need arose.

The Congress had asked its governments in the provinces to resign in protest against the Viceroy's decision to declare war against Germany and other Axis powers. It gave a reason to the British to doubt the assurance of the Congress to support the British in the war. But the British were by now the least bothered as the Indian Army had become the world's largest army in terms of its numbers and was giving a very good account of itself in the war.

In what is considered to be the greatest tank battle ever fought, in North Africa it was the Indian 4th Armoured Division which turned the tide against the Germans and their allies. German armoured forces were led by one of the greatest German officers, General Erwin Rommel. Hitler had specially chosen him, asking him to hold the line and save his friend Mussolini's forces. It was among others the 4th Indian Division which distinguished itself in the battle of El-Alamein in which German and other Axis forces had been outflanked and forced to retreat. General Rommel went back to Germany because of his failing health. The victory of this battle is celebrated to this day and the Indian Army proudly participates there.

With the failure of Cripps Mission, the political situation became very fluid. Congress had no further plan and called for a meeting of the All India Congress Committee in Bombay (now Mumbai) on August 8 1942, to discuss 'What Next'? The Committee met under the Presidentship of Maulana Abdul Kalam Azad to discuss the situation arising out of the failure of Cripps Mission and to decide on the next action. All the Congress leaders were present as was Mahatma Gandhi. The draft resolution had been prepared by Mahatma Gandhi. While rejecting the proposals of the Cripps Mission it declared that the All India Congress Committee (AICC) had come to the conclusion that Britain was incapable of defending India. The resolution further charged that the

British Government had no faith in India's political parties. The army too it said had been maintained to keep India in subjugation. It concluded saying that AICC was of the opinion that the British should withdraw from India.

Following this, the 'Quit India' resolution was moved by Jawaharlal Nehru and seconded by Sardar Vallabh Bhai Patel. It was passed with great enthusiasm amidst shouting of slogans *'Angrezo-Bharat Chhodo'* (British quit India).

In his speech, Mahatma Gandhi did try to explain what he expected of the people of India in this movement calling on the British to quit and asked the people of India to 'Do or Die.' He declared that in the current situation where the whole world is getting involved in a conflagration, 'if I sit quiet in inaction, God will not forgive me. I want freedom immediately, this very night before dawn if it can be had.' He warned the people: 'however gigantic preparations the empire has made, we must get out of its clutches...here is a mantra, a short one, that I give you—the mantra is "Do or Die." We shall either see free India or die in the attempt.'

Clearly, Mahatma Gandhi had called upon the people for violent action for which they had never been asked before.

Before they could take any action to direct the launching of the movement, all the leaders of the Congress party were arrested the very next morning on August 9. They were kept very comfortably by the British in special jails. For Mahatma Gandhi, his wife Kasturba and his secretary Desai, the Aga Khan Palace in Poona was designated a jail. Similarly, the members of the Congress Working Committee which had senior leaders like Nehru were kept in Ahmednagar Fort, and its palace within that was designated jail. All the senior leaders of the Congress Party, Maulana Azad, Sardar Vallabh Bhai Patel, Dr Rajendra Prasad, Dr Syed Mahmood, Shankarrao

Deo were among others detained there till almost the end of World War II.

Jawaharlal Nehru wrote his famous book *Discovery of India* while in Ahmednagar Fort. Apart from writing books, he took keen interest in gardening and set up a rose garden. Maulana Azad too worked on his memoirs and wrote the famous *Ghubar-E-Khatir* (the Dust of Memories).

In Ahmednagar Fort, servants were provided to cook food. A badminton court was laid out for them to exercise. Sardar Vallabh Bhai Patel also took part in gardening. Using the spinning wheel, he spun cloth. Sardar loved the game of cards, Bridge, and played that with others. He read a large number of books that were made available to him as also to others. The authorities were making sure that those detained at the Ahmednagar Fort were comfortable.

The 'Quit India,' 'Do or Die' movement did not last long. In Delhi, as a young boy, I would watch the protest demonstrations in Chandni Chowk, the heart of the city, from the balcony of our house overlooking the street. One was not supposed to stand there. Being a little boy, I would lie down and watch through the grill. Every demonstration would be lathi-charged by the police. If a clash with the police took place, it would finish with the demonstrators arrested. Thereafter both sides would disperse. Same was the case elsewhere in India.

It was on 19 August 1942, in Ballia, in eastern UP, the district that borders Bihar and is the junction of two major rivers Ganga and Ghagra that the Congress declared Independence, which signified a buildup of the Quit India movement . The independence of Balia did not last long even though it was a mass uprising. The British military moved in. Indiscriminate firing followed and several hundred were killed. Balia lost its independence, quickly, much sooner than expected.

According to the available records on the Quit India movement, a total of 60,000 persons were arrested all over India, around a thousand died and nearly 3,000 were injured. It was not long before the agitation died its own death.

The two actions of the Congress, one to ask its governments in the provinces to resign, and the second, to give a call for 'Do or Die' without preparing for it led to all of them being jailed. The two actions also removed Congress from the political field which was left wide open to Mohammed Ali Jinnah. Earlier, Congress had asked its provincial governments to resign. From almost being irrelevant, Jinnah now had all the time to explain his position not just to the British but to Americans, too. He was able to tell them that the Hindu Congress was a leftist organisation inclined towards the Soviet Union. And why it was necessary to have Pakistan. There was no one around from the Congress to refute Jinnah.

Before the end of 1942, the fight for Independence was all but gone, as far as any agitation inside India was concerned. Mahatma Gandhi and the Congress had no further plan of action with their biggest call for 'Do or Die' and 'Quit India' collapsing. Worse, all the Congress leaders were in prison. Considering that the free leaders and revolutionaries like Rash Behari Bose, Ajit Singh, Raja Mahendra Pratap and Netaji Subhash Chandra Bose were in Berlin, and operating from there, the fight for India's freedom was going on from abroad.

In Berlin, however, Subhash Chandra Bose was not eliciting a speedy response to his proposals. He was spending a lot of time with those reporting to Hitler. He was making broadcasts to India to correct the propaganda of the British.

Hitler had been delaying any decision from his side because he considered India as an area of influence of the Soviet Union. But all this changed when Hitler went to war against the Soviet Union.

In Asia, Japan was making astounding advances. Rash Behari Bose was keeping Bose informed. Rash Behari himself was meeting Indians soldiers who were taken prisoners. Most of the British areas in Asia were defended by the Indian soldiers. The Malayan (now Malaysia) campaign by the Japanese and its success could clearly show to Rash Behari that Britain was now facing serious defeats in Asia that would make it impossible for it to rule over India.

In Berlin, Subhash Chandra Bose realised the importance of rushing to Japan and carrying on his fight for freedom of India. He was facing problems finding transport to travel to Japan. The Italians were hoping to send him by air, but were not sure of the safety of the flight. Travelling by ship too was not possible for the kind of checks that were there on the way. Finally, Subhash Chandra Bose and Abid Hussain left by a German submarine on 8 February 1943. It was a long journey that finally brought them to Sumatra. From there they left by air for Tokyo.

Subhash Bose had planned as a first step after getting his brief from Rash Behari Bose that there was urgent need for a provisional Government of India. Soon after his arrival in Tokyo, Subhash Bose was received by Japan's all powerful Prime Minister Hideki Tojo. Unlike Berlin or Rome, he did not have to wait to meet Japan's leaders.

Subhash Bose placed before the Japanese Prime Minister that once the Provisional Government of free India was declared, it should be given recognition by the Axis powers. As a government entity, it would make it possible for it to deal with other powers. Subhash Bose was also confident of support from the large expatriate Indian population living in Asia. Not just simple support, but financial support to make it less dependent or not dependent at all for finance on the Axis powers.

Subhash Bose was greatly encouraged when Hideki speaking in the Japanese Diet (Parliament) declared that Japan was fully committed to throw out the British from India, and ensure that India achieves its full freedom in the true sense of the term. Subhash Bose had waited for over two years for European dictators Hitler and Mussolini to make such a strong commitment.

Another positive thing for Subhash Bose was that he was very well known among the Indian communities abroad. Like many Indians at home, the diaspora also believed that Subhash Bose had not been shown rightful regard by Mahatma Gandhi and other Congress leaders. Thus, Indians in Asia welcomed him with open arms assuring him of all support.

Subhash Bose had also been mentioned by Mohan Singh to the Japanese way back in 1941. The Indian diaspora in Asia beginning from Burma, Thailand, Singapore, Malaysia and Philippines had been expecting him amidst them from the end of 1941. And now that he was among them, he was beginning to move quickly.

Rash Behari in the meanwhile was critical of Jawaharlal Nehru for his anti-Japanese outbursts. Rash Behari had started raising the Indian National Army well before Subhash Chandra Bose arrived in Japan. It was now handed over to Subhash Bose. Taking charge from Rash Behari Bose, Subhash Bose realised the urgency about visiting Singapore and other South East Asian countries with the Indian diaspora— and getting the Indian National Army on the war front towards India.

Subhash Chandra Bose having taken charge of India League from Rash Behari Bose began to study the attitude of the War Department of Japan and its generals towards the way independence was given to Burma and Philippine Islands. Now, convinced that he could handle the relations with Japan, he went on to broadcast to people back home to trust Japan. And that he himself was there to ensure that India's interests were protected.

His appeal to the people back at home was in the absence of all the Congress leaders who had been jailed. He believed that it was time that the people turned the nonviolent disobedience movement into an armed struggle. He assured the people that India would be free before long and then all the sons of India languishing in jails will be free to build a powerful India.

Subhash Chandra Bose realised that he had to allay the Japanese army's fears in case soldiers of the Indian National Army (INA) failed to fight against their former comrades, the men of the British Indian Army. Bose understood the Japanese military's fear, but finally succeeded in getting at least the first regiment of INA to fight alongside the Japanese Army and prove their mettle.

Subash Chandra Bose arrived in Singapore on 2 July 1943 to a huge welcome by the Indian population there. The days following his arrival were spent meeting local Indian leaders. On 4 July at a mass meeting, he accepted the Presidency of India League. He inspected the Indian National Army on 5 July. He spoke as President of the Provisional Government of India and head of the 12,000 strong Indian National Army. He declared that INA would fight by the side of Japan's Army as it made its way to India.

He emphasised that the march towards India was to

liberate the country from the British. It was not just the former POWs from the British Indian Army who were given an opportunity to join INA, but also eligible young Indians settled abroad. Women also came forward to fight under INA and a full-fledged women's regiment was raised. On 6 July, Japan's Prime Minister Hideki Tojo inspected a Guard of Honour from the Indian National Army.

India's fight for freedom now had thousands of unsung, unknown heroes—men and women—leading the battle for freedom of India.

Chapter 13

INDIA INCHES CLOSER TO INDEPENDENCE

Even as the nonviolent movement for India's Independence had all gone quiet at home following a failed 1942 Quit India call, the Japanese army, an ally of the INA, was already knocking close to the doors of India. A highly respected national leader Subhash Chandra Bose was leading the INA, keeping the people of India updated about his army's progress via radio broadcasts from Azad Hind Radio and Ajit Singh from Rome, defying censorship.

On the night of 20 December 1942, suddenly people of Calcutta, India's financial capital and 'city of joy' were woken up by loud explosions. Japan's Air Force had made a successful bombing attack bringing the first signs of war to India.

Calcutta was placed under curfew and blackout at night. Several people started leaving the city or sending their families away from the city. Further air attacks continued almost daily. The night sky was turned into a battle ground between the Allied Air Force and the Japanese. Allies claimed to have destroyed several Japanese fighter planes and bombers in the air battles. The people did not see any signs of that. Japan's air attacks over Calcutta continued till 28 December and later, there were sporadic attacks. In one such attack, the Japanese caused huge damage to the Kidderpore docks of Calcutta. Kidderpore docks were used by the allies to transfer supplies to China. A few thousand people lost their lives when the Kidderpore area was bombed. Several ships anchored at the docks were destroyed.

Then came an air attack on Madras in October 1943. Madras port was bombed. The administration there panicked and ordered a certain amount of evacuation of the city. There was just one attack on Madras, but the city was fearful that another attack by Japan was about to follow. As a matter of fact, a certain amount of panic had spread all over India. This author was only a young school boy at the time, but the British, too, were responsible for creating panic in large parts of India. They had started building and built ARP (Air Raid Precaution) structures on the footpaths for people to take shelter in case of an air raid by the enemy planes. Adding to the fear and panic was the arrival of over a hundred thousand American soldiers with the advance of Japanese and INA forces towards India.

In Madras, a senior Congress leader C Rajagopalachari had not been arrested by the British in the en masse arrests of Congress leaders that followed the call of Quit India. Popularly known as Rajaji, Rajagopalachari took the administration of Madras presidency to task for creating panic by starting evacuation. He told the people that there was little chance of Japan attacking. He called upon the people to be ready to resist the Japanese if at all they came anywhere near.

The war in Europe in the meanwhile was at its peak and going against the allies. The British were afraid that Hitler might attack their island country. They were running out of resources. India was being milked to the maximum. An India which had already been looted by the East India Company was now spending or subscribing more to Britain's war effort. The worst that happened because of this loot was the famine in Bengal during the war in 1942-43.

Winston Churchill, the Prime Minister of Britain and a rabid anti-Indian had made life miserable for the people of Bengal. He caused a huge manmade famine in the midst of the war by moving food from civilians of India for his armed forces. Five million were to die in the famine that hit Bengal as a result of Churchill's action. Like the staff of yesteryear's East India Company, many British bureaucrats made money because of the food shortage. They cornered foodgrains in connivance with the traders to sell at high prices. Subhash Chandra Bose as head of the Provisional Government of India from Singapore made an offer of 100,000 tons of rice for Bengal to fight the famine. The British colonial government, unconcerned with the famine turned down the offer. The result was hunger, misery and death.

With a proclamation by Subhash Chandra Bose on 21 October 1943, the birth of Independent India's provisional government became a reality. In his speech as head of the government, Subhash Bose declared that the provisional government had the full support of the people of India. He told his large audience that he did not have the slightest doubt that once INA crosses into India, real revolution will begin there. And the provisional government of India will be able to take charge of the country as the government of India.

As the ceremony concluded the National Anthem of India, *Jana Gana Mana* from a poem of Rabindra Nath Tagore and set to music by an Indian soldier was played. It is the same anthem that was adopted by the Nehru government when it took charge on 15 August 1947. Everyone stood in honour including the Japanese. There were loud cheers and slogans at the end of the ceremony that had proclaimed the Provisional Government of Independent India.

Subhash Chandra Bose, then made quick visits to the countries of South East Asia as head of the Provisional Government of India. These countries were home to a large Indian diaspora. The idea was to involve them fully in India's fight for freedom, raise money and recruit young manpower from among them for the army. He did not want to be too reliant on Japan for money.

Bose sat down now with Field Marshal Count Terauchi, the commander of Japan's forces for the campaign into Imphal towards India. As the conversation proceeded, the views of Terauchi came as a shock to Bose. Terauchi did not think much of the Indian men or women soldiers. The role suggested by Terauchi for INA and its men was not acceptable to Bose. He wanted the Indian National Army expanded to its maximum and lead the Japanese in the fight for liberation of India. He assured Terauchi that if Indian forces lead the liberation of India, backed by Japan's forces, there will be a huge amount of goodwill earned by Japan. After long discussions, Terauchi agreed to have a division of INA trained to the level of Japanese forces. The rest of INA could then follow.

The discussions between Bose and Terauchi finally led to positive results. He immediately started work to build the first division of INA along the lines of Japan's force. The training of the division started in Malaya (today's Malaysia). INA now had its own Supreme Command Headquarters. Bose was very clear that the training of his men had to be of the highest standards. The enemy that INA was going to face was well-trained and well-equipped. The enemy troops also had the support of Americans. Bose was confident that the very appearance of INA's soldiers on the frontiers of India defeating the colonial army would destroy the morale of the British in India.

Bose was taking personal interest in the training and welfare of the men and women of INA. The salaries of the men were raised. Those he found to be slack in any manner were allowed to go. There was to be a pension for the families of those who got wounded or killed. He made sure that the food served to the soldiers and officers was of good quality. He would give the soldiers a surprise visit and join them in their meal. The Indian National Army was thus raised to the best standards for a fighting force and was not inferior in any manner to the soldiers of the Japanese army.

Subhash Chandra Bose displaying the best of his administrative ability had well-created the structure of the Provisional Government of India.

The Provisional Government was recognised by Japan, Germany and other Axis powers as aslo by Burma, Croatia, Philippines, Nanjing, Italy, and Siam.

As for the financial strength of the provisional government, Bose was dependent to an extent on money from Japan, but he was raising money from the Indian diaspora as well. A system of tax was created, which was imposed on the rich of the Indian diaspora and it worked out to around 25 per cent of the income that the businessmen made. As for money from Japan, he was clear in his mind that it must be repaid by the government in due course.

If we closely look at the structure of the provisional government, it is evident that Bose was building a solid structure that was to one day become the Government of India. The first target he set for India's government was to abolish communalism in the country, create unity and have Hindustani as the national language. In creating the structure of the provisional government, Bose was not enthused in any manner with the colonial government's way of working in India. The culture of the colonial government of India was to lord over the people of India. This was evident even at lowest levels of bureaucracy, be it *patwari* or *tehsildar* in the village or a *babu* (clerk) in the secretariat. Each of the colonial bureaucrats thought of himself as a representative of the Viceroy, the ruler.

Bose wanted the government of the people that was meant to serve the people.

That was going to be the culture of the government when it took charge of India when liberated.

In October 1943, Subhash Chandra Bose flew to Tokyo to meet Japan's Prime Minister Hideki Tojo. He wanted the islands of Andaman and Nicobar already captured by Japan to be transferred to the Provisional Government of India. Prime Minister Hideki Tojo speaking at the East Asiatic Conference declared: 'I have been greatly moved by the fact that the Indian people are all rising in order to obtain their freedom. It should be very obvious that Japan is ready to set India free from the bondage of America and England.' Tojo also announced the return of Andaman and Nicobar Islands to the Provisional Government of India.

This major act by Japan in 1943 laid the foundations of a solid Japan-India friendship that continues.

Subhash Chandra Bose further wanted to make sure that Indian National Army's 1st Division would fight alongside Japan's army when the Burma operation began in the next few months. And that INA would lead the entry of both the *armies into India.* After receiving assurance on all these issues, Bose left Tokyo on 18 November 1943.

Japan's air force had begun attacks on Calcutta during this period. On the way back from Tokyo, he undertook his journey through Shanghai, Nanjing, Manila and Saigon, meeting Indian diaspora and local governments.

Everywhere he received enthusiastic welcomes, not just by the Indian diaspora but by the governments of the countries he visited. In Nanjing, he met representatives of Marshal Chiang Kai Shek.

By mid-1943, news from Europe was disheartening for the Axis powers. In North Africa, Rommel's forces had been beaten and forced to retreat. Indian Army's 4th Armoured Division was winning laurels for itself in this battle of El-Alamein. Germany also suffered its worst ever defeat in Stalingrad when, it is claimed that, nearly 90,000 of its troops died of hunger and an equal number was forced to surrender, thus turning the tide of the war against Germany. This was the biggest surrender of forces during World War II.

Japan, meanwhile, suffered heavy loss of its naval strength in the Battle of Midway against America. This was the biggest naval battle fought between the navies of the two countries, north of Midway Atoll in the Pacific. It inflicted heavy damage on the Japanese Navy so as to almost destroy it. This naval battle gave the Japanese Navy a shocking destructive defeat in the World War, making it indefensible against the US Navy. Japan had earlier destroyed the Pacific fleet of the United States in its attack on Pearl Harbour. The defeat and destruction of the Japanese navy were not good signs for Japan's army that was planning to take an offensive and march towards India. Japan had also suffered heavy air losses. American forces, which had arrived in India in great strength, had well entrenched themselves in North East India. This was not just to defend India in the face of Japan's advance, but later to conduct a Burma campaign against them.

Disappointed with the way the war had gone against the Axis powers in Europe, the Indian National Army and the forces of Japan entered Manipur in March 1944. For the men of the Indian National Army, it was a matter of great joy that they entered the soil of India. The people of Manipur welcomed them happily. A local leader, Guno Singh, who had met Bose in Rangoon, also joined him.

British forces while retreating from Manipur caused a huge damage by following a scorched earth policy. They burnt people's homes, food stocks or anything that could be useful to INA or the forces of Japan. In Europe, the allies under General Eisenhower were preparing to cross the English Channel to oust the Germans from France and march into Germany. Soviet forces had cleared the German army from Belarus in what was yet another big defeat, forcing Germany to retreat.

Both Subhash Chandra Bose and the Japanese commanders were elated by the performance of the Indian National Army and its march into Manipur. The two forces combined had taken on the elements of nature as well in their march towards Imphal. The civil administration staff was equally well-prepared to take over these territories. Tojo had spoken in the Parliament of Japan and made a categorical statement—he had said that the Provisional Government of India would be taking charge of the occupied Indian territories as they moved into India.

Bose had understood from the Japanese commander the problems that the winning force had to deal with when entering enemy territory. Bose had assured him that they would not be entering enemy territory but helping INA to liberate its Indian territory. In the meanwhile, Colonel Loganathan of INA had taken charge as Commissioner of Andaman Islands on behalf of the Provisional Government.

When the march towards Imphal began, Subhash Bose was ready to ensure that civil administration followed. He was not going to rely on any of the staff of the colonial British administration. The commander of Japan's forces Mutaguchi was very confident of an easy victory in Imphal. Bose was not, because of the American support behind the British forces in defending the North East of India.

Americans had built air strips all over North East India to give air support to the men on the ground.

The British had also heavily strengthened the defence of Imphal. The British were aware of the Indian National Army fighting alongside the Japanese. Because of the press censorship, the people of India were unaware of the efficiency, strength or the fighting capabilities of INA or that it had already moved into Manipur. Victory in Imphal was of extreme importance to Subhash Bose to enthuse the people of India. He was very confident of an uprising of the people of India once they got to know that the INA was in Imphal and so was the Provisional Government of Independent India.

When INA and the Japanese forces together began fighting the allied forces for Imphal, it soon became clear to Mutaguchi about how wrong he had been in assessing that it would be an easy one for Japan to beat the allies there. He had been encouraged to believe this by the easy march that INA forces and the Japanese had in Manipur forgetting that it was a princely state. Mutaguchi now had three divisions of Japanese forces assigned towards Imphal, alongwith the one division of the INA that was leading from the front. The allies had been waiting for this offensive and had well prepared the defence of Imphal. Nevertheless, the INA forces were making a very tough but successful march towards Imphal. Colonel Kiani, INA'a commander in the area as also General Shah Nawaz commanding the Subhash regiment in Chin hills kept Bose briefed of the hardships and tough fight that his men were putting up in the face of a huge defence by the enemy. Americans had provided heavy artillery to the British in the area apart from air support. INA's women regiment also fought in this area. Subhash Bose after discussions with the Japanese command moved further reinforcements into the area to strengthen INA forces. Japanese forces were not able to make as quick an advance as had been done by the INA. So confident was he of victory of the Indian National Army that Subhash Bose had made arrangements for supplies and readied the civil administration for Imphal once they liberated the area.

With delays and slow progress of Japan's forces towards Imphal where the INA force was to enter first, Bose was getting worried as the first monsoon rains began. Monsoon in North East of India can be very heavy and stalls everything. With such heavy rains, it becomes the wettest area in the world. The men now had to not just fight the enemy but also protect themselves from snakes and leeches amidst heavy downpours. In spite of all this, the INA men were making excellent progress towards Imphal, and were very enthusiastic as they were to raise the tricolour there.

The World War was going against the Axis powers in Europe. Allied forces, under the command of General Eisenhower, after crossing the English Channel had begun pushing back German forces. Allied air forces were virtually carrying out carpet bombing of German cities, inflicting heavy casualties and destruction on the country. Not only its factories, but residential areas were being flattened.

As the battles continued on the Indian front, once INA and Japanese forces began marching from Manipur, both were handicapped as they lacked any air support. Japan's airpower or whatever was left of it after setbacks in the Pacific and defence of Japan was committed to defending its positions in that area. In Europe by the end of 1944, allied forces were rushing towards Berlin and the German surrender came about on 8 May1945. All of America's and maximum allied power was now directed against Japan. Subhash Chandra Bose was aware of the consequences that were to follow.

After successfully entering Imphal, the battle became virtually house to house and man to man to capture the city. The British forces together with the British Indian Army were defending Imphal with full force. The sprawling bungalow of the district commissioner was the scene of one such man to man fight where the tennis court of the bungalow was changing hands to either side every now and then. If INA forces were beaten back from the tennis court, they would come again till finally INA lost the battle. That so much fight was put up for a tennis court illustrated how INA had to fight for every inch of Imphal soil.

Eventually, the Indian National Army lost the battle for Imphal, largely because Japan had suffered defeats in the Pacific and its air force was not able to help the forces in Imphal. The Indian National Army had suffered heavy casualties in Imphal. Bose still hoped to retain his position in Imphal and continued the fight. A major hit on INA was made by the British forces when they managed to capture three of its important leaders, General Shah Nawaz, G S

Dhillon and P K Sehgal. Their being captured by the enemy gave a severe hit to the morale of their men. Bose was doing his best to assure them that once they capture Imphal, an uprising in India will follow.

The news of the first atomic attack on Hiroshima came as a huge shock to Subhash Bose and to the Japanese commanders in Burma and Southeast Asia. Bose felt the end of the war could not be far as Japan had nothing like an atom bomb to respond with. And the US and allies had already asked for Japan's unconditional surrender.

Bose had organised well the retreat of his forces from Imphal including the women's battalion. Once in Thailand, his concern was to get the women soldiers of INA back to their families, which he managed to do. All this was executed before the formal surrender by Japan.

He, together with some of the Japanese commanders, was making an effort to reach Tokyo as soon as they could. Bose was also aware that the surrender and end of war was not going to finish his struggle for India's Independence. For him the war against Britain would continue. He was keeping a watch on developments in India where Mahatma Gandhi had been released from jail on 6 March 1944 on grounds of health. Lord Wavell was now the Viceroy of India. He was keen to get an interim government organised at the Centre. He was working on what could be the ultimate solution of Indian Independence or home rule. He also wanted his Viceregal Council to be turned into the Cabinet of the Interim Government.

As Mahatma Gandhi came out of jail, he opened talks with Mohammed Ali Jinnah who was now more than ever insistent upon a separate country to be made out of Muslim majority provinces. Subhash Chandra Bose, like all other revolutionaries, was against any division of the country. And for that he had already set an exemplary example of the Provisional Government of India. All he could do was to keep an eye on what was going on, while he dealt with the situation on the war front.

As the date of surrender by Japan neared, one question that cropped up was whether the Provisional Government of India too was to surrender. Bose was clear in his mind that the struggle of the Provisional Government of India against the British would continue. However, he was expected to be in Tokyo. Unfortunately there was no plane available that could carry all the senior members of the Provisional Government of India to Tokyo. He was at that moment in Saigon with his colleagues. There was one plane leaving for Tokyo with Japanese officers. Bose was offered one seat on that plane which he refused. Finally, the Japanese came up with one more. It was decided to accept this offer with Habib ur Rahman to travel with him. The departure was too close for the Provisional Government and its leaders to sit and plan for the future. Taking leave from his colleagues, Bose told them that he expected to see them soon. Bose and Habib ur Rahman left Saigon in this twin engine overloaded bomber in the evening.

Landing at Tourane enroute, the party spent the night there. The flight was resumed the next morning on 18 August and arrived in Formosa (today's Taipei) past midday around 2 pm. After lunch with all aboard including Bose and Rahman, the flight took off on what was an overloaded plane. After it took off, one of its engines lost its propeller and crashed. Many died. Both Bose and Rahman struggled to come out of the wreckage. Bose had suffered serious burns and also had head injuries.

They were taken to the hospital where Bose felt he

could not survive with the kind of injuries and burns he had suffered. According to Habib ur Rahman, the doctors made every effort to save Bose. They were aware that he was the head of the Provisional Government of India. Bose could hardly speak owing to his injuries. But he managed to dictate a message to Field Marshal Terauchi. He is also said to have given a message for the people of India telling Habib ur Rahman to tell them that they will be free soon. Then he went into eternal sleep.

As I close this episode of the death of Subhash Chandra Bose, I must say that events of the plane crash have been surrounded in controversy ever since. Many continued to believe for a long time that he perhaps escaped to the Soviet Union. After all the inquiries it stands confirmed that Bose died in Formosa as explained by Habib ur Rahman.

It is great to see now that the massive contribution that Subhash Chandra Bose made in the fight for India's freedom received recognition finally back home in India. The people of India have always held him in high esteem, maybe more than many others who fought for freedom. In New Delhi, a very fine statue of Bose in INA uniform is installed under the Imperial canopy, where once stood the statue of King George V. It adorns the heart of New Delhi right next to India's War Memorial and is the most sought after place to visit by all Indians visiting Delhi.

As the war ended, Congress leaders were steadily released from jail. In Delhi, the British government put the three senior INA officers, General Shah Nawaz, K S Dhillon and Sehgal on trial at the Red Fort. Now, suddenly all of India became aware of the heroism of the Indian National Army and how close they had been to victory in Imphal. All of India had risen in sympathy for the three INA officers. The

Indian National Congress decided to fight for the defence of the three officers. Congress praised the Indian National Army and called the trial of the three officers and others as an oppression of India's people.

The Indian National Congress, had during the war not approved of the INA fighting alongside the Japanese, condemning the Japanese dictatorship to be as bad as Hitler's facism if not worse. Jawaharlal Nehru was now among the first to declare his support for INA and its men and women. A powerful defence team of advocates was chosen for the three to be led by Bhulabhai Desai who was a leading advocate of India at that time. There were a total of sixteen lawyers. Nehru also joined them making the number seventeen.

The trial of the three officers in the Red Fort was frontpage news in the newspapers all over India with public sympathy rising every day for the men under trial. The witnesses produced by the prosecution were proved by the defence advocates as being tutored and one of them accepted the charge. Bhagat Singh during his trial in Lahore had asserted his right to fight and kill the foreign occupier. In the Red Fort trial, Bhulabhai Desai asserted the right of a country's people to fight for their liberation. Nehru let it be known that the three officers and men of INA had become symbols of India fighting for her Independence. According to Nehru it was now England vs India.

People all over India were demanding release of the three INA officers and other men. When the day of sentence came, all the three officers were sentenced to death. The matter was now to be considered by Field Marshal Claude Auchinleck, Commander in Chief of the Indian army. Without any delay, perhaps not waiting for a formal copy of the order to be in his hands, Auchinleck commuted the sentence and the three were released. There were great celebrations all over India.

This author who was a school lad at that time also went to Delhi's Gandhi ground where the three officers came to be welcomed and honoured by the citizens of the capital of India. The small open ground in old Delhi near the Red Fort and opposite to Gurudwara Sis Ganj Sahib was filled to more than its capacity with people standing on the roads around and on house tops. All I remember is that the vast crowd was chanting *INA Zindabad* and *Victory to INA*. There were slogans for Netaji Subhash Chandra Bose and the three officers. When the meeting ended, there was a huge stampede as the crowds tried to move out via a narrow gate towards Gurdwara Sis Ganj Sahib. I fell on the ground as I tried to come out with the other school boys. God knows how many walked over me and others who had fallen, till a lathi charge by the police cleared the gate and those of us on the ground were rescued. So, this author can never forget that great day of INA and his own survival in a stampede.

The Indian National Congress and Mahatma Gandhi whose last battle for Independence, the 1942 'Do or Die' agitation had failed, now got the people of India rallied again, around the cause of INA and protecting its men.

The people of India were with the Indian National Army. The Congress had no alternative but to support the Indian National Army and protect them. Mahatma Gandhi himself had visited the Red Fort to see where the INA soldiers were kept.

India was now close to Independence.

Chapter 14

INDIA IS FREE BUT PARTITIONED

As World War II came to a close, events began to move fast on various fronts for India. Congress leaders were out of jail where they had been held captive since August 1942. Britain was badly hurt economically by the war expenditure. A vast amount of funds and manpower was needed to rebuild the country from the destruction caused by German air raids and flying bombs. Winston Churchill, the rabid anti-Indian Prime Minister who had led the United Kingdom to victory was defeated in the general elections. Clement Attlee of the Labour Party and wartime deputy Prime Minister succeeded Churchill.

Assessing Britain's precarious condition, Attlee realised it could no longer hold on to India, its colony. Without further ado, Attlee made it clear that the British would leave the country and make India independent.

Among the first acts of Clement Attlee as Prime Minister of Britain was to send a senior delegation of his cabinet ministers under Lord Pethick Lawrence to negotiate the transfer of power to India's leadership. It was Attlee's hope that such a serious action announced by his government may spark unity among the leaders of India and power would be transferred smoothly. The British cabinet mission got to work soon after its arrival in Delhi. With summer setting in, several meetings of the mission with Indian leaders were held in Simla.

The first thing that the mission found was that the Indian National Congress and the Muslim League were poles apart from agreeing, either to the mission's proposals or offering their own proposal, the one that could ensure unity and integrity of India. But Lord Pethick Lawrence was not giving up, as the government in Britain wanted to hand over the country to Indians as soon as possible.

The Viceroy of India Lord Wavell was also very keen on the unity of India. His plan was to club the provinces into groups which would satisfy Jinnah to an extent if Muslim majority provinces were there as such. As the discussions progressed, the Congress finally rejected the proposals in a public speech by Jawaharlal Nehru. Jinnah called Nehru's speech another treachery. The cabinet mission failed to resolve the matter, passing on the buck to the Viceroy.

Lord Wavell, hopeful as he was to maintain the unity of India, announced the formation of an interim government with Nehru as the Prime Minister even as Jinnah refused to participate in such a dispensation. Sidelined by this move by Lord Wavell, Jinnah called his supporters for direct action to secure Pakistan.

This direct action by the Muslim League meant violence. It started on 16 August 1946, resulting in attacks by Muslims, then leading to riots and killings between Hindus and Muslims. Several thousands were killed in Bengal, apart from huge loss of property. The violence didn't help in any way in finding a solution. Significantly, Muslims, too, were split on the idea of Pakistan.

Ultimately, Lord Wavell prevailed upon the Muslim League to give the interim government a chance. Muslim League representatives joined the government on 26 October 1946. Jawaharlal Nehru continued as the Prime Minister. So many reasons have been given, but the primary reason for the Muslim League joining the interim government was not to lose the sympathy of the British government, but to assure them of their loyalty. It all looked good at that moment because the interim government was to take charge of the country.

There was no denying the fact that the transition from a colony to an Independent country was the greatest event in the history of India. A government of Independent India was a cause that would make every resident of the country—under foreign rule for few hundred years—proud.

However, the attraction and goodness of Independence didn't seem to inspire the political class to forge unity among themselves. The Muslim League ministers didn't see eye-to-eye with the Congress ministers, with the result that the interim government was a far cry from a cohesive team.

It did not take long for the interim government to come to a virtual standstill, despite Lord Wavell's best efforts to get the government to work. Nawabzada Liaqat Ali Khan, number two in the Muslim League after Jinnah was the finance minister in the interim government. This meant that the proposals from other ministries, including those managed by the Congress leaders had to go to the finance ministry in case of financial implications.

In a developing nation most proposals have financial implications. All such proposals were not being cleared by the finance ministry or the files were held up, making it impossible for the Congress ministers to carry out any work.

The Interim Government virtually collapsed under these circumstances. It was now clear to Congress that it could not work together with Muslim League. This set the ball rolling for the partition of India.

The British government announced the withdrawal of Lord Wavell and appointed Lord Mountbatten as the Viceroy of India. Mountbatten invited Jawaharlal Nehru whom he had already known to visit him and his wife in Singapore. The British clearly had decided to leave India and were now keen to know who would be the Prime Minister of Independent India.

Jawaharlal Nehru during his visit to Singapore had been welcomed very warmly by the large Indian diaspora there. It is sad that Nehru did not visit the Memorial of the Raising of the Indian National Army in Singapore. It is said that he was asked by Lord Mountbatten not to go there. It is suggested by most historians that Mountbatten had managed to convince Nehru during his stay in Singapore that the solution to India's Independence lay in its partition.

The British Government in London made a public announcement that irrespective of Indian leaders coming to any agreement among themselves on running the country's government or not, it would leave India by 30 June 1948. Basically, it meant they would leave whether Jinnah's demand for a separate homeland for the Muslims of India was agreed or not.

Maulana Azad, who was the Congress president at that time writes in his autobiography, *India Wins Freedom*, that Nehru did not report to him about his discussions with Mountbatten in Singapore when he returned from there. He was entitled to receive a report as president of the Congress party. Maulana Azad held him and Vallabh Bhai Patel as being responsible for the partition of India.

The explanation given by the Congress and Nehru was that the non-cooperative attitude that the Congress faced from the Muslim League in the interim government, would have made it difficult for India to grow and develop. Therefore, they thought it best to agree to the Partition. Then, the two countries governed by the Congress and the Muslim League could develop and grow independently.

Muslims of India who were opposed to such a partition on religious grounds, did not recognise Jinnah as their leader. And they proved their rejection of Jinnah in 1937 when the Muslim League failed to win any Muslim majority in any province where the elections were held. The question that Muslims of India asked was: where were they going to go? This was an unanswered question that bothered them. How could they leave India which was their home for generations and that is where they did all their business. Yet Jinnah was about to be thrust upon them by the British. Hindus were forced to leave the areas that became Pakistan, because it was being said loudly that Pakistan was the home for Muslims.

There were mass demonstrations by the Muslims organised by All India Azad Muslim Conference and several other Muslim organisations in Delhi, appealing to the British and India's leaders not to divide the country. They declared and reminded everyone including the British that Muslim League or its leader Mohammed Ali Jinnah had no right to speak on behalf of Muslims of India. Their concern was the unanswered question why should they leave, giving up their homes, businesses and employment in India.

Azad Muslim Conference opposing the Partition alleged that the idea of dividing India was to keep Muslims backward and suffer economically.

Deobandi scholar Maulana Syed Hussain Madani in his book, *Muttahida Qaumyat Aur Islam*, argued against the idea of Partition. So did Alama Mashriqi who considered separatist leaders as power hungry and misleading the Muslims. He alleged that the separatists were serving the British agenda. The British ignored the fact of massive demonstrations in Delhi including the one by the Muslim weavers of Bihar and Eastern UP against the Partition.

Not just Muslim voices were ignored by the British, but voices of other non-Hindu communities as well. The Akali Party led by Master Tara Singh as also Chief Khalsa Diwan were also opposed to the idea of Pakistan. The Parsi community largely resident in Bombay Presidency, but in smaller numbers all over India was a prosperous one. They were opposed to the idea of Partition. Frank Anthony, leader of the Anglo-Indian community speaking also for the Christians did not approve of Partition. Yet the British were pushing it.

Jinnah had managed to convince the British and the Americans that he alone was their friend in the sub-continent, while the Hindu Congress was left-oriented.

Thus, for the British and the West, in 1946 Jinnah was the voice of the Muslims of India. They ignored all other Muslim voices that actually represented the majority of Muslims living in 1946 India. And there were reasons for such an attitude by the British not known to the people of India. These came out later in Khan Wali Khan's book, *Facts are Facts,* and in the biography of Maulana Azad.

Events moved fast after the arrival of Mountbatten. He advanced the date of British departure from India to 15 August 1947, from 30 June 1948. Why was he in such a hurry? Had he given enough thought to the procedures and problems of dividing a vast country like India, including its assets among two unequal nations? Had the British applied themselves to ensure proper administration of such a division? The Survey of India had not worked out boundaries for the two countries.

Mountbatten invited Cyril Radcliffe, a British advocate who had never visited India and knew nothing of the country to resolve the boundary issue. He did not even know of the issues on which a vast country was to be broken into two. It seems whatever draft boundary may have been worked by the Survey of India was adopted by Cyril Radcliffe. The Radcliffe Award defining the boundaries of the two countries came four days after the two countries were created. What he had really done, and I have no hesitation in writing, drawn lines across and divided India into two.

The concerns and worry that Maulana Azad had visualised about the fallout and reactions to the partition among the people of the affected areas were not ill-founded. In areas defined as West Pakistan and East Pakistan there had been massive publicity given by the Muslim League that Pakistan was to be the country for Muslims. In the villages, Muslims had started telling their Hindu and Sikh neighbours to start leaving, as they won't be allowed to live there.

We all who were living then saw and know what happened when the two countries emerged as a result of Partition on religious basis. History had never seen such a massive movement of mankind. No one is able to give figures of the numbers killed that run into some estimated five million. There is also no information on the number of women kidnapped, raped or converted to Islam forcibly. The country's Independence and Partition came with huge bloodshed. Trains would come from either side loaded with massacred bodies. In the midst of all these killings taking place there were martyrs who tried to stop the fighting and killings. There is a heart-rending martyrdom of one in Multan.

Sardar Nanak Singh

Sardar Nanak Singh was a successful advocate in Multan opposed to Partition. When riots broke out between Muslims and those opposing Partition he tried to cool either side. On 5 March 1947, Nanak Singh got ready as usual in the morning to go to the courts. His wife urged him not to do so as there was tension and some fighting in the city. However, Nanak Singh was confident no harm would come to him.

There was a procession by the students of DAV school calling for no Partition and Akhand Bharat (United India), shouting slogans. As it entered Bohar Darwaza, a narrow street, the young Hindu and Sikh boys were attacked by Muslims with sharp weapons. Many were injured, some killed as they tried to run away. Sardar Nanak Singh reached there and going straight into the middle of the melee, he shouted aloud to stop the butchery of the children. The mob surrounded Nanak Singh. He was assassinated in the most brutal manner, according to eye witnesses.

Nanak Singh left behind a pregnant widow and eight children. There was no future for them in Multan now. The brave Sardarni Harbans Kaur took her eight children aged eight to fifteen years and went to the railway station to board the train going to India. All her attempts to get into the train with her children failed. She broke down not knowing where to go. Seeing her pathetic condition, the train driver held the train and asked her to be seated on the coal in the coal tender. Gratefully accepting that, she and the children sat there.

Covered in black coal dust they arrived at Ferozepur

in India. Here they were met by Sardar Faujdar Singh, her brother and his wife Harbhajan Kaur. At first they could not recognise them as their faces were covered in black coal dust. Later they moved to Patiala where her sister and brother-in-law Samsher Singh lived.

In Patiala, Sardarni Harbans Kaur took control of her life to raise the young family. She took on the job of a teacher. Her children were admitted to schools. They all succeeded in life. Five of them joined India's armed forces as officers. Another became a great educationist in East Africa, later going to London and retiring there. The daughter also pursued her career in education and married an army officer. The youngest son Raminder Singh moved to London. With his great success in business, he, Lord Rami Ranger, is today a member of the House of Lords of the British Parliament.

During his call on Lord Mountbatten before Partition, Maulana Azad had expressed his fears about a fallout of partition, which would mean killings as the people moved from both sides. Mountbatten's reply to him then was that he, being a soldier, would use heavy force and air force if required to curb any violence. Alas had the other leaders including Jinnah foreseen this?

It has been said that Jinnah too was shocked with the killings. Efforts of Nehru in Delhi who himself came to the streets of New Delhi had failed to stop the rioting and killings when these started in the capital.

Independent India stood divided, something that all the revolutionaries were opposed to. The revolutionaries were never in favour of any compromise or negotiations with the British on the issue of Independence, particularly any that would lead to dividing the country. One revolutionary who was alive then and living in Pondicherry, Aurobindo Ghosh issued a statement. He stated loud and clear that he was unhappy at the division of the country. He said that they as revolutionaries had not fought for this.

The fact remains that the division of the country meant the British could continue making money now by selling weapons to the two countries. The tension and enmity between the two countries born from day one meant continuous business for the British.

Following Independence, Khan Wali Khan, son of the Frontier Gandhi Khan Abdul Ghaffar Khan did a thorough research of the British Government papers in London including those that he could access from the British Foreign Office. He was confident that it was something not known to the Indian leadership that led the British to hurry through the Partition of India. After studying the papers and speaking with many British politicians, he then wrote an eye opener book *Facts are Facts*. In this book, he brings out his analysis why the UK, a staunch ally of America, was keen on the creation of a sovereign Pakistan in North India.

He concludes that a country like Pakistan was needed by the West in the Cold War against the Soviet Union that had begun soon after the end of World War II. India's leadership was considered to be left leaning and could not be relied upon. This was something that Jinnah had succeeded in convincing both the British and the Americans, while the Congress leaders were jailed after August 1942. Pakistan was to be a frontline state to stop the movement of the Soviet Union towards the warm waters of the Arabian sea. The Congress leadership did not realise in 1946 that the Cold War had already begun.

Jinnah did not last long after his much dreamt about country, Pakistan emerged on 14 August 1947. He had explained his vision of the new country to the Constituent Assembly when he addressed them on Independence Day. He told the Constituent Assembly that he visualised Pakistan to be a modern nation where every one could practice their religion. He did not mention it as an Islamic state. He expected Pakistan, though Muslim majority, to be a modern, forward looking nation. He perhaps had Mustafa Kemal Atatürk's Turkey in mind.

Suffering from cancer, he passed away on 11 September 1948 hardly a year after Pakistan's birth. He could not build the country of his dreams. He expected the relationship between India and Pakistan to be friendly, if not brotherly. He had asked the Indian government not to take over his house in Bombay, as he expected to return and live there on retirement.

His deputy and the Prime Minister of Pakistan Nawabzada Liaqat Ali Khan too did not last long. He too was in favour of friendly relations with India. He was perhaps as much sad and hurt by the mayhem and murder that followed on the emergence of the two countries. He sat down with Prime Minister Nehru and signed a pact known as the Nehru Liaquat Pact. As per this bilateral pact, refugees were to be allowed by each country to dispose of their property. The looted properties were to be restored, abducted women traced and returned and forced conversions were not to be recognised. In short, the two leaders expressed their desire for friendship and good neighbourliness. This pact was not to the liking of those forces that now controlled Pakistan. The Prime Minister of Pakistan Nawabzada Liaquat Ali Khan was assassinated on 16 October 1951. No one knows till today by whom and why? Thus ended the lives of the two tall leaders and founders of Pakistan.

Then followed years of political turmoil in Pakistan. That is another story. It all resulted in General Ayub Khan emerging as martial law administrator and later President of Pakistan. That country had now gone under military rule forever. A joke in the streets of Pakistan is that usually countries have armies but here the army has a country, Pakistan.

Pakistan, formally joined the grouping of Western nations led by the United States of America against the Soviet Union. The country became a member of the SEATO (South East Asia Treaty Organisation). India was a nonaligned country, remaining aloof from the two blocs fighting the cold war. The objective of the founding fathers of Pakistan, Mohammed Ali Jinnah and Nawabzada Liaquat Ali Khan, eventually landed in the dustbin.

India and Pakistan now drifted apart in their relationship.

It was not before long that America set up a secret air base in Peshawar from where that country's spy U2 planes used to take off to see what the Soviet Union was doing in the field of nuclear development or space research. These planes could fly at a height where Soviet missiles could not hit them. It did not take long for the Soviet Union to develop a missile that hit a U2 plane and its pilot Gary Powers, who ejected, but was arrested by the Soviet Union.

Pakistan was now the frontline state of the western alliance as written by Khan Wali Khan in his book on why India was divided. In the proxy war that the US and its allies, Pakistan and Saudi Arabia, fought against the Soviet Union in Afghanistan from the end of 1979, Pakistan's role was crucial. But that war is now over, as is the Cold War. Even the Soviet Union has gone and Pakistan now stands alone and abandoned by the West.

Coming back to 15 August 1947, India was free. Sadly

for the country, there were no revolutionary leaders around when Independence came. In the absence of Netaji Subash Chandra Bose, rightfully Congress took charge of defending the INA officers. The men of INA who originally belonged to the Indian Army were, however, not given pensions or reinstated in the army.

The history of the Independence struggle as has been written since 1947 gives all credit to nonviolence, non-cooperation and time spent in jail by the Congress leaders. Life in jails for political prisoners was made comfortable by revolutionary Bhagat Singh and his colleagues. The armed struggle fought by the revolutionaries has been downplayed or ignored.

I am shocked when I find that even knowledge about Netaji Subhash Chandra Bose is missing among many of the young. Those living in Bombay (now Mumbai) around Colaba hardly know about the naval mutiny or a small memorial that exists there for those naval officers who lost their lives in fighting for India's Independence. As for the Indian diaspora in particular, the young know very little about the freedom struggle.

It is tragic that Independent India has ignored the revolutionaries. When INA and Netaji Subhash Chandra Bose succeeded in reaching Imphal, the British were alarmed and compelled to think afresh about continuing their rule in India. The naval mutiny in Bombay followed by one in Karachi as also in the Royal Indian Air force was enough to show that forces the British relied on to rule India were going against them.

The British Prime Minister Clement Atlee himself made it clear that the decision to leave India was taken not because of Mahatma Gandhi or the Congress. 'Minimal,' was the exact word he used to describe the influence of the two in the British Raj's decision to leave India.

The fact remains that mass awareness to fight for Independence was inspired by Mahatma Gandhi. His total stress on nonviolence failed to get the people of India to rise and fight when he gave a call for 'Do or Die.' Mahatma Gandhi's exact call to the people was: 'Here is a mantra, a short one that I give you. You may imprint it in your hearts and let every breath of yours give expression to it. The mantra is 'Do or Die'. We shall either free India or die in the attempt. We shall not live to see the perpetuation of our slavery.'

The only people who were doing this long before this call by Mahatma Gandhi were the revolutionaries. While I do not wish to undermine the role of the Congress and Mahatma Gandhi, it is important that we give due credit to all those young and old revolutionaries who fought and died for India.

India was independent and began its journey to work on and implement all that it had promised the people during the fight for Independence. The first and foremost issue was to get the Constitution of India passed by the Constituent Assembly. Prime Minister Jawaharlal Nehru guided the Assembly well, to draft and pass the Constitution of India. Then there were all these over five hundred small areas ruled by the maharajas and nawabs to be integrated into the country. Agriculture had to be looked at afresh to fight poverty and bring about economic growth.

The government got to work on all these subjects in real earnest. We all are aware of how Sardar Patel managed to integrate India and deal with the princes.

The Constituent Assembly passed the Constitution of India on 26 November 1949. It was signed by the members on 24 January 1950, the last day of the Assembly. On 26 January 1950, Dr Rajendra Prasad became the first President of India. India was now no longer a dominion. The goal of complete independence was dreamt and called by Bhagat Singh, and proclaimed by Nehru by raising the Congress flag in Lahore on the last day of 1930.

Tragically there was no living revolutionary joining the celebrations. Those in jails were released. Jogesh Chandra Chatterji was among those who were released from jail after Independence. In his book, *In Search of Freedom*, while describing his life long fight, he complains about the treatment revolutionaries got from Independent India's government. He had himself joined the Congress after Independence, but left it when he found he could not get recognition for the contribution of the revolutionaries or memorials raised for them.

As an example, he states that the British government left four memorials for Lord Hardinge in Delhi, including Hardinge Library and Hardinge Hospital. But Independent India's government did not raise any memorial for the martyrs of the Hardinge bomb conspiracy case, who were hanged apart from Rash Behair Bose, who had escaped to Japan.

In Lucknow it was proposed by the revolutionaries that on 15 August 1947 morning, Congressmen and the revolutionaries should march to the residency, which was occupied by the British since the Mutiny of 1857 and raise the national flag there. The Union Jack used to fly there.

But the president of the Congress Committee, C B Gupta remarked, 'Why on that very day? It may be done later.'

Jogesh Chandra Chatterji writes in his book, 'such attitude clearly indicated the trend of mind of the Congress leaders.' He alleges that the Congress was not bringing about any change in the manner of rule by the bureaucracy. He goes on to write 'Conscious people understood from that very day that power came not for the masses but for a few leaders only.'

Years later in Delhi, it was proposed by the revolutionaries that Delhi jail be preserved. This jail had seen so many revolutionaries imprisoned and hanged.

Prime Minister Jawaharlal Nehru was approached for this, who replied that because Maulana Azad National Medical College was to be opened in that place, a plaque could be put where the gallows existed. After many meetings with various officials and leaders, the Home Ministry under Pandit Govind Ballabh Pant refused to do anything.

The situation, as this author saw in his younger days when the trial of the three INA officers was conducted in the Red Fort, was a complete upsurge of the people of India in sympathy with INA. The British had realised then the time for departing had come. Independent India was able to get France to leave Pondicherry, and other French possessions in India to peacefully integrate with the country.

Independent India's government under Pandit Nehru began its work using the same structure of administration and bureaucracy as was left by the British. The culture of that bureaucracy was to delay response to any representation and behave as though the rulers were doing a favour to the 'subject.' During British rule each and everyone in the bureaucracy thought of himself to be a representative of the Viceroy. As against this, Nehru had declared himself to be the *'First servant'* of the people.

Jogesh Chandra Chatterji was pained to see the ruler-like attitude of the government servants. I, close this chapter with his words: 'As a revolutionary, I was never a believer in compromise, because I was convinced it would degrade the nation. But I could never dream that whatever patriotic spirit we could acquire in the course of our fight for freedom in fifty years, would be totally lost only within eighteen years of Independence. Within such a short time, our national character has been so thoroughly degraded that today we have become a nation of self-seekers. Today, neither the administration nor the Congress organisation has a strong foundation among the people. Only top leadership is there and that, too, is not free from popular distrust. How the nation is to rise again, that question is disturbing the mind of all honest and right thinking Indians.

'I have not the least doubt that a section of the youth of the country would again rise and form the vanguard of revolution and bring about the much desired change in the atmosphere. The sooner it happens the better it would be for the accursed land of ours. I would very eagerly wait for that day before I breathe my last.'

Jogesh Chandra Chatterji passed away in 1969, aged 74 years, sad at the state of the country. The Congress is a shadow of its past. In its long rule, it could not remove poverty from the country. Elections to Parliament have become caste and religion-based. Reservations meant for 'harijans' for ten years, when the Constitution was passed, continue with more demands for reservations from all kinds of sections of society. This has led to a brain drain, another sad story of post-Independence India.

The Bharatiya Janata Party, has been in power since 2014. It is working on schemes that ensure that the poor get benefits meant for them directly into their bank accounts. Basic facilities such as toilets, homes, cooking gas, and electricity are being provided to the poor. Only time will tell how soon India becomes a self-reliant and prosperous country.

Chapter 15

GOA IS LIBERATED

Goa has as much of ancient history as the land of Bharat or India. There are references to Goa in ancient India. It was known as Gomanta or the area of cows. Even today it is claimed that the milk in Goa has the finest quality available in India. There are stories about the land being born when the sixth incarnation of Vishnu, Parashurama asked the sea to recede and was born Gomantak.

Goa today is a vibrant, lively state of India. It attracts tourists from all over the world. It is continuing to grow and is blessed with minerals.

In its long history, from 1498, Goa came under the rule of Adil Shah's Bijapur Sultanate. Fond of the state, Adil Shah treated Goa as his second capital. He built his palace on the banks of River Mandovi. The palace still exists, minus its riches.

The Portuguese army, under the command of Afonso de Albuquerque, first attacked Goa in February 1510, when it had to beat a hasty retreat when the Sultan came after him. But Afonso de Albuquerque came back in November 1510, as soon as he heard that Adil Shah had died and was succeeded by an infant Ismail Adil Shah.

Albuquerque defeated Rasul Khan who defended the territory of infant Ismail Adil Shah. Albuquerque marched victoriously into the city of Ela, Goa, on 25 November 1510. Portuguese rule had now been established and Goa was a colony of Portugal in Europe. But the Portuguese treated the area as an overseas territory of Portugal and called it Estado de Goa India-Portuguesa.

At first Albuquerque did not at all interfere in the religious ceremonies or practices of the Hindus. The only interference, if you call it that, was when he banned the cruel ritual of sati. But he went all out to kill Muslims whom he considered as part of his destruction of Adil Shah. He expanded the territory of Goa capturing the areas now known as Salcete, Marmugao and Bardez, making Goa a jewel of Portuguese overseas territory.

In course of time, Portuguese expanded their rule and began forcibly converting people to Christianity. The Portuguese made full use of Goa, which has India's only natural harbour to base their vessels there. They would attack the Mughal trade or pilgrimage ships when they would leave Surat and collect a heavy levy. The powerful Mughal emperor had no navy to fight them on sea.

Goa was an overseas territory of Portugal with its own culture and civilisation. The people resisted conversion to Christianity, resulting in violence. Then there were other kinds of discrimination against the local people who did not accept Portuguese rule.

As the Portuguese grew stronger, they began a systematic destruction of Hindu temples, intensifying their conversions done with force. Unable to deal with the might of the rulers, many locals would accept Christianity, but continue to observe Hindu rituals and prayers. If found out, such persons suffered terrible punishment amounting sometimes to execution.

In a major incident in 1583 in North Goa, some 300 Hindu temples were destroyed in Cuncolim and other villages around. This was naturally resisted by the local people. It is said the events moved fast.

The villagers attacked those who had come to erect a huge cross and most of those who had come to do so were killed. The Portuguese army had to be called out to recover bodies of the dead including several priests. The Portuguese invited local village chieftains for talks assuring them of safety. Once they arrived, they were all massacred. It is known as the Cuncolim revolt, the first uprising in Goa against Portugal.

In all, nearly 900 big and small temples had been destroyed in Goa.

To raise Christian population, the Portuguese soldiers were encouraged to marry local girls to have children. However the attacks on Hindu temples and loot there as well as killings contributed to the decline of what was once a prosperous and rich territory. When the Portuguese attempted further expansion they faced defeat both at the hands of the Muslim rulers and at the hands of the Marathas.

However, Goa remained under their control. In Goa, the Portuguese were able to further expand the territory under their control moving towards Bicholim, Pernem, Ponda, Sanguem, and Canacona by 1791.

However, by 1835, Hindus were allowed freedom to practise their religion. This ensured peace and contained resistance against the rule. Goa, by then, was like a small country.

The forced conversions of the past apart from voluntary conversions had led to the emergence of a sizeable Christian population in Goa. The clergy, being European coming from Portugal also now had local Christian priests.

The racial discrimination against the local population by the Portuguese continued. Even Goan clergy was not spared. In 1787 two priests Jose Antonio and Caetano Francisco de Couto travelled to Portugal and Rome to plead for appointment of Goan priests as Bishops. This was not done and they continued to be ignored and discriminated against. The priests then decided that there was no alternative, but to rebel.

The two priests concluded that there was no solution anywhere in sight despite negotiations. They had in the meanwhile gained sympathy from the unaffected Christian elements in the army. They then met Abbe Faria, another Goan priest who was a pioneer in the scientific study of hypnotism. The priests now planned a rebellion along with Ignacio Pinto, head of the Pinto clan and several others supported by Abbe Faria. Ignacio Pinto wanted Faria to be installed as future head of the state after victory. They contacted Tipu Sultan, ruler of Mysore for support.

The conspirators planned for the day to start an insurrection. The conspiracy for all this action had been decided at meetings held in the house of Ms Penelope Pinto, great grandmother of the well-known hotelier and businessman of Goa, Ralph de Souza.

Tragic as it has always been in India, all their plans were disclosed to the Portuguese. There was a traitor among them—a Goan Catholic baker. He was expected to serve poison laced bread to the Portuguese soldiers. The first and immediate attack by Tipu Sultan in support of rebels was averted.

As the revolt failed, many fled to British India. However, the Portuguese authorities captured many rebels and punished 47 including the priests. Fifteen priests were publicly executed in an open piece of land in the ward Bairro Sao Tome, Panjim. It is a large open area close to the GPO where executions took place.

The priest Abbe Faria managed to escape and teamed up with French revolutionaries in France.

How suspicious the Portuguese would become of any innocent event after the failed conspiracy is well described by Ralph de Souza. A party was being held in a large house located at Feira Alta in Mapusa by Ralph de Souza's mother, Cristalina and her sister-in-law Eloisa. This was to celebrate the Feast of Our Lady of Assumption. Everyone was happily enjoying and celebrating the feast on the day which happened to be 15 August 1959, India's Independence Day. Someone made a complaint to the authorities that Independence Day was being celebrated with great enthusiasm at the party.

The Portuguese authorities declared the event to be anti-national. Policarpo Vaz, a guest at the party lost his government job, Cristovam and Joaozinho, two brothers from Mapusa were deported to the Atlantic Islands of San Tome where they languished till Goa was liberated by India in 1961. Cipriano de Souza, father of Ralph, lost his mining concession at Sanquelim. Others present at the party were interrogated at the police station and detained for the day. The mining licence of de Souza was renewed only in 1969 long after Goa's liberation.

There were many more who had resisted Portuguese rule. It is unfortunate that their details remain unavailable with earlier records either not being available or all being in Portuguese language.

In the twentieth century, it was Dr Tristao de Braganza Cunha who started a full-fledged independence movement against Portuguese rule after his studies in Paris. He also raised the issue of Indian and Goan independence. Returning to Goa in 1926, he founded Comissao do Congresso de Goa (Goa Congress Committee) in 1928. The Portuguese did not want this. He was pressured by the Portuguese to leave Goa, but continued his work from Bombay.

Returning to Goa later, he organised a huge rally in 1946 at Margao addressed by Dr Ram Manohar Lohia. He was arrested by the Portuguese and kept in a cell in Fort Aguada. He was sentenced to eight years jail and deported to Portugal to be imprisoned at Peniche. After his release in 1954, Cunha returned to Bombay from where he continued his activities to free Goa from Portuguese rule.

Dr Cunha died on 28 September 1958 without seeing the liberation of Goa. Jayaprakash Narayan, great freedom fighter of India was one of the pallbearers at the funeral. The Indian National Congress described him as the father of Goa's independence movement.

The Nehru Government in New Delhi had been making efforts with the rulers of Portugal to peacefully leave the Indian territory in their occupation as the British and French had done. But there was a standard reply from Portugal that they were not in occupation of any Indian territory. They claimed that Goa was an important overseas province of Portugal. Apart from Goa, the Portuguese had small areas of Daman and Diu also under their control.

These two tiny territories are in the state of Gujarat. Daman is more of an industrial town while Diu attracts tourists. In a dry state of Gujarat both the former Portuguese enclaves serve liquor, as it was the assurance of the Government of India to retain Portuguese culture for the local population.

The world was in turmoil since the end of World War II with the cold war. India had adopted a well-considered policy of nonalignment to keep itself away from the cold war. After the Korean war, the US forces were now involved in fighting in Vietnam, Laos and Cambodia. This was all a part of US policy to contain the spread of communism. Fears arose in India that Goa may become one of the R and R (Rest and recuperation) areas for the US troops fighting in Asia. Portugal was an ally of the United States, thus the fears were well founded.

Prime Minister Jawaharlal Nehru did not wish to use force to free Goa hoping to get Portugal to leave peacefully. His Defence Minister Krishna Menon kept pointing out that once US forces begin to visit Goa, the US could develop vested interest in Goa not to be part of India. It was under such circumstances that India decided to eject the Portuguese from Goa, Daman and Diu.

The Indian army in a swift move entered Goa on 18 December 1961. The Governor of Goa Manuel Antonio Vassalo e Silva in his wisdom decided not to put up any fight against the overwhelming power of the Indian Army, Air Force and Navy. He felt that his army, police and people would suffer unnecessary casualties. There was just one Portuguese Naval frigate in Goa apart from a limited number of troops. The Portuguese army did put up small fights in some areas and took other steps to stall the progress of the Indian attack. They decided on destroying some of the bridges. Lacking enough trucks they forcefully took these vehicles from Goans, among them Cipriano de Souza whose mining lease had been cancelled earlier.

Egypt's President Gamal Abdel Nasser, a great friend of Nehru had not allowed the Portuguese naval ships to enter the Suez Canal on their way to Goa. It was in a matter of hours that the Indian Army led by General Choudhury got surrender from the Portuguese in the evening. Goa was now a part of India.

This author was present at the surrender, arriving in Goa independently of the army. In those days the Indian army still implemented censor rules of World War II. Thus, I had to find my own way to cover the event. That is another story.

It would be dishonest of me if I were not to say that many Goans were unhappy at the defeat of Portugal and Goa becoming Indian. The Portuguese who came in 1510 were gone in 1961 after a rule of 450 years.

I have given the known names of unsung heroes who fought for the independence of Goa to be part of Mother India. There are tens of them who remain anonymous. Goa is now a vibrant state of India whose face is totally changed with growing prosperity from tourism and other industries.

As Goans say: 'Viva Goa.'

> Supplement

Allies Hold Trials of Japanese War Crimes
India Sends Judge Radhabinod Pal

World War II was over. Netaji Subhash Chandra Bose couldn't reach Tokyo to meet leaders of Japan before surrender to the allies. After the surrender, Japan was now occupied by the allied forces, mainly the Americans. The Emperor of Japan continued in his position as head of his country. However, General MacArthur was in control of the country as a ruler. He ordered the arrest of Japan's political leaders, including the Prime Minister Hideki Tojo. He also ordered the arrest of Japan's military commanders who had led the country's armed forces during the war.

On 19 January 1946, General MacArthur ordered for an International Military Tribunal for the trial of Japan's wartime leaders and military commanders. The tribunal was mainly composed of European and American judges. After protests from Asian countries that had also fought against Japan, a judge from the Philippines and one from British India were invited to join the tribunal. From British India, Justice Radhabinod Pal from Calcutta High Court joined the tribunal. The tribunal's charter had been copied from the

Nuremberg trials of German leaders and military men. There was really no comparison if one considers what Hitler did to the Jews. Japan's army or the country's political leaders did not commit any such racial atrocity or war crime.

Japan had been very friendly with the freedom fighters from India. Many of them had taken refuge there. The most prominent was Rash Behari Bose. Japan was first among those countries that had recognised the Provisional Government of India headed by Netaji Subhash Chandra Bose. Netaji was able to build a very close relationship with the Prime Minister of Japan Hideki Tojo, who had agreed with Bose that when the time came to enter India the joint forces of Japan and Indian National Army would be led by INA. It was to let the people of India know that 'their liberation army' had entered India to throw the British out. Prime Minister Tojo had commended his country's relationship with the Provisional Government of India. That friendly relationship continues since.

Rash Behari Bose and several other freedom fighters were still in Japan when the country surrendered and the Tokyo trials were announced by MacArthur.

On arrival in Tokyo, Justice Radhabinod Pal found that those European and American judges had already taken certain decisions on how the bench would proceed with the trial. Justice Pal was surprised at this and told them bluntly that he is not a party to such a decision. And that he would take his own consideration of the case against the accused.

Justice Pal believed that the Tokyo trial was in many ways a major trial which could not be compared to the Nuremberg trial of Nazi leaders and military men. Defence advocates for Japan's leaders and army men had taken a stand that Japan had not indulged in the extermination of any race as had been done by Nazi Germany to the Jews. Japan had fought a war. According to the Japanese, the war too had been forced on them and they had fought according to the rules of war.

Author Gary J Bass in his book, *Judgement at Tokyo,* has thoroughly discussed the making of the Tokyo Tribunal. He brings out the fact of racist views of Americans and others, notably Australians, against the Japanese. It was hatred by the American Whites of the coloured people. He also refers to jealousy on the economic and military success of Japan. The prosecution team he points out was headed by a *blundering alcoholic,* America's Kennan whose arguments and performance had embarrassed every one. Bass makes special reference to Justice Pal for his line of reasoning and rejection of the tribunal itself. Bass gave a very balanced account of Justice Pal's dissent with the other judges. Pal had pointed out racism and hypocrisy in the trial. Nevertheless, the trial proceeded despite all these doubts. MacArthur was hoping for a quick judgement but the trial ran for over two years.

Justice Pal was born on 27 January 1886 in Salimpur, Bengal. Salimpur is now in Bangladesh. His early education was in Rajshahi. He has been described as a hardworking person who worked in Allahabad before he took his degree in law in 1911 at the age of 25. Justice Pal practised for some time at Mymensingh. While practising there he further improved his qualifications, passing and securing a degree of LLM from Calcutta University. He was now highly qualified as an advocate. Apart from law, he was always interested in mathematics, though he was pursuing his career in constitutional law.

The government took notice of him as an expert and of his high qualifications in law. He was appointed as legal adviser to the Government of India. He became a Judge of the Calcutta High Court in 1941. The young lad from Salimpur had come a long way to reach this position. Not just that, he became the Vice Chancellor of India's finest university then—the Calcutta University. Independent India's government honoured him with Padma Vibhushan.

Justice Radhabinod Pal was thus the best legal mind to represent India at the Tokyo Trial. He saw the whole trial in balance. When he arrived in Tokyo he was told by the Tribunal President Justice Sir William Flood Webb of Australia on how the judges had agreed to conduct the trial. To Justice Pal, this sounded strange! Perhaps he felt this to be justice of revenge by the victors in the war. He was insistent upon a fair trial and looked at all aspects including how the war started between America and Japan.

In colonial India, Justic Pal had served as a judge and had as much knowledge of British law. Therefore, in Tokyo he made it clear to the other judges from day one that he was not just a token judge from Asia. He reasoned well and raised doubts among other judges with their line of thinking and reasoning. Like him, the judges from the Netherlands and France were now going with their own line of reasoning.

To start with, Justice Pal reasoned that the Tokyo Trial could not in any manner be compared with the Nuremberg trials of Nazi leaders. Second, there was the issue of who started the war. The chief prosecutor Joseph Keenan was seeking punishment on the basis of war crimes, crimes against humanity and peace. All these charges had been picked up from the Nuremberg trials, which had no relevance or comparison to what was sought to be achieved against Hideki Tojo, the war-time Prime Minister of Japan and a highly respected figure of the country. Where was any order by him to exterminate the Chinese? When questioned, the prosecution could not produce any. Others being tried with him and respected leaders of Japan were Heitaro Kimura and Iwane Matsui. They were both generals in the Japanese army.

As the trial started questions rose from the very start over the legality of the court.

Then questions arose about the selection of judges. Two of them, Mei Ruao from China and Delfin Jaranilla from Philippines had suffered during the war like other people did. They were both full of bias and anger against those charged in the trial for they held them responsible for what they suffered during the war. Then came the issue of who started the war? The American view was that Japan's attack on Pearl Harbour started the war. The defence presented documents and notes that had been exchanged between the two nations and Japanese feared attack by America. All these papers were seen by the judges. Defence also pointed out the fact that in 1919 when the League of Nations was formed, the demand from Japan of racial equality in the Covenant of the League of Nations was denied.

When Justice Pal had come to Japan to join the tribunal, India was a colony of the British. While he was in Tokyo, India became free and he was now a judge from Independent India, a sovereign country. The defence had been alleging racial bias of some of the countries, including Australia and USA towards Japan and against those put on trial by them.

When finally the day of judgement came, it was not unanimous as expected by America. This was unlike the judgement in Nuremberg which was unanimous. Six out of the eleven judges submitted their own independent judgements. Their views differed. Justice Pal from India was clear in his judgement, acquitting all those who had been charged. Pal had not affirmed all the actions but was of the view that the actions were not illegal. Those were the actions that any nation takes to achieve victory in war.

Justice Pal presented a historical perspective that justified Japan's actions in protecting itself from the manner in which Western colonial powers, Britain, Dutch, and French were spreading in Asia. Indonesia, Singapore, Malaysia, and the Philippines were all colonies of these Western nations. He mentioned how colonial British had used Indian troops to fight for them to preserve the British Empire. In his well-reasoned judgement, he rejected the prosecutor's claim and charge that the Japanese ruling class had conspired to wage the war.

Justice Pal had no doubt assailed the European powers for their actions in Asia. He also accused the United States for the manner in which it had destroyed the cities of Hiroshima and Nagasaki, using atomic bombs, a huge crime against humanity during World War II.

Justice Pal in his judgement did not condone what had been alleged to have been done in Nanjing, China. Those acts he believed should have been classified and punished under categories which covered conventional war crimes. Justice Pal certainly had sympathy for the way he stood against the West. He defended Japanese actions legitimately against the communist revolution in East Asia.

Justice Pal had argued it all in a 1,230-page judgement copies of which he gave to the fellow judges of the tribunal when acquitting all in the Tokyo trial. People in Japan have praised him and respect him as the champion and friend of the people of Japan. Former Prime Minister of Japan Shinzo Abe when visiting India in 2007 specially flew to Calcutta to meet Justice Pal's son Prasanta Pal and convey the regards that people of Japan had for his father. Shinzo Abe and the party also visited Netaji Research Institute in Bhowanipore before taking off for Japan.

In 1966, Justice Radhabinod Pal, then retired, visited Japan and in a speech told the audience that he had admiration for Japan from an early age for being a nation that stood up to the West. He thanked the people of Japan for looking after India's freedom fighters. The Emperor of Japan bestowed on him, the First class of the Order of Sacred Treasure.

Pal is respected and revered by the people of Japan. A monument stands in his honour in the grounds of the Yasukuni Shrine. A sculpture of the bust of Justice Pal also stands in Calcutta High Court.

Independent India waived all reparation claims from Japan that had been raised by the British on behalf of British India. Justice Pal died on 10 January 1967, leaving behind a great legacy of his judgement at the Tokyo Trial, that also cemented the relations between India and Japan.

The Burden of Gujarat

Sixteen Pages   Reg. No. B. 1922

Subscription { Single copy as. 2 / One year Rs. 5 / Six months Rs. 3 }
Foreign Rs. 7, 12s., & 3

Young India

A Weekly Journal   Editor: Jairamdas Daulatram

Vol. XII   Ahmedabad: Thursday, June 12, 1930   No. 24

'Exemplary Behaviour of the Police'

During these days when the authorities in Whitehall and Simla are never tired of extolling the behaviour of the police, I thought I would go and see for myself how far exemplary behaviour has affected the Satyagrahis for …sans.

…at …ulsar at mid-day on 6th, just as the wound… being brought in there from the "raid" of that …ning. Many of them were being carried in on stretch…, others could just struggle from the motors to the hospital wards.

'The beating and torturing has been most merciless to-day!' said the doctors and attendants. I proceeded round the rooms to visit the Satyagrahis more closely, and to take notes from the doctor as to the nature of their wounds.

Literally I felt my skin to creep and my hair to stand on end as I saw those brave men, who, but a few hours previously, had gone forth absolutely unarmed, vowed to non-violence, now lying here before me battered and beaten from head to foot.

Here was a young man with his shoulders and buttocks so beaten that he could not be on his back, yet his arms and sides were so damaged as well, that he did not know how to turn for rest. There was another gasping for breath with his chest badly battered; and nearby was a tall, strong, Mussalman lying utterly helpless.

'What are his damages?' I asked.

'He has received fearful blows on the stomach, the back and right leg.,' they replied. 'Also his testicles are both swollen having been badly squeezed by the police.'

We went on upstairs. — here my attention was attracted by the sound of sharp drawn whistling breathing, intermixed with heart-rending groans. It was a young man writhing in agony. He kept catching at his stomach, and at intervals he would suddenly sit up as if he were going to go mad with the pain.

'He has had a deadly blow right on the abdomen,' they said; 'and he has been vomiting blood. He has also had his testicles severely squeezed, which has shattered his nerves.'

They fetched ice, and applied it to the head and damaged parts, which gradually soothed him.

And on we went from this house to another, where we found still more and more wounded.

Everyone to whom I talked gave the same description of fiendish beating, torturing, thrusting and dragging, and one and all spoke with burning horror of the foul abuse and unspeakable blasphemy which the police and their Indian and English superiors had poured upon them.

So this is some of the exemplary behaviour of the police, of which the English lords and gentlemen are so proud. Do they not know what is going on? No, that surely cannot be, for such high-placed English officials as the Commissioner N. D. and the Collector of Surat have been all along on the field of action.

What, then, has become of English honour, English justice?

No amount of argument can excuse what they have been doing at Dharasana.

The object of the Satyagrahis has been a civil breach of the Salt Laws (which are universally admitted to be unjust). The Satyagrahis were ready to accept unresistingly the legal punishment of arrest and imprisonment, but the authorities thought it preferable to employ other methods. Then, on 22nd May, perhaps to try and lend a shade of legality to their actions, the authorities brought in to force Section 144, making any gathering of more than four persons an unlawful assembly.

With this emergency law in force, it might be argued, by the official world, that it is justifiable to try and disperse a collection of people by *lathi* charges, if they refuse to go away when ordered, even though the individuals are absolutely non-violent, and known not to be going to hurt a single person.

That much brutal argument one might understand from their point of view.

But nothing could excuse the manner in which they have actually dealt with the Satyagrahis.

Who could dare to uphold as a means of dispersing a non-violent gathering:—

1. *Lathi* blows on head, chest, stomach, joints;

2. Thrusts with *lathis* in private parts, abdominal regions, chest etc;

3. Stripping of men naked before beating;

4. Tearing off of loin-cloth and thrusting of stick into *anus*;

5. Pressing and squeezing of the testicles till a man becomes unconscious;

6. Dragging of wounded men by legs or arms, often beating them the while;

7. Throwing of wounded men into thorn hedges or into salt water;

8. Riding of horses over men as they lie or sit on the ground;

Young India reading how Salt Satyagrahis were beaten

Fort William, Calcutta